SEKHMET & BASTET
THE FELINE POWERS OF EGYPT

SEKHMET & BASTET
THE FELINE POWERS OF EGYPT

LESLEY JACKSON

Published by Avalonia
www.avaloniabooks.co.uk

Published by Avalonia

BM Avalonia, London, WC1N 3XX, England, UK

www.avaloniabooks.co.uk

SEKHMET AND BASTET: The Feline Powers of Egypt

© Lesley Jackson, 2017

First published by Avalonia, March 2018

ISBN 978-1-910191-06-4

Typeset and design by Satori.

Cover design by Satori. Illustrations by Brian Andrews © 2017. Photo by bunebake/Shutterstock.com.

Illustrations by Brian Andrews, © 2017

British Library Cataloguing in Publication Data. A catalogue record for this book is available from the British Library.

DEDICATION

This book is dedicated to Sekhmet, the Lady of the Original Power,
to Bastet, the Goddess Great of Festivity,
and to my late brother Julian.

BIOGRAPHY

Lesley Jackson has always had an interest in, and a yearning for, the mysterious geographical; be it lost worlds, otherworlds or the sacred places of this world. A career in IT was merely a logical façade. Many years of involvement in the local archaeological society deepened her interest in ancient cultures and their religions.

Since being blessed with early retirement, Lesley has devoted much of her time to researching and writing about early religion and mythology. Ancient Egypt is an enduring passion, but other paths are always beckoning from around the misty hills. She is the author of *Thoth: The History of the Ancient Egyptian God of Wisdom* (Avalonia, 2011), *Hathor: A Reintroduction to an Ancient Egyptian Goddess* (Avalonia, 2013) and *Isis: The Eternal Goddess of Egypt and Rome* (Avalonia, 2016).

She lives in the remote East Riding with a tolerant husband and an ever-increasing volume of books and rocks. Any remaining spare time is spent travelling or baking and making chocolates.

ACKNOWLEDGEMENTS

No study of Egyptian religion would be possible without access to their writings. I am indebted to all of those who have studied these ancient languages and have provided translations for the rest of us to use.

I would like to thank the British Library, and the Egyptian Exploration Society and the University of Hull for the use of their libraries.

TABLE OF CONTENTS

CHAPTER 1

INTRODUCTION

"Her majesty came down as the potent and prospering Eye to join the world through her to the Spirit of God. At peace, to dwell in Isheru in her form of Sakhmet, Mistress of the Two Lands."[1]

Sekhmet and Bastet are well known and popular Goddesses today, and much of their appeal lies in their feline iconography and characters. They, and the other less well known Feline Goddesses, are inseparable from the concept of the Solar Eye Goddess who is the visible solar disc and the Daughter of the Sun God. This fuels both their character and their strong duality. But there are other major Goddesses, Hathor and Mut, who are Solar Eye Goddesses without feline characteristics despite having one of the Feline Goddesses as an alter ego.

It has proved difficult to study Sekhmet and Bastet in isolation. They may stand dominant but feline power spreads across Egypt like the rays of the rising sun. So I have included all aspects of feline power in this book whilst trying to answer the main questions that the feline deities pose. Why is there such a predominance of Goddesses? Why are they so

---

[1] *Hymns, Prayers and Songs*, Foster, 1995:70

interchangeable in the myths and are frequently angry or benevolent forms of each other? Finally, what about the Feline Gods of Egypt? Why aren't they particularly feline in character and why don't they dominate given the importance of the lion as a symbol of the king? I have excluded the sphinx despite its feline association as it really is a topic in its own right.

CHAPTER 2

THE IMPORTANCE OF FELINES

"When they wish to symbolise spiritedness, they draw a lion...it has fiery eyes...its mane radiates from about it, in imitation of the sun."[2]

Animals and the Egyptians

The natural world and especially the animals in it were very important to the Egyptians. All ancient societies had a much closer link to the natural world than we do if only through the fact that they were predominantly rural societies, but for the Egyptians, animals were an integral part of all aspects of their lives. Over 20 percent of hieroglyphs are connected with animals, and they form a significant part of Egyptian iconography.

The Egyptians were very much aware of the natural world around them. Many animals became significant because they had some feature, such as fertility or hunting skills, which was admired. This power manifested more in the specific animal than in people. Being generalists, we can do what most animals can but not as skilfully. Because of this

---

[2] *The Hieroglyphics of Horapollo*, Horapollo & Boas, 1950:56

animals were seen as a link to the various deities and emblematic of their powers. The desert was seen as the refuge of wild animals compared to the civilised cultivated land. Wild animals represented the dangerous forces of chaos which could only be pacified or controlled through sacred rites and royal intervention. Felines are one of the most iconic of Egyptian symbolic animals. Their major areas of symbolism are listed below and will be dealt with in depth in the relevant chapters.

The Family *Felidae*

The feline family is divided into *Panthera* which contains the big cats (lion, leopard and so forth) and *Felinae* which contains all others. Felines are the most specialist of the carnivores and are exclusively meat eaters. They are adept at prowling and stalking and their speciality is hunting at night. The vast majority of the species are solitary. Unfortunately all species are classed as vulnerable by the IUCN.

The Natural History of Lions

The lion, *Panthera leo*, is the largest African feline and originally there were a number of different species. They were widespread in Europe, the Near East, South West Asia and all of Africa. The Egyptians will have encountered species from North Africa (the Barbary lion) and the Near East (the Asiatic lion) as well as the African lion. Today these species are mostly eradicated with only the African lion remaining in the wild and confined to sub-Saharan Africa. Hunting, disease and loss of habitat and prey caused their decline with hunting rising to obscene levels with well-armed trophy hunters.

It is thought that lions were originally quite abundant in Egypt in the semi-desert areas to the east and west of the Nile and in Sinai. They appear to have drifted south during the Pre-dynastic Period as a result of climate change and increasing human population density and were uncommon during the Pharaonic Period. There may have been a small population still surviving in Egypt during the Ptolemaic Period but it isn't known when they became locally extinct. Tomb chapels in the Old and Middle Kingdoms frequently depict lions hunting in the desert, but that doesn't mean that they were commonly seen rather that they were a popular motif through their symbolism.

Whilst obviously a feline, lions do have some significant differences compared to the other felines. With the exception of feral cats, lions are the only feline to live in large groups. Lionesses inherit their territory and form the core of the pride; hunting, feeding and raising their young together. The male will defend his pride and territory. Lions don't have a breeding season and the females often ovulate and conceive at the same time and raise cubs communally, something which few mammals do. Roles within the pride are not fixed, females will defend territories and males hunt. They are the only felines which display such a noticeable difference between the sexes. The mane is the lion's most distinctive feature, along with its tufted tail. The healthiest male has the largest mane, lionesses often have a short mane or ruff which is similar to that of an adolescent lion. The roar of a lion is an impressive, if terrifying, sound.

The Symbolism of Lions

As predators ourselves, humans have always been fascinated by large predators so, given the lion's grace and striking appearance, it is not surprising that lions command such fascination and importance in people's lives. Although other dangerous animals, predators or otherwise, are revered, we have a widespread affinity with lions. Was this because humans evolved on the East African savannah which is prime lion habitat?

Symbolism in the Pre-Dynastic and Early Dynastic Periods

Although lions were more widespread in Egypt in the early Pre-dynastic Period they are seldom depicted on rock art or pottery. The predominant species portrayed were ostrich, hippo, elephant, ungulates and fish. During the latter part of the Pre-dynastic, the Naqada II (Gerzean) Period, these creatures were replaced by the lion, baboon and falcon. Power had become centralised, the state of Egypt was being established, and new symbols were required, ones which were not encumbered with meanings of an older and very different culture. The new favoured species all had royal and solar connotations. Lion symbolism in particular became important very quickly for this reason.

This change of symbolism is illustrated by comparing ceremonial palettes. These were installed in shrines, and their overall theme is that of bringing control to places and situations which were out of control or hard to dominate; such as the desert or enemy tribes. The late Pre-dynastic Hunter's palette shows two groups of hunters attacking two lions and capturing other animals. It has been suggested that this symbolises victory over the Libyans. The Battlefield palette from the same period shows defeated enemies being devoured by lions and birds of prey. Another palette shows a lion shot with arrows which represents a king strong enough to defeat another king. This decoration contrasts with that of earlier palettes, such as the Narmer palette, where hunting dogs are shown as the symbol of control. This could be because a pack of dogs reflected and emphasised teamwork, hence when the kings became more powerful and absolute rulers they moved towards lion imagery. Now one animal alone, the lion, stood for the power of the king and the rest of his group were not depicted. By the Pharaonic Period the hunting dog imagery had disappeared.

Lion Symbolism in the Pharaonic and Greco-Roman Periods

The tawny coat of the lion may provide a link to the sun, but many animals have a similar coloured coat, so more is needed for the lion to become the ultimate solar animal. Felines have specialised eyes enabling them to see in near darkness, requiring only one-sixth of the light that humans do. They cannot see in complete darkness but give the impression that they can. A reflective layer at the back of the eye allows them to capture as much light as possible and also makes their eyes shine at night. It was believed that their eyes reflected the sun even at night which made them very symbolic, aligning them with the Sun God and his nightly journey through the underworld.

The Egyptians were not alone in choosing the lion as a symbol of kingship. Many areas in Africa had a strong connection between lions and kings, and it became a universal symbol of royalty in Europe. Lions are dangerous, powerful and very distinctive making them an excellent symbol of royal authority. They are social animals, and the lion as leader of the pride made them comparable to the king as the leader and protector of his people.

Lion hunting was reserved for royals and the elite and was of great importance in emphasising the king's power and prowess. It was as much a propaganda exercise as it was a sport. Whether it was a genuine hunt or was staged leaving little to chance is not known. That may have depended upon the ability of the specific king and on the availability of wild lions in the area. The kings often recorded their hunts on commemorative scarabs, over 137 of these have been found. The earliest recorded royal hunt was that of Amenhotep III (18th dynasty). The *"number of lions taken by his majesty with his own shooting"* was said to be 102 in the first ten years of his reign.[3] Thutmose III (18th dynasty) was said to have killed five in a single outing.

Lion imagery was prominent during the reign of Amenhotep III, especially on monuments in or relating to Nubia. Amenhotep III was particularly fond of the Lioness Goddesses and feline symbolism but the importance of the lion to the Nubians is also likely to have been an influence. On *stelae* recording his Nubian campaigns he is referred to as the *"fierce-eyed lion"* and the *"lion of rulers"*[4]. Jar seals from Buhen show him as a lion attacking his enemies. Texts on the Soleb lion (Nubia) say that the lion is the king's *"living image on earth"*[5] which is very similar to the concept of an animal being the deities living image while on earth. The *nemes* headdress worn by royals was made of striped, stiffened linen giving the suggestion of a lion's mane.

Lions were kept as royal pets. Rameses II (19th dynasty), Rameses III and Rameses VI (20th dynasty) kept tame lions as did Tutankhamun (18th dynasty). A temple relief from Beit el-Wali (Nubia) shows Rameses II with his pet lioness, called *"slayer of his enemies"*, next to his throne.[6] In some Ramesside battle scenes lions are shown running beside the king or in his chariot. They are referred to as *"battle lions"*.[7] It is unlikely that they were actually present in the battle. A frightened lion would not know which side a person is fighting on and would probably just try to escape the melee. A more likely explanation is to show the presence of Sekhmet inspiring the king. Berenike II, the wife of Ptolemy III (246-221 BCE), had a pet lioness. She ruled during her husband's absence and it was said

---

[3] *Egyptian Scarabs*, Wilkinson, 2008:43
[4] *Egypt's Dazzling Sun: Amenhotep III and his World*, Kozloff & Bryan, 1992:67
[5] *Egypt's Dazzling Sun: Amenhotep III and his World*, Kozloff & Bryan, 1992:220
[6] *The Animal World of the Pharaohs*, Houlihan, 1996:93
[7] *The Mammals of Ancient Egypt*, Osborn, 1998:116

that "*her bravery and strength is that of Neith, her courage that of Bastet-Sekhmet*".[8]

Kings are shown receiving tribute from the south, including lions, on an 18th dynasty tomb chapel at Thebes. Lions were occasionally imported from Syria. A relief from the tomb of Horemheb (18th dynasty) shows several large felines on leashes, at least one being a lion. In the Old Kingdom royal women were associated with the lioness and this link was strengthened during the Middle Kingdom. The queens were shown in sphinx form, as lions with human heads, and their feline qualities emphasised by wearing cat or lion claw amulets.

"*Braver were their hearts than lions.*"[9] The lion was a general symbol of protection due to its strength and ferocity. Like many of the dangerous creatures of Egypt, the lion wasn't demonised and its power was channelled for good purposes as a guardian and protector. As well as repelling physical enemies they could drive away evil spirits, the evil eye and diseases. "*The lion while on guard closes his eyes, but when sleeping keeps them open...they place lions as guards in the court-yards of the temples as symbols.*"[10] The sacred temple areas needed to be protected from anything evil or profane in the outside world. The use of lions as gate guardians was widespread because the gateway is the weakest part of any enclosure and needs strong guardians. The door bolts of the Horus temple at Edfu were decorated with lions.

A red terracotta lion once guarded the temple Horus at Hierakonpolis. It is thought to date to the 6th dynasty but it is in a Pre-dynastic style. The lion is seated and has a heavy mane which is neatly cut forming a bib on its front.[11] A pair of red granite lions guarded the gateway to the temple of Amenhotep III at Soleb. Their pose is unusual for Egyptian sculpture of that date. They have their paws crossed and heads turned towards the viewer as if to warn anyone who approaches the temple. This pose was more common during the Greco-Roman Period. The Romans adopted the lion as a guardian of temples and palaces and also incorporated it into locks and gargoyles, and with the Roman Empire it spread across Europe.

---

[8] *The Story of Egypt*, Fletcher, 2015:325
[9] *Ancient Egyptian Literature*, Foster, 2001:10
[10] *The Hieroglyphics of Horapollo*, Horapollo & Boas, 1950:56
[11] *Egypt: 4000 Years of Egyptian Art*, Malek, 2003:88

From the Old Kingdom gargoyle spouts on temples often had lion heads to repel storms sent by the Chaos God Seth (the often malevolent brother of Isis and Osiris). They also allude to the inundation which occurred as the sun entered the constellation of Leo. Plutarch (46-119 CE) said *"they honour the Lion, and ornament the doors of the temples with gaping lions' mouths; since Nilus overflows: When first the Sun doth with the Lion join"*[12]. On a more domestic level, lions were often carved on furniture and used as amulets to provide protection.

Lions were a popular motif in funerary decoration as they combined apotropaic qualities with a strong solar association. They lived in the desert margins to the east and west of the Nile and so were considered the guardians of the eastern and western horizon and thus of the Sun God on his nightly journey. This connected them to the cycles of death and rebirth. Funerary biers and embalming tables were decorated with lion legs, paws and heads.

The Natural History and Symbolism of the Leopard

The leopard (*Panthera pardus*) is solitary, shy and nocturnal and probably more dangerous than the lion. They are good climbers and swimmers and have a wide range of prey and habitat. They were originally found in Egypt and appear on the Naqada II palettes but are thought to have been eradicated in areas north of the First Cataract as early as the 2nd dynasty due to human settlement and hunting. The pattern on the leopard's coat is very distinctive with its rosette of black spots, and for that reason it is unfortunately very much desired. Its skin is valuable and of high status throughout Africa being worn by royals, priests and the elite of many cultures. In Egypt leopard skins, both real and imitation, were worn by priests and kings as status symbols on special occasions. They were brought to Egypt from the south either as trade or tribute; leopard skins are depicted on some tomb reliefs which show tribute being gathered. The *sem*-priests were high-status priests associated with funerary rites. They were identified by the leopard skin draped over their shoulders or worn as a robe. The 4th dynasty Prince

---

[12] *Plutarch: Concerning the Mysteries of Isis and Osiris*, Mead, 2002:219

Nefertiabet is shown on a *stele* wearing a leopard skin robe.[13] Some have suggested that a leopard skin garment was originally worn by shamans.

Leopards appear in Egyptian art, but it is not always clear whether it is a leopard or cheetah being depicted despite their very different appearances. The leopard was a prestigious animal to keep as a pet and had the added bonus of being a very useful method of intimidation. The 5th dynasty tomb chapel of Ptahhotep II at Saqqara has a relief which shows hunters returning with a captured lion and leopards in a cage. Another tomb chapel relief of the 5th – 6th dynasty shows pets being exercised; these are two hunting dogs, a leopard and a monkey. Our sympathy lies with the monkey.

The hieroglyph of the leopard was used convey the concepts of strength and violence. "*With the strength of the leopard he threw down the rebel.*"[14] The male leopard was associated with Seth and his uncontrollable rage but females had a more protective role. There is a gilded statuette of Tutankhamun standing on the back of a striding leopard. Here the leopard appears to be an afterlife protector, similar wooden leopards were found amongst the funerary equipment of other kings in the Valley of the Kings.

The Natural History and Symbolism of the Cheetah

The cheetah (*Acinonyx jubatus*) is the least feline of the family. It is very slender with a long tail and legs, and its claws are not retractable. Cheetahs are usually solitary and unlike the other cats are daytime hunters, as they chase their prey at high speeds they need to be able to see clearly. They are very fast but as a result have little stamina being sprinters rather than long-distance runners. Their coat has solid black spots so is not as distinct as the leopards and doesn't seem to have been valued as much. The eye markings are pronounced with thick black tear markings from the eye to the mouth. Cheetahs live in open country and semi-desert areas and were found in northern Sinai and the northern part of the Western Desert. They are now confined to East Africa and parts of southern Africa. They are classed as a vulnerable species due to overhunting and the taking of cubs for the international pet trade. It is

---

[13] *The Use of Leopard Skin in Ancient Egypt,* van Ryneveld, 2008:30-32
[14] *Ancient Egyptian Literature,* Foster, 2001:105

not known when they became extinct in Egypt. Like leopards, they will have been imported from the south. During the New Kingdom they were popular royal pets and are shown on leads in some tomb paintings from the period.

There appears to be no symbolism attached to the cheetah which is strange given its distinctive appearance and characteristics. Was this because it was rarely seen in Egypt when the important religious symbols were developing? The fact that cheetah has some canine attributes may have been significant. There is little symbolism attached to wild or domestic dogs except for jackals who have an important afterlife role. Cheetahs are much less aggressive than lions and leopards, and this might have had an influence.

Where are the Leopard and Cheetah Deities?

Mafdet (see chapter 5) is sometimes depicted as a leopard or cheetah and her epithet of *"runner"* does suggest the cheetah. She has an amorphous feline iconography rather than being aligned to any species in particular; she is also depicted as a lioness and a mongoose. Seshat is frequently depicted wearing a leopard skin dress. She is the Goddess of numeracy, notation and writing. A consort of Thoth, she is the patron of architects and surveyors. Mafdet and Seshat are both Pre-dynastic Goddesses so the leopard and cheetah symbolism may have been a characteristic of the early deities before it was superseded by lion symbolism in the Dynastic Period. Pinch suggests that depictions of the God Ruty (see chapter 8) might derive from earlier images of a pair of leopards who represented the sky. By the New Kingdom they were depicted as spotted leopard-lions.[15] Why wasn't the less aggressive Bastet given the symbol of a cheetah? Perhaps it was because cheetahs appeared less feline. A cat is a lot closer in appearance and character to a lion than a cheetah is.

Neither animal appears much in the mythology, probably because their related deities were either never very dominant or had adopted the lion symbolism. There is one story of how Seth disguised himself as a leopard to try and approach the body of Osiris. Anubis (the jackal-headed God of the Afterlife) caught him and as punishment branded him with a hot iron bar, thus explaining how the leopard got its spots. He then flayed

---

[15] *Egyptian Mythology*, Pinch, 2002:133

Seth and wore his skin as a warning to others, which may explain why *sem*-priests wore a leopard skin. This association with Seth could also be a reason for the lack of leopard deities. The character of the leopard may not have been thought suitable for a more benevolent deity. They are solitary creatures and are considered vicious compared to the more social lions. Leopards do not display sexual dimorphism and apart from their pelt are less distinctive than the lion and lioness. They are largely nocturnal and this will have reduced their solar association.

Becoming Divine

With so much inherent mystery, majesty and symbolism it is not surprising that the felines, lions in particular, became associated with deities and became divine themselves.

CHAPTER 3

THE NATURAL HISTORY AND SYMBOLISM OF CATS

"O cat, your eyes are the eyes of the Lord of the Glorious Eye, by whose eyes the Two Lands are lighted and who brightens the face on the dark road."[16]

The Wild Cats of Egypt

What are termed the small cats belong to the genus of *Felis* in the family of *Felinae*. The Egyptians didn't differentiate between the wild and domestic cat using the same onomatopoeic word for both - *mii* or *miu*. *Miit* is the female version and has the literal meaning *"she who mews"*.[17]

In Egypt there were two species of wild cat; the swamp or jungle cat (*Felis chaus*) and the African wild cat (*Felis silvestris lybica*). The swamp cat is indigenous to Egypt and, as its name implies, prefers a marshy habitat with dense vegetation. It will have been common in the papyrus thickets of the Delta and along the wetlands of the Nile Valley. Its coat is

---

[16] *The Metternich Stele*, Scott, 1951:201-217
[17] *The Cat in Ancient Egypt*, Malek, 1993:25

usually plain and it has a relatively short tail and long tufted ears. The African wild cat has a lighter build and a longer tail. The colour of its coat varies and it can have distinct markings. They are mainly nocturnal and spend the day hidden in trees, dense vegetation or in rock shelters. Wild cats are widely distributed throughout Africa and are only absent in the Sahara desert and the tropical rainforests. As well as in the marshes the Egyptians would have encountered them in the Western Mediterranean and Sinai coastal deserts, in both rocky and agricultural areas.

There are no known rock drawings of wild cats but their remains have been found in the Pre-dynastic sites of Merimde-Benisalama in the western Delta, Nabta Playa in the Western Desert and the Bashendi site at the Dakhla Oasis. The earliest remains of a wild cat were found with a gazelle in a burial of a craftsman near Asyut and date to around 4,000 BCE (the Badarian Period). Excavations of a late Pre-dynastic settlement at Abydos uncovered skeletons of cats which are thought to have been wild cats kept as pets.

The Serval

Felis serval has a slender build and very long legs, ears and tail. Its coat has spots and stripes giving it a very distinctive appearance. They prefer habitats with tall reeds or grasses and capture their prey by leaping on it. Servals are depicted in tomb paintings but they are not attested to before the 18th dynasty and it is thought that they were imported from sub-Saharan Africa. One Ramesside tribute list records cats from a place in Nubia called Miu but this may be only because of the pun on the place name. In some Ramesside vignettes the cat depicted does show a more serval form so the two species may have been used interchangeably.

The Caracal

Caracal caracal is of medium build, with a short tail and long legs and ear tufts. It is solitary, nocturnal and an excellent climber. Its habitat ranges from savannah to semi-desert especially rocky and mountainous areas. Caracals are shown on some tomb paintings.

The Domestication of the Cat

The Egyptians kept a variety of wild animals as pets, and this included wild cats. The oldest evidence of the relationship between humans and wild cats dates to the Pre-dynastic Period, but there is a difference between keeping wild animals as pets and domesticating them. An individual wild animal may be tamed and get used to being around people but domesticated animals have their behaviour and often physical attributes permanently altered, intentionally or otherwise, and inherit a predisposition towards humans. The wild cat (*Felis silvestris*) is widespread in Eurasia and Africa but it is ferocious and untameable. The progenitor of the domestic cat is believed to be the North African variety (*Felis silvestris lybica*) which is much more gentle and friendly. Academics agree that the cat was domesticated in Egypt, there is no evidence that the domestic cat was introduced into Egypt.

Egypt was an organised agrarian society which meant that a lot of grain was stored. This attracted vast numbers of unwelcome vermin such as rodents and small birds. Rubbish dumped in and around settlements would also have attracted vermin. It is possible that wild cats moved into villages to hunt these creatures. Snakes would have been attracted by the same creatures and also would have sought out the higher ground during the inundation but the potentially poisonous snakes would have been less welcome. The fact that wild cats killed the creatures who posed the two main threats to life and prosperity, snakes and grain-eating animals, would have made them very popular with the residents who would have encouraged them to remain in the vicinity. According to a New Kingdom dream interpretation papyrus, seeing a large cat was a good omen foretelling a large harvest. Cats are territorial so are easy to keep in an area once they have become attracted to it, they then accept the humans within their territory. People may have left out scraps to encourage the wild cats and persuade them to take up residence. This would have quickly developed into a symbiotic relationship as cats are very good at taking advantage of situations.

Through diet and selective breeding, probably unintentionally, wild cats became domesticated. Unlike other domestic animals, the cat changed very little under human influence, probably because its breeding was seldom controlled by humans. Domestic cats became slightly smaller with a wider variation in the colour and length of their coats, they have adapted to urban environments, and they breed more rapidly than wild cats. They became moderately social but essentially remain independent and predatory. The cats of Ancient Egypt were not so varied in appearance as cats are today and were slightly larger.

The mongoose is also an expert hunter of snakes and would have been viewed as a very useful animal to have around the village. They can be kept as pets but they were not domesticated. For the cat to become domesticated it was almost certainly seen as an object of affection as well as being very useful to have around the house and village. In present-day hunter-gatherer societies, in places such as Borneo and the Amazon, women and children adopt newly weaned animals which have been taken from the wild and keep them as pets. This seems to be a global human trait. The animals are often driven away, or eaten, once their cuteness fades or they become a nuisance. They are only kept if their usefulness outweighs any disadvantages. Kittens are highly attractive so it is easy to imagine children finding them and bringing them home where they could entertain the adults and work their spell on them.

The dog was domesticated very early on in human history as it was useful to hunters, pastoralists and nomads. The cat only became important when agriculture became dominant and with it the associated vermin. This will be one reason why the cat has little religious significance in the earlier periods, but it does raise the question of the comparative lack of canine symbolism in that period. The time of the domestication of the cat is not clear and will in any case have occurred over a long period: most authors tend to agree that cats weren't fully domesticated until the 18th dynasty although some suggest the 21st dynasty. Domesticated cats are rarely shown before the 18th dynasty but it difficult to know if the cat depicted is domesticated or not, even if it is shown in a domestic context. Art was not a photographic record of what was there at the time, and the animal's symbolism was the most important aspect for the Egyptians.

There are no representations of cats before the 5th dynasty. In the Old Kingdom there are some depictions of cats in the marshes or in desert environments on tomb-chapel and temple walls, such as the 5th dynasty tomb-chapel of a vizier at Saqqara, but these show wild cats in their natural habitat. There is one reference to *"Cat Town"* on a wall relief from el-Lisht. If its dating to the Old Kingdom is correct then it is the oldest example of the cat hieroglyph. The first definitive reference to a domestic cat is considered to be in the 11th dynasty rock-cut tomb of Baket III, an official from Beni Hassan. Here a vignette depicts a female cat confronting a large rat. A 12th dynasty relief from Koptos shows a cat under the chair of a woman. In Abydos a small 12th dynasty tomb was found which contained the skeletons of 17 cats and a row of small offering bowls. The bowls may have contained milk, if so this is the earliest record of cats drinking milk. "*To the cats and ichneumons, they give bread soaked in milk*" reported Diodorus Siculus (80-20 BCE).[18]

The Rise of the Cat

Originally domestic cats would have been rare, and early on the population probably wouldn't have been self-sustaining and domestic cats would have interbred with wild ones. Over the next 500 years the domestic cat took a much more prominent role in life in Egypt. Bradshaw debates whether the veneration of the cat and the breeding of cats in temples gave the species time to evolve into a fully domesticated animal. Selective breeding could have produced animals more comfortable in confined spaces and in close proximity to other cats. It is possible that some of the cats would have evaded sacrifice either through escaping or being bought as pets. These would have interbred with the local cats in the villages.[19] Once established, the popularity of cats as pets increased rapidly to reach a peak in the Ptolemaic Period. No myths have been found concerning the first contact between cats and humans or their domestication. For such an important creature you might expect at least one myth, but any such stories were probably unrecorded folklore. The *Return of the Distant Goddess* myth, in which the Goddess is first estranged from and then reunited with the Sun God, can be read in part about the evolution of the peaceful cat from the wild cat. (This is discussed in detail in chapter 12.)

A number of cats are referred to as Tamyt which means female cat and may be our equivalent of kitty or pussy. An 18th dynasty tomb refers to one cat as "*the Pleasant One*".[20] The Crown Prince Thutmose (18th dynasty) is best known for the burial of his pet cat at Saqqara. The mummified cat was treated to a human burial, complete with funerary texts on the coffin where the deceased cat is referred to as "*the Osiris, She-cat*".[21] The deceased cat is shown sitting in front of an offering table

---

[18] *The Historical Library of History of Diodorus Siculus*, Diodorus Siculus & Booth, 1814:87

[19] *Cat Sense*, Bradshaw, 2014:57

[20] *The Animal World of the Pharaohs*, Houlihan, 1996:85

[21] *Egypt's Dazzling Sun: Amenhotep III and his World*, Kozloff & Bryan, 1992:425

and a *sem*-priest. Behind the deceased cat another cat stands upright mimicking a human posture. This is a very rare occurrence of a pet receiving a human burial. Words for cats were used in personal names for both men and women from the Old Kingdom. A popular nickname for young girls was *miw-sheri* meaning Little Cat. Pamiw's (22nd dynasty) name translates as tomcat. There are records of some of the foreign wives of Amenhotep III taking Egyptian names which included two which translate as *"the Catlike One"* and *"Hot-tempered like a Leopard"*.[22]

The Symbolism of Cats

The role of cats in domestic life and art becomes prominent in the New Kingdom. They appear in paintings and towards the end of the period cat amulets become very popular. Some of the symbolism of cats is shared with lions but there are some noticeable differences. They have no royal association which isn't surprising. Cats were viewed as a smaller, tame version of a lion and so were not considered as good a symbol for the elite and powerful. They have a strong connection with fertility and women which is not found with lions despite the preponderance of Lioness Goddesses.

Like the rest of the felines, cats were considered solar animals for the same reasons. They are often depicted with solar images such as the winged scarab or *wedjat* eye. Horapollo, an Egyptian writing in the 4-5th century CE, said that the cat's pupils changed according to the time of day. *"For they say the male cat changes its pupils with the course of the sun. For they widen out towards morning at the rising of the god. And they become round like a balloon at noon, and they appear somewhat faint as the sun is about to set. Wherefore in Heliopolis the statue of the god is in the form of a cat."*[23] However, Plutarch reported a similar feature but this time in sympathy with the phases of the moon. The fact that cats kill snakes makes them a highly symbolic creature especially as the main enemy of the Sun God is the Chaos Serpent Apophis. *"The cat likewise is very serviceable against the venomous stings of serpents, and the deadly bite of the asp."*[24] Archaeologists in Egypt in the1930s reported sightings of cats killing horned vipers and cobras. The mongoose is the

---

[22] *The Story of Egypt*, Fletcher, 2015:208
[23] *Hieroglyphics of Horapollo*, Horapollo & Boas, 1950:48-49
[24] *The Historical Library of History of Diodorus Siculus*, Diodorus Siculus & Booth, 1814:87

more skilled specialist snake hunter, but the popularity of the domestic cat ensured their place in snake-killing symbolism. Their well-honed hunting instinct was a major influence in the development of cat-related mythology. Cats hunt for entertainment as well as to feed themselves. Cats appear as apotropaic symbols on Middle Kingdom magical knives and wands where they are shown attacking snakes. They are also important in the afterlife both as guardians and demons, probably influenced by the fact that they have reflective eyes and can see in apparent darkness. In some tomb scenes they have a gilded coating on their eyes depicting the way their eyes shine in the darkness and emphasising their ability to see evil creatures.

Cats enjoy a noisy sex life which quickly made them symbols of sexuality and its consequential fertility. Female cats are capable of producing up to twelve kittens per year. For an agricultural society fecundity is much valued in all species, vermin excepted, and the cat was a popular symbol of fecundity. The cat was seen as a renewer and protector of life due to its fecundity and the fact that it hunted the vermin which pillaged the grain stores. Peace and prosperity were symbolised by the cat who protects, confirms and renews life.

Cats have had a strong association with women from the beginning in all cultures. Even today there is a tendency to think of dogs as male and cats as female and to be preferred by the respective genders. Whether this is born out in actuality I do not know. Certainly amongst my family and friends about half the cat-lovers are male and half the dog-lovers are female. In Egyptian art it is usually women who are depicted with cats. The symbolism of women and cats in paintings is discussed in chapter 21. The cat's association with sex and fertility is cited as the reason for this relationship. There is some misogyny in that the fact that the female cat's active and assertive sexual role aligned them to women. The inference is that the woman were the sexual predators of the reluctant males. Another suggestion for the close link to women is because cats constantly groom themselves. Others are more tenuous suggesting that cats stay around the house compared to dogs. Some societies view dogs as more 'manly' companions but a cynic could say that there is some male hostility towards cats because they can't control them.

Non-Egyptian Attitudes Towards Cats

The Greeks were impressed by the domestic cat as they had only known the untameable wild cat. Domestic cats began to spread around the Roman Empire and into Asia but in very low numbers. Cats were present in Roman Britain, their remains have been found along with paw-prints on tiles laid out to dry. They didn't become common in Europe until the Middle Ages. The Greeks assigned lunar symbolism to cats, but as they first encountered the domestic cat in Egypt it is surprising that they didn't adopt the Egyptian symbolism. During the Greco-Roman period the cat was closely associated with Bastet and Isis, and the Greeks viewed all Goddesses as lunar. Their associated sacred animals were thus considered lunar creatures as well.

The Egyptians were well known for revering cats and the Classical writers commented on this. Herodotus reported that when a house was on fire *"it is only the cats that matter"*[25] and that all the inhabitants of a house mourn when their cat has died. The 2nd century CE Macedonian Polyaenus wrote about the battle of Pelusium in the Delta in 525 BCE and said that the front rank soldiers carried cats and the Egyptians wouldn't attack in case they hurt the cats. This is considered unlikely to be true. Apart from specific individuals most non-Egyptian cultures, especially in Europe, didn't view the cat as benevolent. Given the nature of many of the Greco-Roman spells involving cats it is not surprising that the cat could be associated with evil powers by other cultures (see chapter 17).

Cats were strongly linked to Isis in her cult outside of Egypt and then became associated with other European Goddesses. This strong association with paganism, and Goddesses in particular, brought them into conflict with Christianity which demonised them. This led to persecution by the church which was particularly unpleasant and widespread during the superstitious Medieval Period. Cat worship was outlawed in Ypres in 962 BCE which is a good indication that the Goddess and her cats were still popular at this time.[26] Dogs fared much better for a number of reasons. They had been part of European culture for millennia, were trainable, and able to carry out a number of roles such as hunting, herding or guarding. Although they did have an association with some pagan deities, this wasn't as strong as the cats'

---

[25] *The Histories*, Herodotus & Selincourt, 2003:122
[26] *Cat Sense*, Bradshaw, 2014:59

link to the Goddess. The fact that dogs were seen as masculine creatures will have carried much weight in a male-dominated society. Cats fared much better in Islamic cultures being viewed as a clean creature compared to dogs who were considered impure.

Cats are self-contained and enigmatic which has associated them with the divine and also meant that they were credited with uncanny abilities – cats love to stare into space or chase imaginary or invisible beings to entertain or spook their owners. The Egyptians didn't have an ambivalent attitude towards cats, they saw them as benevolent and divine and any aloofness or strange behaviour merely emphasised the divine link.

Some Non-Felines

The Egyptians appear to have considered the mongoose and the genet as similar species and gave them feline symbolism, so I have included them in this chapter. Surprisingly, given the great accuracy with which other species are portrayed, the Egyptians didn't always give an accurate rendition of the mongoose. Its features are sometimes muted so they are not always easy to distinguish, especially for the non-naturalist. It is thought that some have been wrongly interpreted as the genet or weasel. Did the Egyptians consider the mongoose and the genet as the same type of animal? In some depictions there are several species combined into one image. Was this because the artist hadn't seen the animal? Although the mongoose and genet are very different creatures the Egyptians didn't always differentiate between them and the cat which suggests that the symbolism was so close that it didn't matter exactly which species was shown. If it had have been important then the specific species would have been made obvious.

The genet (*Genetta genetta*) is a small carnivore which is now extinct in Egypt. They have a cat-like appearance with long, slender bodies and long tails. Their legs are short and they have retractable claws. Genets are nocturnal hunters with a wide range of habitat and prey but prefer vegetated slopes particularly near water. They are expert climbers. Tomb scenes show them climbing papyrus stalks to get to bird nests, although they are too heavy to be supported by the single stem they are often depicted on. Genets are said to be tameable and may have been kept as rodent and snake killers but domestic cats proved more able at the job and more attractive as the genet has an unpleasant smell. Genets may have been cult animals of the Goddess Mafdet as similar-looking animals appear on some of her cult objects.

Sometimes referred to as the ichneumon, the mongoose (*Herpestes ichneumon*) belongs to the Herpestidae family which consists of small carnivores native to southern Eurasia and Africa. They have a slender body, similar in form to a weasel, but are not as cat-like as the genet. Mongoose live in a range of environments, including swamps, and they can swim. Like the genet they are depicted in hunting and fowling scenes. Their diet includes eggs, carrion, insects, rodents, lizards and birds and they are excellent killers of snakes. Mongooses are one of the few mammals that have an inbuilt resistance to snake venom. They have not been domesticated but can be tamed and because of their snake killing abilities are actively encouraged in many places in Africa and India. One factor against them is that they will take poultry eggs.

Becoming Divine

Like lions, cats have an inherent air of mystery and aloofness which makes them ideal candidates for representing divinities. By the time the cat was domesticated the Egyptian religion was well established which is why there are fewer cat deities. In addition, they had to compete as a symbol with the more impressive and majestic lion.

CHAPTER 4

SEKHMET

"Hail to you, Lady of Plague, Sekhmet the Great, Lady to the Limit!"[27]

The Lioness Goddesses

There are a number of Lioness Goddesses. Some we know virtually nothing about, others have their own distinct personality and can sometimes be an aspect of another Goddess. They are all similar in appearance and personality and are all viewed as Solar Eye Goddesses namely Daughters of the Sun God and the Eye of the Sun (the visible solar disc which is discussed in chapter 10). Lionesses are rarely depicted in the Pre-dynastic Period yet early in the Pharaonic Period the Lioness Goddesses are well established and important. They were widely venerated, feared and respected and Sekhmet is still popular and venerated today. All have a strong polarity and can be both malign and benign, and all are associated with the power of the sun. The lioness is a fierce protector of her cubs, but this is not a trait confined to felines so cannot by itself explain the Lioness Goddess. The dangerous aspect of

---

[27] *Voices from Ancient Egypt*, Parkinson, 1991:127

the Lioness Goddess will be investigated in later chapters, but it is important to note that no matter how dangerous and malign they could be they were never demonised. After all, what the Lioness Goddess depicted was the uncontrollable heat of the sun, and that could never be evil as it was essential for life. Their anger was accepted as part of the natural order and was balanced by a benevolence that led to them being held as popular protectors at all levels of society.

Sekhmet

Sekhmet is the most important and enduring of the Lioness Goddesses. She is the major manifestation of the Eye of the Sun God and closely linked with the fire-breathing *uraeus* (the protective cobra on the head of deities and kings). Sekhmet is never anything but a Lioness Goddess always remaining true to her nature and along with Pakhet (see chapter 5) is the most leonine of the Goddesses. She is sometimes viewed as a Goddess in her own right but at other times seen as the aggressive aspect of Hathor or Mut or the aggressive side of the dual Goddess Sekhmet-Bastet. Personally, I see her as a unique Goddess, and the Egyptians were quite happy to hold both views simultaneously, seeing each as equally valid. In the same inscription Sekhmet and Hathor can be addressed both as individual Goddesses and as the composite Sekhmet-Hathor. The concept of Sekhmet personifying divine power and rage was in place by the early Old Kingdom. Over time she became increasingly independent as her personality developed.

Name and Epithets

Sekhmet's name reinforces her nature – the Powerful or Mighty One. Many of her epithets are generic ones shared with all the other Goddesses; Lady of Heaven, Mistress of the Two Lands, Mistress of the Gods and the Great One. Like the other Feline Goddesses, she is also the *"Eye of Ra, upon the sun disc"*.[28] The one specific to Sekhmet is Beloved of Ptah (her consort). Many allude to the nature of the *"Lady of Many Faces"*. She is *"Mistress of Flame"* and *"Mistress of Heat"*. In her benevolent aspect she is the *"Good Eye who gives Life to the Two Lands"* and *"Lady of the Bread Offerings"*.[29] Some of Sekhmet's names reflect her

---

[28] *Popular Religion in Egypt During the New Kingdom*, Sadek, 1988:35
[29] *Sekhmet et la Protection du Monde*, Germond, 1981:349 (My translation)

dangerous side; such as "*Smiter of the iwnty.w*" (probably a nomadic people),[30] "*Lady of darkness*" and "*She who brings death*".[31] Her varied powers led to conflicting feelings, those of fear and horror set against those of awe and hope. At Edfu one inscription refers to the "*Lady of all manifestations of Sekhmet*". [32]

Many of Sekhmet's names are geographical. She has epithets relating to her cult centres, such as Sekhmet of Sahure and Mistress of Ankhtawy. The later means Life of the Two Lands and is an area of Memphis. She is "*Sakhmet who is in Bubastis*" and "*Sakhmet the great who dwells in the city*".[33] The latter is probably a reference to Thebes. At Abydos she was "*Sekhmet on her mountain*". A list of the cults of Abydos includes "*the goddess Sekhmet in the valley*". With Pakhet she shares a number of variations of the phrase "*at the head of the valley*" inspired by sightings of lionesses at the entrances of wadis (dry river valleys which flood after heavy rains). Although she is not a Lioness Goddess Hathor also had the epithet "*Mistress at the mouth of the valley*" at Tehna.[34]

As Sekhmet is sometimes considered the alter-ego of Hathor or Mut she can take epithets more suited to them. One such is a reference to Sekhmet as the Lady of the Acacia, on a *stele* from Memphis, although Sekhmet has no Tree Goddess aspect herself. Hathor is often referred to by this epithet as well as Lady of the Sycamore in her afterlife aspect. Acacias were planted for Sekhmet, and Queen Hetepheres (4th dynasty) had the title "*Leader of Slaughter in the Acacia House*".[35] She was responsible for meat offerings to Sekhmet. "*You will smell the odour of fat from the goats and pigs when Sekhmet is appeased along with her emissary demons.*"[36]

---

[30] *Hathor Returns to Medamud*, Darnell, 1995:47-97

[31] *Sekhmet et la Protection du Monde*, Germond, 1981:349 (My translation)

[32] *Sekhmet et la Protection du Monde*, Germond, 1981:108 (My translation)

[33] *Egyptian Healing Statues in Three Museums in Italy (Turin, Florence, Naples)*, Kakosy, 1697:65 & 106

[34] *Le Role et le Sens du Lion dans L'Egypte Ancienne*, de Wit, 1951:286-287 (My Translation)

[35] *The Story of Egypt*, Fletcher, 2015:67

[36] *Traversing Eternity*, Smith, 2009:416

1 - Sekhmet (Seated)

Iconography

Sekhmet is usually depicted as a lioness-headed woman wearing the solar disc draped by the *uraeus* and a long tripartite wig. When she is combined with other Goddesses her crown will vary, for example as Sekhmet-Mut she usually wears the double crown of Egypt. Sekhmet is never shown in human form and only occasionally as a lioness. Sekhmet is depicted as a lioness in some healing statues; one shows her recumbent upon a pedestal wearing the *atef*-crown and sun disc. The *atef*-crown is the White Crown of Upper Egypt with two feathers.

Sekhmet usually carries the *ankh*, the symbol of life, and the papyrus stem sceptre, which is a symbol of her native Lower Egypt. The papyrus sceptre is an ancient symbol, first seen in the 2nd dynasty where it was held by Wadjet (see chapter 10). It is held by Hathor and Bastet in the 5th dynasty. Depictions of Sekhmet in the Old Kingdom don't often have the papyrus sceptre, but by the Ramesside Period all the Lioness Goddesses carried one. It is thought to have originated in the cult of Hathor who had a close connection to the papyrus. This was gathered and presented to the Hathor Cow to remind her of her home in the marshes. The papyrus has connotations of flourishing life, satisfaction and support which alludes to Sekhmet's more benevolent nurturing and sustaining aspect. It is also a symbol of rebirth appearing in funerary scenes. *"High is Sekhmet, glorious is she...her joy is in her papyrus-wand."*[37] Her dress is long and often red reflecting her epithet Lady of the Bright Red Linen. This could be a reference to her warlike nature, with blood-soaked clothes, to fire and or to the colour of the crown of Lower Egypt.

There is probably no more famous or widespread Egyptian statues than those of Sekhmet commissioned by Amenhotep III (18th dynasty) for his mortuary temple and the Precinct of Mut at Karnak. He had over 700 statues sculpted, and these are now found in museums across the world. The statues are of granodiorite and are about 2m high and weigh 2 tons. The stone was all quarried at Aswan but many different types of granodiorite have been identified which implies that they were from a large number of different quarries and workshops. The colour of the stone varies from deep black to a brownish-red. Black represented the fertile earth whilst colours such as red and gold referred to the sun.

---

[37] *Temple Ritual at Abydos*, David, 2016:220

Under a certain light the statues shimmer so they will have sparkled in the sunlight when they were newly polished. The layout and function of these statues is discussed in chapter 19.

Half of the statues depict Sekhmet standing with her left foot forward. She holds the papyrus sceptre across her body emphasising her authority as well as Lower Egypt. The other statues show her seated on a low-backed throne. Most have decorations on the sides of the throne, frequently including the entwined lotus and papyrus as the combined symbols of Upper and Lower Egypt. Her feet are together and her hands rest flat on her knees, in her left hand she holds an *ankh*. The head is a combination of the features of a lioness and an adolescent lion. Very skilled sculptors have perfectly conveyed the identifying features of the lion; eyes with a teardrop curve in the corner, round ears, a flat wide bridge nose and clearly defined cheekbones. The faces of the finest statues include whiskers shaped like daisy petals with little drilled dots near the point of each one and talon shaped hooks inside the corner of each eye. Sekhmet has a stylised mane, onto which is carved the rays of the sun, which extends into a long wig falling to her breasts. Each statue will have worn the solar disc and *uraeus* but as these were made separately and attached many are now missing. Fragments of one head shows a crown composed entirely of *uraei*. Sekhmet's posture suggests composure and stability. This alludes both to *maat* and to the stillness of a watchful predator.

Her ankle length dress is tight fitting with a broad strap over the shoulders. The design is slightly old-fashioned for the period, to the Egyptians this was considered appropriate with old being seen as more superior and dignified. Some of the best statues have a rosette over each breast. These were a popular motif in the New Kingdom, and it is thought that by emphasising her breasts it will have emphasised her more benign aspects of fertility and abundance. Others believe that it represents the pattern of the shoulder hair on lions or the shoulder star of the constellation of Leo as shown on the astronomical ceilings. Sekhmet wears a broad collar with many rows of beads called a *wesekh*-collar and in many of the statues she wears bracelets or anklets. It is thought that the statues were painted as traces of paint remain. The eyes of some of the statues were tinted red. Recently excavated statues at Amenhotep's mortuary temple have remains of blue and red paint on the bracelets.[38]

The Aspects of Sekhmet

Sekhmet is a purely Solar and Lioness Goddess. Her two major roles are a reflection of her ambivalent nature; she is both a bringer of war and disease and a protector and healer. Sekhmet is She "*who presides over the desert*"[39] representing the desiccating influence of the sun and the dangerous chaos of the desert regions. The hot desert winds were said to be the "*breath of Sekhmet*".[40] She is also present in the afterlife. In the *Book of the Dead* she has a more celestial abode. The deceased says "*I am Sekhmet, and I sit beside Her who is in the grand wind of the sky*".[41] Another spell says that she is found in the constellation of Orion. As with all the feline deities introduced in the following chapters Sekhmet's major aspects will be covered in greater detail in the relevant chapters.

Isis and Hathor have a long and close association with royalty and especially the king and both ensure his right to rule and his protection. Sekhmet, and to a lesser extent Bastet, also ensure the inheritance and transmission of royal power as well as protecting the king's body and authority. Sneferu (4th dynasty) was a devotee of the Lioness Goddesses. A relief from his temple at Dahshur shows a lioness-headed Goddess with her muzzle next to the king. He is breathing in the life force she is breathing out. She may be Sekhmet, but there is no inscription. Sneferu planted sacred groves of sycamores for Hathor and acacias for Sekhmet and provided meat offerings for Sekhmet and dancing for Hathor. His consort Queen Hetepheres was closely aligned with Hathor and Sekhmet. Another Queen Hetepheres, the wife of Djedefra (4th dynasty), was also closely associated with Hathor and Sekhmet. She was depicted as a crouching lioness with her human head as the first known sphinx.

The role of Sekhmet in the monarchy becomes increasingly important in the New Kingdom, especially during the 18th dynasty. Reinforced by her association with Mut, Sekhmet becomes one of the

---

[38] *Travellers from an Antique Land: Statues of the Goddess Sekhmet in the British Museum*, Draper-Stumm, 2012.
[39] *Men and Gods on the Roman Nile*, Lindsay, 1968:200
[40] *The Complete Gods and Goddesses of Ancient Egypt*, Wilkinson, 2003: 181
[41] *How to Read the Egyptian Book of the Dead*, Kemp, 2007:81

principal deities protecting the king. The kings claimed many Goddesses as their mother. Rameses II (19th dynasty) was the son of Sekhmet while Thutmose III (18th dynasty) was *"the fierce lion, Sakhmet's son"*.[42] Sety I's (19th dynasty) temple at Abydos records Sekhmet giving him dominion over foreign lands. He refers to her as his mother and calls himself beloved of Ptah and Sekhmet. Sekhmet says *"I give thee kingship...I am with thee in all that thou hast done"* in another relief she holds the *ankh* and *menat* to his nose saying *"I protect thee a million times"*.[43] She presents him with two staffs entwined with snakes who wear the red and white crowns of Egypt. The papyrus *Harris* refers to Rameses III (20th dynasty) building a secret stone shrine at Elephantine for Ptah, Sekhmet and Nefertem. He is depicted offering flowers to Ptah and Sekhmet. Amenemope (21st dynasty) offers lotus and papyrus to Sekhmet and Sheshonq IV (23rd dynasty) is shown offering wine to Sekhmet, Shesmetet, Bastet and Wadjet.

These are just a few of the hundreds of reliefs depicting exchanges between the Lioness Goddesses and kings. The kings make offerings and in return receive protection and the authority to rule. Arguably this is more like a business transaction than an act of devotion, but the Egyptians were practical and had similarly minded deities. Anything at a more mystic level either wasn't recorded or we can't recognise it.

Her Consort

Sekhmet's consort is Ptah of Memphis. He is an ancient God attested to in the 1st Dynasty and is depicted as a man wearing a tightly wrapped cloak and skull cap. He carries a sceptre which is a combination of the *djed* (denoting stability), the *ankh* (life) and the *was* (denoting dominion). His face is often blue symbolising the sky. Ptah is the Creator God of the Memphite tradition where he created all things through his heart (symbolising creative intelligence) and his tongue (using the magical power of the spoken word). The *Opening of the Mouth* ceremony, which allowed the deceased to be reborn and which animated the cult statues, was said to have been invented by Ptah. He was the patron God of craft workers; in particular masons, builders, sculptures and metal workers. He watched over them as they continued his work of creation. Ptah was

---

[42] *The Literature of Ancient Egypt*, Simpson et al, 2003:73
[43] *Temple Ritual at Abydos*, David, 2016:36

considered one of the 'hearing deities' that is he listened to people's prayers and responded.

Why was he considered the consort of Sekhmet? Was it just because she was an important Goddess in the area around Memphis? That alone was a major factor, the two main deities in a region (or their priests to be more honest) would want to join forces to improve their status and power. Ptah is not a Solar God so has no connection to Sekhmet as the Eye Goddess. One reason may have been to counterbalance the increasing dominance of the solar tradition. She also brought her element of fire to balance the more air-like element of Ptah. There might have been a myth explaining their union but if there was it is now lost. Whatever the reason Sekhmet was the considered *"the Beloved of Ptah"*[44] and *"the Heart of Ptah"*.[45] Triads, a grouping of three deities, became very popular during the New Kingdom and it was at this time that the Memphite triad of Ptah, Sekhmet and their son Nefertem (see chapter 8) was established.

Ptah was also associated with the other Daughters of Ra; Bastet, Tefnut, Mut and Maat. In the mortuary temple of Sety I there is a reference to *"Mut, Mistress of the House of Ptah"* and at Karnak Maat is referred to as *"Ptah's beloved"*.[46]

Other Relationships

Sokar is the hawk-headed God of the Memphis necropolis and was linked to Ptah so Sekhmet can also be his consort. One epithet on a Sekhmet statue is *"Daughter of Osiris"*.[47] This probably arose with the merging of the Solar and Osirian theologies in the New Kingdom. As Osiris increased in popularity and power previously unrelated deities started to be associated with him. Four Lioness Goddesses guarded the body of Osiris; Sekhmet, Shesmetet, Bastet and Wadjet. Some other epithets of Sekhmet suggest that she had taken on Thoth's role as mediator and peacemaker between Horus and Seth. She is the *"Pacifier of Horus and Seth"* and *"Friend of the Two Gods"*.[48] There is logic in this

---

[44] *Ancient Egyptian Literature Volume II*, Lichtheim, 2006:101
[45] *Excavations at Armant, 1929-31*, Myers & Fairman, 1931:223-232
[46] *The God Ptah*, Holmberg, 1946:224
[47] *Les Statues Thebaines de la Desses Sakhmet*, Gautier, 1920:117-207 (My translation)
[48] *Les Statues Thebaines de la Desses Sakhmet*, Gautier, 1920:117-207 (My translation)

role: she is mirroring the actions of her pacifier Thoth, and as a previously Angry Goddess the pacified becomes the pacifier and furthers the cause of *maat* and a return to order and the healed eye (see chapter 12).

Her Alter-egos

Sekhmet was created from the anger which came forth from Hathor. *"Hathor has power over those who rebelled against her father in that her name of Sakhmet."*[49] As such, Sekhmet can be viewed as the angry aspect of Hathor which, when pacified, is reabsorbed into the benevolent Hathor. The papyrus *Jumilhac* tells how Hathor of the Two Braziers transforms into Sekhmet to destroy Seth and his followers. A number of *stelae* from Serabit depict burnt offerings of wildfowl in a pair of braziers. Wildfowl were associated with the forces of chaos suggested by the calling, wheeling flocks in the marshes. Sekhmet can also form the composite Sekhmet-Hathor. The foundations of a temple to Sekhmet-Hathor were found in Kom el-Hisn in western Delta. It probably dates to the New Kingdom or later. Two statues of Rameses II were found, dedicated to *"Sekhmet-Hathor Mistress of Imu"*.[50] The order of the names may be important. Sekhmet-Hathor may refer to Sekhmet with a gentler nature whilst Hathor-Sekhmet may imply Hathor as Sekhmet and a more aggressive aspect. New Kingdom and Greco-Roman inscriptions reinforce the association of Hathor and Sekhmet. Both were considered responsible for the arrival of the inundation, the renewal of universal cycles and the king's power and legitimacy. Offerings considered suitable for Sekhmet were similar to those offered to Hathor; geese, antelope, beer, wine, *sistra* and sceptres. Sekhmet can also be viewed as the angry aspect of Mut. She is also paired with Bastet who can be seen as the pacified aspect of Sekhmet.

The Origin and Evolution of Her Cult

When the cult centres of the Lioness Goddesses are plotted on a map, it is clear that there is a concentration in Lower Egypt, predominantly in the Delta region. It is probable that the main cult

---

[49] *The Bremner-Rhind Papyrus II*, Faulkner, 1937:10-16
[50] *Preliminary Report on the Survey of Kom el-Hisin, 1996*, Kirby, Orel & Smith, 1998:23-43

centres were where the deity originated, but this cannot be proved. At first thought it might be expected that a Lioness Goddess was more likely to originate in the south of the country, but lions may have been more prevalent in the north. During the early periods lions were widespread in North Africa and the Near East. Since Pre-dynastic times the population of the Delta was more mixed than that of Upper Egypt, and its position meant that it was open to outside influences especially from neighbouring Libya and traders from the east. Is there a non-Egyptian influence on the early Lioness Goddesses? It is hard to tell given that lion symbolism was strong across the region. One of Sekhmet's epithets is Sekhmet of the Libyans. Does this hint at a foreign origin or just that she was popular with the Libyans who had settled in the Delta region? The depictions of lions before the 3rd dynasty certainly show a Near Eastern style but was this because the lions in the area where the objects were created were the Barbary or Asiatic Lions rather than the African ones? (This is discussed further in chapter 21.) If there was a non-Egyptian influence it has been lost until we get to the Greco-Roman Period.

Memphis was the main cult centre of Sekhmet. Narmer (1st dynasty) was said to have founded the temple to Ptah and Sekhmet on the site where the first land emerged at creation. The many epithets of Sekhmet means that it is very difficult to determine her origins. Germond suggests that she probably originated in the 4th dynasty in the Memphis region. Sekhmet has a strong link to the 2nd and 3rd *nomes* of Lower Egypt, which are on the western side of the Delta. Sekhmet was worshipped with Ra at Heliopolis since the early Old Kingdom. In the 12th dynasty, Sekhmet's influence spread and she was introduced to the Theban region. Her cult was very important in the Theban region during the 18th dynasty, and there are 22 epithets referring to her sanctuaries in this area.

The New Kingdom, and the 18th dynasty in particular, was a golden age for the Feline Goddesses. This was driven by a number of the kings who were particular devotees. Hatshepsut (18th dynasty) was especially devoted to the powerful Solar and Lioness Goddesses as was Thutmose III (18th dynasty). Amenhotep III (18th dynasty) was particularly devoted to Sekhmet and Mut as was Sety I. The expulsion of the Hyksos who occupied Lower Egypt during the 2nd Intermediate Period and the reestablishment of Egypt's' southern border against the invading Nubians could be seen as a victory for Sekhmet. The rulers in the New Kingdom came from Thebes and the Theban triad of Amun, Mut and

Khonsu became increasingly important. They began to absorb the attributes of other deities, and Sekhmet was increasingly viewed as the aggressive manifestation of Mut. One of her epithets from Karnak was "*She who is united with Mut*".[51] Mut is a southern Goddess and is depicted wearing the crown of Upper Egypt. Establishing a close relationship between Mut and Sekhmet was also a way of emphasising the unity between Upper and Lower Egypt. Sekhmet's associated with Thebes is emphasised in a hymn to Thebes. "*Pleased to dwell by the waters of Asheru in the likeness of Sakhmet, Mistress of Egypt. How strong she is! Without contender...sharp-sighted, keen as God's protector, Right Eye of Re.*"[52]

Thutmose I (18th dynasty) was the first Egyptian king to sail as far south as the Fifth Cataract. His official fleet included his wife Ahmose and his daughter Hatshepsut. They represented the protective female and feline powers of Hathor and Sekhmet, something which was vital in this dangerous border region. Hatshepsut needed strong divine allies when she became the ruler of Egypt. She took Amun-Ra as her father and Mut as her mother and was a devotee of Hathor, Sekhmet and Pakhet. It was Amenhotep III, the "*beloved of Mut*",[53] who showed his devotion to Mut and Sekhmet in the largest possible way, including his famous statues of Sekhmet. His wife Tiy was closely associated with Hathor and Sekhmet and was identified as the Eye of Ra and Sekhmet at her temple at Sedinga, Nubia.

Sekhmet the Beloved

Sekhmet might have been greatly feared, but she was never demonised and had many devotees among the ordinary people. Like all the Feline Goddesses she is a formidable protector when she is on your side. Her devotees petitioned her with the usual requests. "*Favour and love, a sound mouth, and youthful limbs for this life, and a good burial and old age.*"[54]

---

[51] *Sekhmet et la Protection du Monde*, Germond, 1981:179 (My translation)
[52] *Echoes of Egyptian Voices*, Foster, 1992:65
[53] *The Story of Egypt*, Fletcher, 2015:208
[54] *Popular Religion in Egypt During the New Kingdom*, Sadek, 1988:35

CHAPTER 5

INTRODUCING THE OTHER LIONESS GODDESSES

"Pakhet the Great, whose eyes are keen and whose claws are sharp, the lioness who sees and catches by night."[55]

Introduction

There are two types of Feline Goddesses; those who are predominately feline in nature (such as Sekhmet and Bastet) and those who have a feline aspect or alter-ego such as Hathor and Mut (who will be covered in chapter 7.) Bastet was originally a Lioness Goddess before she metamorphosed into her more well-known Cat Goddess form and is covered in detail in chapter 6.

---

[55] *The Ancient Egyptian Coffin Texts Volume II*, Faulkner, 2007:105 spell 470

Mehit (Mekhit or Mehyt)

The origin of Mehit's name is not known. Like all Goddesses she can be *"Mistress of Heaven, Mistress of the Gods"*.[56] Mehit is usually shown as a lioness-headed woman but she can also be shown as a recumbent lioness with three bent poles projecting from her back. She is depicted in this way on a number of early dynastic seals, and her image always precedes the depiction of the typical Upper Egyptian shrine, a square topped by a sloping roof. This suggests that she may have been a protector of sacred places. The poles on her back may represent the flagpoles placed outside the shrine.

She was a Goddess of Upper Egypt associated with Hierakonpolis and the district of This (near Abydos). *"Mehit, Mistress of This, residing in eastern Behedet."*[57] The 20th- 21st dynasty *Berlin* papyrus refers to a woman who was a *"worker of the domain of Mehit"*.[58] There is a Ptolemaic *stele* of Petearpocrates who was the king's scribe and a prophet of Mehyt-in-Abydos. One of her priests left a statue of himself with an inscription explaining that he would act as an intermediary with the Goddess. *"I hear your requests...I convey them to Mehit"* in return for *"offerings on every feast day in the land of Mehit"*.[59]

Mehit is most often known as one of the Distant Goddesses discussed in chapter 12. As well as an Eye Goddess she can also be the *uraeus* and was viewed as a Warrior Goddess. One inscription says that *"Mehyt is behind those who attack her"* which could refer to her sending disease-bearing winds.[60] She has a strong protective role especially in the afterlife. The Temple of Horus at Edfu has a chapel called the *Throne of Ra* where his soul was said to sleep each night and from where he rose each morning. It is decorated with images of Mehit in her lioness form. She protects both the temple and the roads that the Sun God and the deceased have to travel along. The sacred barque on the left side of the chapel describes her as angry and aggressive whilst the barque on the right describes her as peaceful and beneficent. She also protects Osiris.

---

[56] *The Epigraphic Survey of Samanud*, Spencer, 1999:55-83
[57] *Le Role et le Sens du Lion dans L'Egypte Ancienne*, de Wit, 1951:287 (My Translation)
[58] *Two Oracle Petitions Addressed to Horus-khau with Some Notes on the Oracular Amuletic Decrees (P. Berlin P. 8525 and P. 8526)*, Fischer-Elfert, 1996:129-144
[59] *The Gods of Ancient Egypt*, Vernus, 1998:165
[60] *Two Oracle Petitions Addressed to Horus-khau with Some Notes on the Oracular Amuletic Decrees (P. Berlin P. 8525 and P. 8526)*, Fischer-Elfert, 1996:129-144

The Chamber of Behdet at the temple of Edfu contains an image of *"the goddess Mehit and the Divine Ennead, who watch over Osiris"*.[61]

Mehit is associated with two consorts, the main one being Onuris whom she had a cult centre with at This and Samannud (Sebennytos) where the local mythology was centred on Onuris-Shu and Mehit. The temple of Onuris-Shu at Samannud was built between the 30th dynasty and the early Ptolemaic Period. Mehit is depicted on a number of the fragments of granite reliefs. A king makes an offering to *"Mehit...mistress of heaven"* and to Onuris-Shu who wears a four-feathered headdress. An unnamed lioness-headed Goddess with a sceptre is described as the *"Daughter of Re, ruler of Sebennytos...begotten of Re, ruler of heaven, ruler of all the gods"*. There are many fragmentary inscriptions to Mehit including one referencing Nekhtnebef the High Priest of Onuris. One of his names was the *"excellent offspring of Mehit"*.[62] In all the depictions Mehit wears the *atef*-crown. This was the commonest form of crown for the king and all the deities in depictions in this area. The mythology of Onuris and Mehit was much expanded in the Late Period and Mehit was given a Nubian origin. Samannud was the home of the 30th dynasty kings which will have been an influence, and there was also a heightened interest in Lioness Goddesses during the Late Period.

At Esna Mehit was associated with Khnum (the ram-headed Potter God associated with the Nile cataracts). The Goddess Menhyt was a consort of Khnum at Esna which may be the source of this association. Both Goddesses have similar names, and it is not always clear which version of the translated name refers to which Goddess. Khnum was usually associated in a triad with the Goddesses Anukis and Satis (chapter 7). Nekau II (26th dynasty) dedicated an altar at Deir al-Abiad. Much of the inscription is lost but it refers to him as *"beloved by Mehit the great, mistress of Behedet"*.[63]

Menhyt

Little is known about Menhyt. She is named as one of the epithets of Mut in a Ramesside hymn. This hymn addresses ten Goddesses and personifies Menhyt as the *uraeus*.[64] She was worshipped in the Edfu

---

[61] *The Temple of Edfu*, Kurth, 2004:58
[62] *The Epigraphic Survey of Samanud*, Spencer, 1999:55-83
[63] *The statue BMEA 37891 and the Erasure of Necho II's Names*, Gozzoli, 2000:67-80
[64] *Mut Enthroned*, Troy, 1996:313

region and also in the Delta where she was associated both with Neith of Sais and Wadjet. The Ptolemaic temple at Esna depicts her as the consort of Khnum.[65] Trajan (81-117 CE) and Hadrian (117-138 CE) are depicted dancing before Menhyt as part of a ritual to propitiate her.[66] Whether they actually danced before her is not known, possibly the ritual was carried out on their behalf as they wouldn't have known how to perform it properly and it is unlikely that the Emperors of Rome would have submitted to teaching or indeed to performing in the temples.

Mestjet

Mestjet is known as the Eye of Ra from a single inscription on a 21st dynasty *stele* from Abydos and is considered to be a local form of the Eye Goddess. Here a woman and her daughter are depicted offering to a lioness-headed Goddess. She wears the solar disc draped with a *uraeus* and carries an *ankh* and papyrus sceptre.

Pakhet (Pasht)

Pakhet "*who tears (her prey) asunder*"[67] is the most aggressive of the Lioness Goddesses and does not take a benevolent form. Her name means Tearer, or She Who Scratches. Lioness Goddesses were frequently worshipped at the entrances of wadis as this was where lions came out of the desert to drink or hunt. Pakhet's epithets, some of which she shares with Sekhmet, reflect this. She is referred to as Mistress (or Goddess) of the Valley, Mistress at the Head of the Valley and Mistress at the Mouth of the Valley. The "*Goddess at the mouth of the wadi...who opens the ways of the stormy rains*".[68] Pakhet was believed to roam the wadis and scratches on the rocks (caused by floodwater) were seen as the marks left when she sharpened her claws.

Usually depicted as lioness-headed, Pakhet has no special iconography. Depictions of a Lioness Goddess standing over prostrate captives are thought to represent her. A lioness-headed barque of Pakhet escorts the solar barque in a vignette from the *Book of the Amduat*. Like all the Lioness Goddesses she could also appear as the *uraeus*. She was

---

[65] *The British Museum Dictionary of Ancient Egypt*, Shaw & Nicholson, 2008:169
[66] *The Secret Lore of Egypt: Its Impact on the West*, Hornung, 2001:70
[67] *The Sungod's Journey Through the Netherworld*, Schweizer, 2010:71
[68] *Gods of Ancient Egypt*, Watterson, 2003:167

very much a local Goddess and was not widely depicted. The Greeks associated her with Artemis, the Goddess of the Hunt, and called her temple Speos Artemidos – the cave of Artemis. Pakhet is local to the Beni Hasan area in the Eastern desert. She is first attested to in the Middle Kingdom, but there is no evidence of her cult before the early New Kingdom. Pakhet does not appear in any of the Eye Myths, probably due to her limited sphere of influence.

Seret

Seret is a little-known Lioness Goddess. There is an obscure 5th dynasty inscription which references her in the 3rd *nome* of Lower Egypt. This area had a predominantly Libyan population in the early dynastic, so it is possible that she is of Libyan origin. Some translations refer to her as a Goose Goddess but Wilkinson says that this is an error in the understanding of her name.[69]

Shesmetet

This Lioness Goddess is usually considered a manifestation of Sekhmet and sometimes Bastet. She is an ancient Goddess, attested to in the early Dynastic Period when she may have been more independent. One of her epithets is Lady of Punt which hints at a southern origin as well as also being an epithet of Hathor. From the 5th dynasty she is depicted as lioness-headed or as a lioness.

She was associated with, or personified, the *shesmet* girdle from which her name derives. This is an elaborate beaded apron, with a beaded tail at the back, worn on the hips. It was worn by the Hawk God Sopdu (Soped) and must have been of cultic significance as Sopdu has the epithet Lord of the Shesmet. The Egyptian name for *shesmet* may be related to that of malachite. The green colour of malachite gives it symbolism pertaining to life, vegetation growth and rebirth. It was often associated with Hathor. The *shesmet* was part of the symbolic attire of the early dynastic rules. Djoser (3rd dynasty) is depicted wearing one and it might allude to the bull-like strength of the king. The *shesmet* was also worn by women, perhaps to invoke Shesmetet. Could it have had a protective function for the reproductive organs and during pregnancy?

---

[69] *The Complete Gods and Goddesses of Ancient Egypt*, Wilkinson, 2003:183

An elite woman buried at Lisht during the Middle Kingdom wore a *shesmet* as well as necklaces, bracelets and anklets. One interesting feature of this burial was that her grave goods also included stone maces, bows and arrows and a copper knife. A fitting tribute if she had been a devotee of a Lioness Goddess.

At El Kab in Upper Egypt there is a rock-cut sanctuary of Shesmetet. Her protective role is also apparent in the afterlife. She joins the other deities in the Solar Barque as protection against Apophis. *"You stand in the boat of your father, felling the malicious one."*[70] In the *Pyramid Texts* Shesmetet is said to give birth to the king. In the later *Book of the Dead* Shesmetet is considered the mother of all the deceased and thus their protector. In one spell for the *Last Day of the Year* she is invoked against the slaughtering demons aligning her closely with Sekhmet.[71]

Tefnut

In the Heliopolitan theology Tefnut was the daughter of the Creator God Atum and wife of her brother Shu. Creation is often described in mystical or intellectual ways, but in the Heliopolitan one it is basic and biological with Atum either masturbating or spitting to create these first twin deities. It is thought that her name was onomatopoeic in imitation of this expectoration which is, to my mind, an unpleasant and undignified name for a Goddess. Tefnut can be depicted as a woman with a long wig and solar disc and *uraeus*, a lioness-headed woman or a lioness. Shu can also be depicted as a lion and according to one myth they were created as a pair of lion cubs so she is portrayed in this form with Shu in dual-headed designs. Other depictions include a lion-headed cobra and a rearing cobra on a sceptre.

There are few references to Tefnut in the Old Kingdom, but she was a popular image on plaques and amulets in the New Kingdom as the Distant Goddess who transformed into Bastet. Her main cult centre was at Heliopolis where she had a sanctuary with the other members of the Ennead, the nine deities associated with the Heliopolitan theology. Tefnut probably meant little to the ordinary people, and her worship by them was restricted to a few local areas around her cult centres.

---

[70] *Death as an Enemy*, Zandee, 1960:214
[71] *Ancient Egyptian Magical Texts*, Bourghouts, 1978:12-13

At first sight Tefnut is an unusual Goddess to take lioness form as she has a strong water element. Shu is the God of sunlight and air and Tefnut the Goddess personifying moisture. One suggestion is that she represented the atmosphere of lower world and Shu the upper. In one *Pyramid Text* spell she creates pure water for the king and as the pacified Distant Goddess she brought the inundation. Gargoyle spouts on temples often had lion heads which might also be a link to Tefnut in her role as Goddess of moisture. As the daughter of the Creator Tefnut is an Eye Goddess and so contains a strong fire element. *"Tefnut, daughter of Re in Bigga, the great uraeus of Harakhti, the powerful Neseret, mistress of the demons who burns the rebels with the blast of fire in her mouth."*[72] Shu is described as being *"Shu of the House of Flame of his sister"*.[73] Her dual water-fire aspect is reflected by the fact that she is the Solar Eye but does at times take on the role of the Lunar Eye.

According to the Memphis texts Atum is the manifestation of Ptah, but a later tradition says Tefnut is the tongue of Ptah. The tongue is the command which gave rise to creation, which makes Tefnut a Creator Goddess. Tefnut and Shu are the parents of the Sky Goddess Nut and the Earth God Geb. They have important afterlife aspects either as individual deities or as Ruty, the Double Lion, and are covered in this aspect in chapter 8.

The Partially Feline Mafdet

I have included Mafdet for the sake of completeness. Even though she isn't a genuine Feline Goddess she shares some of their traits and the Egyptians didn't categorise animals to the extent that we do. Mafdet is an ancient Protective Goddess and is first attested to in the 1st dynasty. The origin of her name is not clear neither is the animal she is associated with. Some texts (or just the translations) call her a Panther Goddess (meaning a leopard) others associate her with the mongoose or another feline. The type of animal she's depicted as isn't always clear. Sometimes it seems to be clearly feline other times it is a mongoose or similar looking species. This variation may be significant as the Egyptians depicted some species very accurately. Mafdet probably combines the characteristics of

---

[72] *The Ptah-Shu-Tefnut Triad and the Gods of the Winds on a Ptolemaic Sarcophagus*, Kakosy, 1996:221
[73] *Le Role et le Sens du Lion dans L'Egypte Ancienne*, de Wit, 1951:333 (My Translation)

many felines and the mongoose. It isn't clear why; perhaps she was a shape-shifter but the associated mythology is lost. She is particularly associated with prevailing over scorpions and snakes, in line with the talents of the mongoose. There is a named representation of her as a cheetah or leopard on a stone vase from the Early Dynastic Period from a royal tomb at Abydos. Another identifies her as a standing lioness.

Mafdet was important during the 1st dynasty. Part of a seal from Den's tomb shows her insignia. On the Palermo stone Den is depicted fashioning or dedicating an image of Mafdet. An inscription from his tomb at Abydos refers to a year in his reign as "*the year of depicting an image of Mafdet*".[74] Mafdet didn't have a cult of her own, but given her prominence in the 1st Dynasty she might have originally had one. Mafdet loses importance throughout the Pharaonic Period until the Late Period when the mongoose rose in popularity as a sacred, protective animal associated with all solar deities. She was mentioned in temple inscriptions during this period.

Mafdet was important in kingship, possibly responsible for the physical well-being of the king. One of her epithets is "*Mistress of the Estate (House) of life*".[75] She might have been a protector of the living or storage areas of the court and may have been associated with the mongoose and wild cat who killed snakes and scorpions. Or she could have been allied with a tamed big cat, possibly a leopard, who escorted and protected the king as well as symbolising his power and strength. She is mentioned in conjunction with the *House of Life* four times in the *Pyramid Texts,* where she is said to dwell, and she kills snakes with her paws. This reflects the practice of keeping mongooses in the palace to kill snakes. "*Mafdet leaps at the neck of the in-if-snake, she does it again at the neck of the serpent with the raised head. Who is he who will survive? It is I who will survive.*"[76] Her defensive role in the afterlife will be covered in chapter 16.

She has a more dangerous aspect as a punisher of criminals. This is an early role of hers; she is pictured with Den leading away captives. Her standard consists of an instrument used for executions and she is seen as a manifestation of judicial authority. It is a curved pole with a knife lashed to the top, representing her claws, and is based upon one used to decapitate captives. Often a mongoose-like creature is shown running

[74] *Early Dynastic Egypt*, Wilkinson, 1999:259
[75] *Early Dynastic Egypt*, Wilkinson, 1999:288
[76] *The Ancient Egyptian Pyramid Texts*, Faulkner, 2007:88 utterance 295

up the pole. One version shows a lioness but is inscribed as Mafdet. Her scratch was considered lethal to snakes, so the barbs on the king's harpoon were equated to her claws. *"Take this favourite harpoon of yours...whose points are the claws of Mafdet."*[77] She joins in the fight against Apophis whose *"heart is cut out by Mafdet"*.[78] During the Middle Kingdom Mafdet was depicted on magical objects as an apotropaic deity. She was invoked in everyday magical rituals, especially against ghosts and demons. In one example from the 21st dynasty the spell is spoken over a loaf of bread which is then wrapped in fatty meat and given to a cat. As the cat eats the food so Mafdet destroys the malevolent power.

Reflecting the Great Lioness

The pre-eminence of Sekhmet has overshadowed the other Lioness Goddesses. There may have been many more local ones whose names we do not know, most depictions of lioness-headed Goddesses are unidentifiable without an inscription. Some may just have been the local names of a more regional Goddess. As they all share the same characteristics and often the same epithets, the Egyptians would have regarded them as interchangeable. They were one of the many incarnations of the Great Lioness.

---

[77] *The Ancient Egyptian Pyramid Texts*, Faulkner, 2007:193 utterance 519
[78] *The Evil Eye of Apophis*, Borghouts, 1972:114-150

CHAPTER 6

BASTET FROM LION TO CAT

"Bastet, the Great One, the Lady of Busbastis, the Eye of Ra, who is in Behedet, who sits on the throne, who smites the enemies, who is protected by the gods".[79]

Introduction

Today Bastet is widely known, and revered, as a Cat Goddess but she was originally the lioness-headed *"daughter of Atum, the first daughter of the All Lord"*.[80] Although having a similar character to the other Feline Goddesses she doesn't seem to have been as aggressive, possibly having a less dominant solar aspect. In many ways the story of Bastet parallels that of the myth of the Distant Goddess and the domestication of the cat. Because she is so well known Bastet is the deity who is immediately associated with the cat. Other Goddesses can be represented as cats or cat-headed but this is less common. In some vignettes of judgement scenes from the *Book of the Dead* there is a cat-headed woman. She is usually nameless but some authors suggest that

---

[79] *Goddess on the Water: the Sacred Landscape of Bubastis*, Lange & Ullmann, 2015:17-19
[80] *The Apotropaic Goddess in the Eye*, Darnell, 1997:35-48

she is Mafdet. Mut and Hathor are associated with cats but they are not Cat Goddesses. The cat's late arrival meant that most feline deities were too strongly associated with the lion to move towards cat imagery.

Bastet's Name and Epithets

Bastet's name gives no clue to her origins or even her character. It translates as "*She of the ointment jar*".[81] The name is written phonetically using the hieroglyph of a sealed perfume jar. Why would a Feline Goddess be associated with perfume? Was her original fetish a jar or does it allude to the ritual purity of cult? Or is it just that Bastet, like Hathor, enjoys perfume and her name alludes to the pleasures she both brings and enjoys? However that comment is made with the hindsight of her later character, originally she was a much fiercer Lioness Goddess. Some earlier translations give her name as Bast and her name to mean "*She of Bubastis*" which is now not considered accurate. The epithets of Bastet tend to be either geographical or generic such as "*Bastet Lady of Ankhtawy*"[82] or Bastet the Great. An Old Kingdom text calls her "*Mistress of Habes. Mistress of the Two Lands in All her Places*".[83]

Iconography of the Lioness Bastet

Bastet's original depiction was as a lioness-headed Goddess. She was not depicted as a lioness as far as we are aware. In this form there is little to distinguish her from the other Lioness Goddesses, she wears the sun disc and *uraeus* and carries an *ankh* and papyrus sceptre. Some examples are on an 18th dynasty *stele* of Parachutes from Sedment and Middle Kingdom depictions at Armant and Koptos.[84] The lioness-headed Bastet was the only form depicted in temples.

Bastet's Cat Iconography

In later periods Bastet was shown as either cat-headed or as a cat. She is immediately recognisable in her cat-headed form and can appear as a cat, but not every cat is Bastet. There are many thousands of bronze statuettes of the cat-headed Bastet and most are small. Some have

---

[81] *The British Museum Dictionary of Ancient Egypt*, Shaw & Nicholson, 2008:55

[82] *The Gayer-Anderson Cat*, Spencer, 2007:28

[83] *Texts From the Pyramid Age*, Strudwick, 2005:86

[84] *The Cat in Ancient Egypt*, Langton, 2002:64

general inscriptions on such as *"may Bastet give life"*.[85] Others are inscribed with New Year greetings or dedicated for a specific festival. Many just invoke the Goddess and occasionally contain a request. They range in date from the Late Period to the Greco-Roman Period. Most of these will have been votive offerings left at her temples. Excavations at places such as Saqqara and Bubastis have uncovered caches of such offerings. A number were dedicated by people with Greek names hinting at her wide-ranging popularity. Recent excavation at the temple of Heliopolis has uncovered a workshop with practice pieces and a bronze figurine of a cat-headed Bastet.[86]

One common form of statue is patronisingly referred to as the 'housewife Bastet' as she doesn't wear a crown or headdress. In these she wears both Egyptian and Greek-style dresses. The dresses vary from long to short and kilted, and there are different designs of cape and sleeves. Over 20 elaborate patterns on the dresses have been noted.[87] This wide variation in dress seems peculiar to Bastet, but when depicted in her lioness-headed form her dress conforms to the style normally worn by all Goddesses.

In these statues Bastet doesn't carry an *ankh* or sceptre, as these denote sovereignty and in her cat-headed form Bastet allies herself with ordinary people. Some statues show her carrying a small figure of her son Nefertem or a basket. The reason for the basket is not known. It might be used to carry cats or their food and is probably similar to baskets carried by women of this period. It doesn't represent the equivalent of the Classical cornucopia as Bastet does not have any connection with the harvest or plenty. Bastet is shown standing or striding. There are often kittens or a small cat on the plinth the statue stands upon. Are these her sacred cats or does it allude to her fertility and maternal aspects? Does the cat depict her *ba*? We cannot tell, possibly all of these or one of them depending on the situation. The word *ba* is usually translated as the soul of a deity or person; we don't have an equivalent word. A deity's *ba* can reside in an animal or statue, and the *ba* is often depicted as the human-headed *ba*-bird.

Bastet often holds a combination of *sistrum*, *menat* or an *aegis* of Sekhmet. An *aegis* is the Greek word for shield and it refers to a model of a broad collar surmounted by the head of a deity. This is normally one

---

[85] *The Life of Meresamun*, Teeter & Johnson, 2009:40
[86] *News*, Griffiths, 2016:6-14
[87] *The Cat in Ancient Egypt*, Langton, 2002:66

of the Eye Goddesses (Hathor, Tefnut, Sekhmet, Mehit or Bastet) but Isis is sometimes depicted. They had a protective function and are often placed on the prow and stern of sacred barques. One golden *aegis* has the head of Sekhmet but she has pointed ears like a cat. Does this indicate her more benevolent aspect? Bastet is the only Goddess who carries an *aegis*. Perhaps it alludes to her role as the pacified, benevolent form of Hathor or Sekhmet.

The *sistrum* was originally closely connected with Hathor and was an important cult instrument. It is a type of rattle used by her priestesses, when shaken it produces a tinkling sound believed to be soothing to her as it mimicked the sound of rustling papyrus and so reminded her of her home in the papyrus swamps when in her Cow Goddess form. It also drove away evil. The *sistrum* consists of a curved band supporting cross-bars fitted with small metal discs which are attached to a handle. They are normally made of metal and there are some very ornate ones. *Sistra* were popular votive offerings. In the New Kingdom *sistra* were often decorated with cats. Bastet wasn't routinely depicted as cat-headed until the 3rd Intermediate Period but it does suggest that the cat was beginning to be associated with her and Hathor at this period. Hathor has a strong sexual and fertility aspect, so the cat was a good choice of symbol. It was also a solar animal and so a reference to Hathor's solar aspects. When both lions and cats are depicted it is thought that this alludes to the Distant Goddess in both her angry and pacified forms. Through her association with Hathor and the Eye Goddess as well as her Cat Goddess form Bastet soon became associated with the *sistrum* as well. Sekhmet is never depicted with the *sistrum*. It is used to pacify the Goddess and when in her aspect of Sekhmet she is not pacified.

Bastet is also associated with Hathor's other cult object, the *menat*. This is a multi-strand necklace with a large counterpoise of metal, wood or stone. It was usually carried by royal women and priestesses and was connected with pacification rituals, particularly towards the dangerous Feline Goddesses. It too was used as an instrument and shaken. In depictions it is either worn or carried and could contain or channel some of the power of the Goddess. The roundels were sometimes decorated, one example depicts cats wearing *menats*. One

2 - Bastet, Standing with Sistrum

from the 3rd Intermediate Period depicts a Child God offering a *sistrum* and *menat* to an enthroned lioness-headed Goddess labelled Mut-Sekhmet-Bastet.[88] Sekhmet, Mut and Tefnut can also wear or carry the *menat.*

Combined Lion and Cat Iconography

As Bastet has both cat and lioness symbolism both creatures can appear together to represent her, it is usually in the form of a lioness-headed Goddess accompanied by a cat. The lioness is also used to represent Sekhmet showing the relationship between the two. One Late Period amulet depicts Bastet as a walking lioness-headed Goddess with a seated cat.[89] In the Egyptian Museum (Cairo) there is a statuette of Bastet as a seated lioness-headed Goddess with a cat on her lap.[90] A Ptolemaic amulet shows a lioness-headed Goddess with a cat on each shoulder next to a mummiform Osiris with a cat at each side. Without an inscription the Goddess is impossible to identify, but Langton suggests that she is Sekhmet as she wears a sun-disc and *uraeus.* There are also statues of a lioness-headed Goddess with one or two cats on her head.

A fragment of a relief shows the feet of a Goddess who is trampling on two prone captives. A seated cat looks over its shoulder as if to turn its back on the scene. Is this Sekhmet or Pahket trampling the enemies and the benign Bastet turning away? Is the cat on the lookout for more enemies? Is the cat Ra disassociating himself from the carnage? Without further information we can only speculate.

Bastet as a Lioness Goddess

Bastet didn't take the role of the Distant Goddess but was sometimes seen as her pacified aspect, usually in contrast with Sekhmet. Like all the Lioness Goddesses she was the *"Eye of Ra who protects her father Ra"*[91] and was an aggressive protector. She could also be the knife-wielding cat fighting Apophis. Bastet displayed the same ferocity as the other Feline Goddess being invoked as a War Goddess. Battle texts of

---

[88] *Gifts for the Gods: Images from Egyptian Temples*, Hill, 2007:104
[89] *Further on Some Egyptian Figures of Cats*, Langton, 1936:54-58
[90] *Notes on Some Small Egyptian Figures of Cats*, Langton, 1936:115-120
[91] *Egyptian Mythology*, Pinch, 2002:115

Amenhotep II (18th dynasty) describe his enemies being slaughtered like the victims of Bastet. Her dangerous aspect dominates in the *Coffin Texts*, the *Book of the Dead* and in medicinal spells where the "*slaughterers of Bastet*" inflict plague at the end of the year. In some spells the person identifies themselves as her son in an attempt to avoid catching the plague. Gifts, such as small blue glazed flasks and amulets or statutes of cats, were exchanged at New Year and the name of Bastet is often inscribed on them. One is inscribed "*may Bastet give a Happy (New) Year to Pedubaste*".[92] As Bastet and Sekhmet were associated with this dangerous period it was appropriate to thank them once it had passed and a new year began again.

As an Eye Goddesses Bastet could be an agent of divine retribution. The story of Prince Setna comes from the Late Period. He becomes infatuated with Bastet-Taboubu, the daughter of a priest. They meet in the temple at Memphis and she makes him sign a deed handing over all of his possessions. In his blind lust for her he even lets her kill his children. When Setna finally embraces her he finds it has all been a dream and he is lying naked on the highway. This was his punishment for stealing a magical book from a tomb. Bastet-Taboubu may have been a manifestation of Bastet. One of her original roles was to punish those who had offended the deities. In the *Bremner-Rhind* papyrus there is the statement "*as to any servant who shall serve his lord, there shall be no prophet of Bastet against him*".[93] We know nothing more about priests of Bastet as agents of vengeance. In the *Pyramid Texts* she can be the protector, mother and nurse of the king. A relief at Karnak shows a king taking part in ritual races in front of Bastet. Here she is called the Ruler of the Divine Field, meaning Egypt.[94] Bastet played a role in the afterlife which is discussed in chapter 16.

Bastet is the mother and protector of the king but this is not as pronounced during most periods compared to the other Feline Goddesses. At the temple of Sahure the king is shown "*Offering mimi to Bastet*". This is thought to be a grain-based food offering. Bastet replies "*To you I have given all life and dominion, all health, and all joy forever*".[95]

---

[92] *Notes on Some Small Egyptian Figures of Cats*, Langton, 1936:115-120
[93] *The Bremner-Rhind Papyrus II*, Faulkner, 1937:10-16
[94] *The Routledge Dictionary of Egyptian Gods and Goddesses*, Hart, 2005:46
[95] *Texts From the Pyramid Age*, Strudwick, 2005:86

At the Bubastis chapel of Pepy I (6th dynasty) he is shown with Hathor receiving an *ankh* from a lioness-headed Bastet who is *"giving all life"*.[96]

The use of the epithets Son of Bastet in royal names corresponds to the late 22nd dynasties reflecting their affiliation with Bastet. Son of Bastet is used primarily by the kings of this dynasty; Osorkon I and II, Sheshonq III and V and Pimay. Nectanebo I (30th dynasty) was also the Son of Bastet. On one statue Osorkon II asks for protection from the *"censure of Amun, Pre, Ptah, Bastet, Lady of Bubastis, Osiris, Horus, Isis"*.[97] Did he have a guilty conscious about something? These are the deities who are meant to be his protectors.

The Transition to a Cat Goddess

It is not known when Bastet started to become associated with the cat, or even why. A 17th dynasty scarab with the name Bastet incorporating the hieroglyph of a cat is the first evidence of her association with the cat, but this might have been as her cult animal rather than implying Bastet as a cat. The earliest depiction of a cat-headed Goddess who we know is Bastet appears on the 21st dynasty papyrus of *Dirpu* where she leads the deceased into the Judgement Hall.

The domestic cat initially had no religious significance and Bastet was well established as a Lioness Goddess. Was associating her with the cat a way of differentiating her from the other Lioness Goddesses, in particular Sekhmet who had a very dominant personality? Bastet may have been seen as a less aggressive form of Sekhmet from the early periods but until the cat was domesticated there wasn't another creature who could represent her feline but friendly character. Certainly the cat provided a good illustration of the gentler pacified Goddess compared to the angry Goddess depicted in the form of a lioness. However, Hathor was regarded as the gentler form of Sekhmet so why was Bastet needed? This was partly geographical. In areas where Hathor was preeminent she took the form of the pacified

---

[96] *Texts From the Pyramid Age*, Strudwick, 2005:92
[97] *The Inscriptions on the Philadelphia: Cairo Statue of Osorkon II*, Jacquet-Gordon, 1960:12-23

3 - Bastet, Cat Goddess

Goddess, but in the Delta it was taken by Bastet. Although Hathor was an Eye Goddess she wasn't particularly feline in aspect, unlike Bastet.

As her iconography changed to more cat-like Bastet was viewed as more benign. When the cat became widespread and popular its religious and symbolic importance developed and it must have become a symbol in need of a deity. Until the 3rd Intermediate Period Bastet always manifested in, and was depicted in, lioness form although she was associated with the cat from the Middle Kingdom. She did not lose her lioness-headed form and this continued to be used in temples whilst her image for domestic religion changed into the cat-headed or cat form. The Late Period *Brooklyn* papyrus describes a statue of Bastet as "*a statue of a woman with the face of a lioness*".[98] The cat form was obviously considered only suitable for domestic worship, a lesser form which didn't fully depict the Goddess as officially viewed.

Bastet's popularity increased and during the Late and Greco-Roman Periods she was very popular and enjoyed great status especially in the Delta. In the Ptolemaic Period Bastet was the second most popular element in personal names. Osiris was the most popular. A few examples are Bastetirdis and Pedibast meaning "*(s)he whom Bastet gave*" and Senobastis meaning the son or daughter of Bastet. There is also Ankh-Bastet "*may Bastet live*" and Nakhtebasterau "*Bastet is powerful against them*".[99]

The Aspects of Bastet as a Cat Goddess

As Bastet became increasingly associated with the cat, her character became more gentle and friendly. Did the character of the domestic cat influence how Bastet came to be perceived or did she always have a gentler side and the presence of the cat emphasised it? I suspect the latter, in her angry aspect she never seems as dangerous as Sekhmet. Certainly the lioness traits of Sekhmet and the other Goddesses are often absent.

The child-bearing and nurturing instincts are a dominant aspect of the later Bastet and her fertility and fecundity symbolism is important. She was a protector of pregnant women and women in childbirth. She

---

[98] *Goddess on the Water: the Sacred Landscape of Bubastis*, Lange & Ullmann, 2015:17-19
[99] *The Cat in Ancient Egypt*, Malek, 1993:99

retains her protective role in line with the cat's symbolism without the dangerous aspect inherent in the Lioness Goddess. It is easy to see why she appealed to the ordinary people and became increasingly popular. In her cat form she mingled with the people rather than having the more exclusive, remote association with lionesses and royalty. She may have been seen as a 'safer' Goddess than Sekhmet, which is fairly obvious, but she was also in competition with Hathor and especially Isis who was in her ascendance during the Late and Greco-Roman Periods.

Bastet the Cat Goddess shows a number of traits reminiscent of Hathor. They have a number of shared aspects; love, fertility, motherhood, protection and a love of the sensual in perfume, music and dance. For some reason Bastet is not associated with the love songs which were very popular. This was probably because Hathor had such a close association with love and sex and Bastet only assumed these aspects at a later date. Bastet is the *"Goddess great of festivity"*.[100] Enjoyment of life isn't a totally new aspect for Bastet. A text from the 11th dynasty says *"so that you will be happier than the Mistress of Bubastis"*.[101] Perfume was very important to the Egyptians. It was considered a gift from the deities who could be recognised by their divine scent. As well as being used for personal hygiene and pleasure perfume was an important ingredient in medicine and vast amounts were offered in temples. Bastet can be considered a Goddess of Perfume through her strong association with perfume.

Perfume containers were made from a variety of materials such as alabaster, faience, wood and glass. Animal shapes were popular especially felines because the hieroglyph which represented Bastet was that of sealed alabaster perfume jar, the *bas*. The earliest three-dimensional representation of a cat on a larger scale is an alabaster jar in the shape of a cat from the 12th dynasty. It was probably used to store cosmetic oil or medicine. Its eyes are of rock crystal inlaid over copper with a painted pupil. Incised lines on the body suggest tabby markings.[102] Lions were also a popular form especially on royal jars. An alabaster jar from the tomb of Tutankhamun (18th dynasty) has a reclining lion on the lid. A jar from the Late Period is carved in serpentine, a lion of the same height sits beside the jar holding it with his front

---

[100] *Mut Enthroned*, Troy, 1996:311
[101] *Letters from Ancient Egypt*, Wente, 1990:15
[102] *The Cat in Ancient Egypt*, Malek, 1993:52

paws.[103] A lion graces the lid of another alabaster cosmetic jar. He has his front paws crossed and his red tongue hangs out. The jar is decorated with depictions of Asiatic captives.[104]

Cats are the protectors of the grain supply so it is surprising that Bastet plays no role in the harvest or the protection of the granaries. This role is taken by the Cobra Goddess Renenutet and reflects the late arrival of the cat into the mythology as snakes would have been the original protectors preying on the vermin. However, roles were fluid in Egyptian religion, so it is strange that Bastet didn't adopt this role. Possibly by the time of her ascendance Isis had assimilated Renenutet and already taken on this aspect.

Her Relationships

As well as being the daughter of Amun-Ra, Bastet can also be his consort, and their son is the savage Lion God Mahes. Nefertem was usually considered the son of Sekhmet and Ptah. In the Delta he was the son of Wadjet although Bastet is occasionally said to be his mother. He is the God of the Primeval Lotus from which the sun rose and is associated with perfume making, both of which link him to Bastet. Horus is usually the son of Isis but has a number of other mothers including Bastet. This is an unlikely relationship but it does ally her to the important kingship myth and she is one of the mothers of the king.

Hathor had a close relationship with the dwarf God Bes, and Bastet seems to have acquired this as well. They had shared attributes of music and dance, fecundity and childbirth. In the funerary papyrus of *Dirpu* the deceased is shown being led into the judgement hall by a cat-headed Bastet accompanied by a dwarf. A Saite Period bronze (26th dynasty) depicts Bastet as cat-headed but also with the legs and tail of a cat. She wears a short tunic. On her right is Bes playing the lyre. It might depict a ritual of feeding temple cats as one is shown biting the head off a bird. In another section Bes plays a lute and two cats sit at his feet.[105]

---

[103] *Oils and Perfumes of Ancient Egypt*, Fletcher, 1999:51
[104] *Artefacts of Stone*, Duffy, 2012:44-49
[105] *Further on Some Egyptian Figures of Cats*, Langton, 1936:54-58

Alter Egos

The Eye Goddesses all have strong links to each other and Bastet is usually seen as the pacified version of the Eye Goddess Hathor or Sekhmet. Hathor's sensual aspects connect her with Bastet, but she does not have the same relationship with Bastet as she does with Sekhmet. Hathor and Bastet can be complementary through some of their shared aspects. A hymn to Hathor in the papyrus *Bremner-Rhind* says "*Gold rises beside her father in this her name of Bastet*".[106] In the New Kingdom Bastet could be associated with Mut of Thebes. In Bubastis there was a triad of Atum, Bastet and Horhekenu (a version of Horus).

Isis assimilated many Goddesses, especially during the Greco-Roman Period, and Bastet was no exception. An inscription from the temple of Edfu states that the soul of Isis is present in Bastet and in the Kyme *aretalogy* Isis says that "*for me was built the city of Bubastis*".[107] As soon as Isis adopted the *sistrum* as a cult object the connection between the two Goddesses was emphasised by the cat imagery on these objects. The Greco-Roman *Book of Hours* refers to Isis-Bastet.[108] Isis was identified as the *Uraeus* and the Eye of Ra in the hymns, and one hymn from her temple at Philae identifies her with Sekhmet to emphasise her warlike aspect. Overall though, the Lioness Goddesses were not in keeping with Isis' character. Bastet, with her gentler aspects, and her popularity with the ordinary people was a much more suitable match.

The Origin and Development of Her Cult

It is generally assumed that Bastet originated in the Delta and her most important cult centre, Bubastis, was in the north-east Delta. This was an important settlement during the Pre-dynastic and by the end of the 2nd dynasty power became centralised in the Delta region. It is likely that Bastet was a local Goddess adopted by these early kings, but they may have imported deities as part of their state policy. At the start of the 3rd dynasty Bastet is linked with other places especially Memphis (probably via Sekhmet), Heliopolis (as the daughter of the Creator and Sun God Atum) and with Herakleopolis. It is probably safe to assume

---

[106] *The Bremner-Rhind Papyrus II*, Faulkner, 1937:10-16
[107] *Hymns to Isis in Her Temple at Philae*, Zabkar, 1988:140
[108] *An Ancient Egyptian Book of Hours*, Faulkner, 1958:13

that the domestic cat will have originated in the Delta region given that scientists believe that its ancestor was the North African variety of the wild cat.

Bastet, in her lioness-headed form, became prominent during the 2nd dynasty. The earliest depiction of Bastet is on stone vessels from Saqqara which refer to Hetepsekhemwy (2nd dynasty). She is shown as lioness-headed with a *uraeus* on her forehead and she holds a sceptre and an *ankh*. She also appears inscribed on stone vessels of two other 2nd dynasty kings, Raneb and Nynetjer. The later provided priests responsible for the cult of Bastet. There is also a reference to a priest of Bastet at the end of the 2nd dynasty on an incised stone vessel in the tomb of Khasekhemwy.[109]

Incised stone vessels from the step pyramid complex of Djoser (3rd dynasty) depict a lioness-headed Bastet holding a *was*-sceptre next to the king's cartouche.[110] Excavations at a prominent outcrop near Saqqara revealed a rock-cut chamber in the centre of the slope. Inside were statues modelled in clay, terracotta and wood. Most of these depicted Lioness Goddesses but were unnamed. Some were inscribed to Khufu (4th dynasty) and Pepy I (6th dynasty).[111] The Valley Temple of Khafra (4th dynasty) at Giza depicts and names only two Goddesses on the façade; Hathor who represents Upper Egypt and Bastet who represents Lower Egypt. In the geographical lists in the 12th dynasty chapel of Senusret I Isis and Bastet are referred to as the two main deities of the Heliopolitan *nome*.

The cult of Bastet showed a marked rise in popularity during the 3rd Intermediate Period and the first depiction of a cat-headed Bastet is from this period. Was this paralleled with a rise in the popularity of the cat? During this period Egypt was in turmoil, it was a time of uncertainty and disunity. A more benevolent Cat Goddess obviously filled a need but why wasn't this taken by one of the other protective and motherly Goddesses such as Hathor or Isis? One answer was that the 22nd dynasty kings of the period came from Bubastis and they were very devoted to their local Goddess. At the end of the New Kingdom Rameses III (20th dynasty) defeated the Libyans and their allies the Sea-people who had invaded the western Delta. The captured Libyans were placed in military settlements

---

[109] *Early Dynastic Egypt*, Wilkinson, 1999:282
[110] *Early Dynastic Egypt*, Wilkinson, 1999:262
[111] *An Early Cult Centre at Abusir-Saqqara? Recent Discoveries at a Rocky Outcrop in Northwest Saqqara*, Kawai,2011:803

within Egypt and Bubastis was one of the main ones. The later 22nd dynasty kings were descended from these Libyans who had long ago adopted the Egyptian religion. These kings chose Bubastis as their power base and Bastet as their main deity. They also favoured her son, Mahes.

Despite her northern origins Bastet found favour with the Nubians. The Nastasene *stele* lists the wrongdoings of the nomadic Madjay which includes *"they took...property of things that come to Bastet who dwells in Tarae"*.[112]

Bastet and Sekhmet were still popular in the Late Period but were overshadowed by Isis who had begun her rapid rise to prominence. The Ptolemies both respected and adopted the Egyptian deities but the Feline Goddess were less popular. Bastet was largely assimilated by Isis who was at the height of her popularity and power, and she and Serapis became the official deities of the Ptolemies and the state.

The Silent One

With such a popular Goddess as Bastet you would expect to find a lot of primary source material about her, especially as her popularity peaked in the later periods where more evidence has survived. This does not appear to be the situation with Bastet, probably because she was favoured by the ordinary people who left little written trace of their worship. The high volume of cat-related artefacts have to stand as testimony to the Egyptians' love of her.

---

[112] *The Image of the Ordered World in Ancient Nubian Art*, Torok, 2002:342

CHAPTER 7

THE NON-FELINE EYE GODDESSES

"The Mistress of the horizon at her beautiful rising at dawn."[113]

Introduction

The Eye Goddesses are always Daughters of the Sun God but not every Eye Goddess is feline. Hathor and Mut are the main Goddesses in this form, and both are strongly associated with Sekhmet as their angry aspect. Although both have a wide range of aspects they are very different especially in terms of the extent of their cult.

---

[113] *A Crossword Hymn to Mut*, Stewart, 1971:87-104

Hathor

Her Names and Epithets

Hathor's name means *"House of Horus"* and she is the Sky Goddess in which the Hawk God Horus (the Elder) resides. Her name can also be interpreted as the *"Womb of Horus"* emphasising her maternal aspects. Hathor is strongly associated with gold, especially from the New Kingdom when she was called *Nwbt "the Golden"* and similar epithets. This is gold both as the metal and as the colour of the sun.

Hathor was the *"Great One of many names"* and like Isis she assimilated, and was associated with, many other Goddesses especially the Eye Goddesses. In a hymn at Edfu she is referred to *"in your name of"* Mut, Tefnut and Sekhmet.[114] At Karnak there is a list of Hathor's epithets and here she is Mistress of the Mouth of the Valley and Mistress of the Eastern Wadi. All these are epithets of Sekhmet and Pakhet. At Gebelein she is Hathor of the Two Mountains, the mountains of the horizon. Many epithets refer to locations of her cult sites or are the generic titles of all Goddesses, such as Mistress of the Two Lands and Lady of Heaven. Others relate to her aspects or to her relationships with other deities.

Iconography

Hathor is normally depicted as a woman or as a cow, rarely as a cow-headed woman. In both these forms she normally wears a crown consisting of cow horns supporting the red sun disc which emphasises her two most important aspects of Cow and Solar Goddess. In later periods she sometimes wears the vulture cap of Mut and in her afterlife aspect of Goddess of the West she may wear the hieroglyph sign for the west (a falcon on a pole). She can appear as a winged Goddess, unlike the Feline Goddesses. This is probably because her protection is of a gentler form than theirs. Hathor is one of the few Goddesses who carry the *was*-sceptre, as does Sekhmet. She also carries the papyrus sceptre.

One depiction of Hathor is immediately recognisable and distinguishes her from all other deities – her Hathor Head form. In this her face is shown facing forwards, an unusual pose in Egyptian art, and she has cow ears. Her head is depicted in this way on objects such as

---

[114] *Egyptian Mysteries: New Light on Ancient Knowledge*, Lamy, 1986:82

mirrors or when it forms the capital of a pillar. Hathor Head pillars have been used since the Old Kingdom. A number of explanations have been put forward for the Hathor Head including its origin as her Pre-dynastic symbol of a cow skull mounted on a pole. Showing her complete face could allude to the sun disc which is always complete unlike that of the moon (ignoring eclipses). Hathor can also be depicted as a tree but not as a lioness-headed woman as that would indicate that she was in her Sekhmet aspect.

Aspects

Hathor is an ancient and universal Goddess and thus has many aspects some of which have little in common with the Feline and Eye Goddesses. She plays an important role in the afterlife, most often in her Cow or Tree aspect, where she provides food for the deceased and protects them. Hathor is a Sky Goddess but is more the diurnal sky than the starry night sky of the Sky Goddess Nut. Her epithet Lady of Turquoise can refer to the sky as well as the precious stone. Her sky aspect comes largely from her role as the Celestial Cow. This concept was established in the Pre-dynastic when the Celestial Cow became a symbol of creation and the sky.

Hathor is a very physical Goddess, very much of the earth and enjoying its pleasures. Her sensual aspect covers drink, music, dance, perfume, love and sex. Following on from the latter she has fertility aspects, in both humans and in general, and is involved in pregnancy and childbirth. All these ally her closely with the pleasure-loving Bastet. Despite her caring personality Hathor has little involvement in healing and this is probably because it is so strong in Sekhmet.

Her main connection with the other Feline Goddesses is in her role of Solar Goddess. This was an early role. By the 5th dynasty Hathor was worshipped in solar temples and her relationship with Ra was established in myth and ritual. Her crown, with the solar disc usually draped by the *uraeus*, emphasises this connection.

Hathor and Ra

Hathor's main relationship with Ra is as his daughter, the *"Eye of Ra upon his disc"*.[115] It is in this role that she displays her Sekhmet

---

[115] *A New Temple for Hathor at Memphis*, el-Sayed, 1978:1

persona. *"Ra exalts without ceasing, His heart rejoices when he joins his daughter, he swims his firmament, in peace."*[116] It is Ra's love for his daughter which enables him to journey across the sky every day. She is his protector and is often in the Solar Barque. At Dendera Hathor is *"The Eye of Re which illuminates the Two Lands with her rays since the child opened his eye within the lotus-flower".*[117] A hymn to Hathor at Edfu emphasises her solar aspect. *"O Golden One...Uraeus of the Supreme Lord...Luminous One who thrusts back the darkness, who illuminates every human creature with her rays."* She can also be Ra's mother or his partner. As a Sky Goddess it is a simple progression to being the mother of the sun. She is *"Hathor who nurses the dawn".*[118]

The northern tradition held Hathor to be the daughter of Ptah. As part of her *Festival of the Beautiful Union* Hathor of Dendera is reunited with her husband Horus of Edfu. As part of this the statue of Ptah at Edfu was taken to visit his daughter whilst at Memphis Ptah visited Hathor of the Sycamore.

Hathor and Cats

In some parts of Egypt, during certain periods, Hathor was closely associated with cats and did appear to have a cat form. Kings are shown offering to Hathor in her woman and cow form but never as a cat. The cat was considered too domestic to contain the power of the Goddess in royal or official situations. There are a number of factors which could explain Hathor's relationship with cats. The Distant Goddess could take the form of a cat as well as a lion. Bastet has a strong association both with cats and with Hathor and Ra is the Great Cat who kills Apophis. The sexual and fertility symbolism of cats also links them to Hathor who has strong sexual and fertility aspects.

Votive offerings excavated from a number of Hathor temples have yielded cat figurines and objects depicting one or two cats. The earliest precisely datable one is with a cartouche of Amenhotep III (18th dynasty).[119] Pinch has studied votive offerings to Hathor at six sites; Deir el-Bahri in Egypt, Faras and Mirgissa in Nubia, Serabit el-Khadim in Sinai, Timna in the Negev and Gebel el-Zeit near the Red Sea coast. All sites have some representations of cats, but cat votive offerings dominate

---

[116] *Hathor Rising*, Roberts, 2001:60
[117] *The Evil Eye of Apophis*, Borghouts, 1972:114-150
[118] *Ancient Egyptian Literature Volume I*, Lichtheim, 2006:94
[119] *Votive Offerings to Hathor*, Pinch, 1993:189

at temples outside of Egypt especially at Serabit el-Khadim and Timna. She suggests that this is because the Distant Goddess is visualised in cat form outside Egypt. The Egyptians viewed desert areas as hostile and on the edge of chaos, and this might be one reason why they invoked Hathor as a fierce and protective cat rather than in her more usual cow form. The natural environment was also more suited to a cat than a cow.

The blue and green faience plaques have drawings of cats, usually sat on a plinth facing right. Two species are shown, the domestic cat and what appears to be the serval. The plaques date from the 18th to the 20th dynasty. Pinch concludes that these cat plaques represent Hathor, Lady of Mefkat (Turquoise) in cat form. At Deir el-Bahri the cat form of Hathor is comparable to her cow form and associated with the cycle of birth-death-rebirth.[120] The Funerary papyrus of *Nespehergan* depicts a cat seated on a plinth which is decorated with the *wedjat* eye. "*Cat of Lapis Lazuli, great of forms...Mistress of the Good House, grant the beauteous West in peace unto the Osiris.*"[121] Lady of Lapis Lazuli was an epithet of Hathor of Serabit which suggests that this cat was a form of Hathor. A number of faience plaques depicting a serval were found at the temple of Hathor at Serabit el-Khadim. It is thought they are linked to a particular local cult of this region. Some these have the cartouche of Hatshepsut (18th dynasty) and Thutmose III (18th dynasty).

Faience bowls with marsh decorations sometimes have a cat or a pair of cats. Given the popularity of cats in the marsh scenes of tomb paintings, this is not unexpected. Hathor has a strong link with the marshes through her Cow Goddess aspect. Two faience rings decorated with cats were found at the Mirgissa site. At Timna three amulets were found depicting a lioness-headed Goddess. These probably represent Sekhmet or Tefnut. There is a 19th dynasty *stele* dedicated by a couple from Deir el-Medina which depicts two cats flanking a Hathor Head. A fragment of a relief from the 30th dynasty tomb of Kasa and Bukhanef shows two cats sat on either side of a Hathor Head. The cats' heads are turned so they look back towards the Hathor Head which is a very unusual posture. Malek says the context suggests Hathor rather than Bastet, but as it is from Bubastis does it link Bastet with Hathor?[122] Cat decorations appear on *sistra* from the New Kingdom throughout all of Egypt. It is strange that cats should dominate on Hathor's cult *sistrum*

---

[120] *Votive Offerings to Hathor*, Pinch, 1993:196
[121] *The Funerary Papyrus of Nespeher'an (Pap. Skrine, No. 2)*, Blackman, 1918:24-35
[122] *The Cat in Ancient Egypt*, Malek, 1993:93

when her link with cats is quite weak and geographically specific. Probably their important solar and fertility symbolism was the reason for their inclusion.

As cats are sacred to Bastet can we assume that they are also sacred to Hathor? It would appear not and none have been described as the cat of Hathor. There isn't any evidence of many temple cats at Timna or Serabit. Pinch suggests that there might have been one in which Hathor could manifest but all cats depicted on the votive offerings are shown on plinths which suggests statues of cats rather than the cats themselves.[123]

Is Hathor a Feline Goddess?

Hathor has a much wider range of aspects than the other Feline and Eye Goddesses but she does share many traits, in particular her dynamic and independent personality. Like the other Feline Goddess, and the sun, she is essential to life but can also be deadly because of the intensity of her power. She is volatile and needs constant pacification but is loyal to her father, the Sun God, and protects and invigorates him ensuring the continuation of both creation and life. Despite this, Hathor does not come across very strongly as a Feline Goddess. There are two reasons for this; her other aspects are more dominant and when she is at her most powerful and active as a Feline Goddess she assumes her Sekhmet persona. Sekhmet is such a strong Goddess that this removes much of Hathor's feline personality. However, Hathor is unceasing energy. Without her the Sun God is devoid of power, and the cycles of life in all forms depend upon her pulsating energy. With this energy she demonstrates her feline aspects without appearing outwardly feline.

Mut

Name and Epithets

The Great Goddess of Thebes is not particularly well known and it is largely her relationship with Sekhmet, and in particular the vast numbers of Sekhmet statues in her temple precinct at Karnak, that give her visibility today. Her name, *Mwt*, has the same root as that of 'mother' suggesting a role either as Mother Goddess or mother to the king. Her

---

[123] *Votive Offerings to Hathor*, Pinch, 1993:190

name is usually written with the bread and vulture hieroglyphs but the cat hieroglyph is sometimes used. Like many queens and Goddesses she usually wears a vulture headdress. This does not imply that she is a Vulture Goddess. The word for vulture is *nrt*. Vultures were ambivalent symbols for the Egyptians being a carrion eater associated with death and the destruction of the corpse. They were all considered female and were a symbol of motherhood and hence protective. *"The noble vulture of which no male exists."*[124] The word for mother is always written with the vulture hieroglyph.

Mut's epithets are the usual ones of Goddesses. A *stele* of Ptolemy VIII (170-116 BCE) and Euergetes II refers to her as *"Mut, the great, Lady of Xois, Eye of Re, Lady of Heaven, Mistress of all the gods"*. These epithets are exactly the same as those of Tefnut on a *stele* found in the quarries of Maasara.[125] Other generic epithets are *"Lady of the Two Lands...lady of Isheru, Eye of Ra without her equal...Mistress of the House of Amun, Mistress of all the lands"*.[126] She was also the *"Mistress of peace...Lady of Joy"*.[127]

Iconography

Mut is usually depicted as a mature woman, unlike the other Goddesses, to emphasise her political authority and wisdom. She wears a sheath dress, often in blue or red with a featherlike pattern, a long wig and the vulture headdress and the combined crowns of Upper and Lower Egypt. She carries the lotus sceptre of Upper Egypt. As befits an Eye Goddess she was shown as lioness-headed and until the New Kingdom was only depicted in these two forms. She is depicted as lioness-headed on the hypostyle at Karnak and on a statue from the reign of Ramesses II (19th dynasty) she is called *"Mut, the Great, Eye of Re"*.[128] In later periods there are a few depictions of Mut as a vulture and during this period she began to be depicted as a cat. Excavations at the temple of Mut recovered a statue of Mut in cat form. One vignette on the Metternich *stele* is of a cat seated on a shrine labelled *"Mut, Mistress of*

---

[124] *The Goddess Mut and the Vulture*, te Velde, 2008:244

[125] *A Xoite Stela of Ptolemy VIII Euergetes II with Cleopatra II (British Museum EA 612)*, Lezno, 2015:217-237

[126] *Popular Religion in Egypt During the New Kingdom*, Sadek, 1988:149

[127] *Excavating the Temple of Mut*, Fazzini & Peck, 1983:16-23

[128] *Le Role et le Sens du Lion dans L'Egypte Ancienne*, de Wit, 1951:350 (My Translation)

Asheru".[129] Mut also has a fearsome aspect as a winged ithyphallic woman with three heads; that of a lion, a vulture and a woman. In the *Book of the Dead* (spell 164) she is invoked in this form by the deceased to save them from a second death. The spell is recited over a statuette of the three-headed Mut.

Aspects

A lot of the information we have about Mut comes from fragments of a crossword hymn to Mut dating to the 20th dynasty. In a crossword hymn the text reads the same in two directions. Stewart (1971) gives a full translation of this hymn.

Mut is the bearer of the crowns of Egypt. "*The crowns of Upper and Lower Egypt being established on her head.*"[130] Her role is that of regent rather than a personification of the crowns and like Isis she can be seen as a manifestation of the throne "*being under the king as the throne*". Her authority to rule comes directly from Ra "*she has ruled because of him*". This automatically aligns her with kingship and Mut can be another of the king's mothers. "*The kingship comes into being in her name.*"[131] A relief on the doorframe of the temple of Mut shows Hatshepsut offering to Mut who is depicted as a woman. It was during Hatshepsut's reign that Mut became really prominent and was depicted with the double crown of Egypt. Hatshepsut aligned herself with Mut's fierce and powerful aspect reminding people that she wasn't to be crossed.

The Kushite kings of the 25th dynasty associated themselves with Mut and Amun, particularly emphasising Mut's regal association and their right to rule. They carried out extensive work on her temple and their royal women were heavily involved in Mut's cult. A fragmentary scene from the Luxor temple shows Ptolemy XII (80-51 BCE) worshipping Mut and her entourage. An enthroned Mut is accompanied by Hathor, Isis and a Goddess with the Red Crown. Mut holds an *ankh* in her right hand and a papyrus sceptre in the other. The text is fragmentary but above Mut it reads "*recitation by Mut...Raet in the circuit of the sun disk... (she of) the Two Ladies of the double crown*".[132]

---

[129] *The Metternich Stele*, Scott, 1951:201-217
[130] *A Crossword Hymn to Mut*, Stewart, 1971:87-104
[131] *Mut Enthroned*, Troy, 1996:302-303
[132] *A Fragmentary Scene of Ptolemy XII Worshiping the Goddess Mut and Her Divine Entourage*, Johnson & McClain, 2008:137

Mut is described as the Daughter of Ra and can take on the role of the Distant Goddess. The Eye Goddesses are all considered the visible manifestation of the Sun God, namely the solar disc, but this role is particularly emphasised with Mut. She is *"great of sunlight, who illuminates the entire land with her rays"*.[133] Her face is described as the sun disc and she is the *"goddess in the sun disk, the sole one who encircles what is below"*. In this imagery she has almost taken over the role of the Sun God. As the Eye of Ra Mut can be the Distant Goddess and also the *uraeus*. *"The coiled one, the fearsome one, the foremost of awe...the one who overthrows the rebels for her father."*[134] She is also *"Wadjet who is united with his brow"*.[135]

In texts at Karnak Mut is given a celestial character and she is identified with the sun, again taking over the roles of the Sun God. *"Arise in Glory, O Manifest One...the Great Ennead and the Little Ennead are pleased with the perfume of her fragrance, happy with that which the Eye of Horus, the Bright One did. The gods come into being from her tears and Atum is vivified in her flesh. This incense is for Mut as a gift of king Memere."*[136] In the accompanying relief she is depicted as lioness-headed wearing the solar disc and *uraeus*.

In the crossword hymn Mut takes on the role of Creator. *"Everything came into being because of her...mankind and gods are her offspring...everyone is united to her ka."*[137] She created through visualisation and particular emphasis is placed on her role as nourisher of vegetation. She made the *"papyrus and the fruit tree through her wish"*. Mut is the one who *"spits out the Nile...placed plants on the entire land"*. Through her light *"all good plants are born"*[138] and she brings prosperity to the land. Her responsibility for the essential food crops emmer and wheat are specifically named in the hymn. As the solar disc, Mut takes on the role as preserver of life for without her there would be no life. She is also referred to as Lady of the Sea and this water aspect links her to Tefnut.

---

[133] *A Crossword Hymn to Mut*, Stewart, 1971:87-104
[134] *Mut Enthroned*, Troy, 1996:302-304
[135] *The First Pylon of the Mut Temple, South Karnak: Architecture, Decorations, Inscriptions*, Fazzini & van Dijk, 2015:19
[136] *Certain Reliefs at Karnak and Medinet Habu and the Ritual of Amenophis I (Concluded)*, Nelson, 1949:310-345
[137] *Mut Enthroned*, Troy, 1996:304-305
[138] *A Crossword Hymn to Mut*, Stewart, 1971:87-104

Mut's Relationship with Ra

"His daughter of his two eyes, she having appeared as his mother, through whom he is protected."[139] As with Hathor, Mut can be both the mother and daughter of the Sun God. Like the other Eye Goddesses Mut has a close, if somewhat fraught, relationship with her father. Mut is not identified with the sky or the heavens but is found within them; they are a place where she reigns, which was given to her by Ra. In this she acts as her father's heir. It is important to remember that this interpretation is based on the crossword hymn which may have emphasised certain aspects or introduced new ones. Without other hymns to compare it to it is difficult to know if this was the understanding of Mut in the earlier periods.

Her Relationships with Other Goddesses

Mut has the dangerous aspects associated with the Eye Goddesses but, as with Hathor, Sekhmet tends to take over this role and Mut is seen as the benevolent, pacified Eye Goddess. Sekhmet is *"the flame of Mut"*.[140] The return of the Distant Goddess was re-enacted in the temple of Mut and when Sekhmet bathed in the temple lake she was transformed into Mut. An 18th dynasty statue refers to her as Mut-Sekhmet. At Memphis Mut rather than Sekhmet could be the consort of Ptah. Mut is also paired with Bastet. The *Crossword Hymn* calls her *"Mut-Bastet, mistress of the Two Lands, Ruler of the banks, great of might in the bark of Re"*. At times she was paired with Hathor and Isis. She is described as being in the company of Neith and allied to Nekhbet and compared with the *"likeness of the lady of justice"* namely Maat.[141]

The Origins and Extent of the Cult of Mut

Mut keeps her secrets. There is no reference to her until the Middle Kingdom but by the New Kingdom she formed the Theban triad with Amun and their son Khonsu. Triads became popular in the New Kingdom and some have suggested that she was invented as a more suitable wife for Amun, others that she was a minor local Goddess of Thebes who rose to prominence. Amaunet was one of the original deities of creation which formed the Ogdoad. They represent pre-creation aspects, those of

---

[139] *Mut Enthroned*, Troy, 1996:302
[140] *The Story of Egypt*, Fletcher, 2015:208
[141] *A Crossword Hymn to Mut*, Stewart, 1971:87-104

Amaunet being hidden power. It is not surprising that Amaunet lost her place to a Goddess with a more concrete personality. Details of a Mut ritual from the *Berlin* papyrus suggests that her cult was founded upon the myth of *the Return of the Distant Goddess*.[142]

Apart from her cult and temple at Karnak Mut had sanctuaries at Tanis, Giza and Heliopolis. There is a Middle Kingdom reference to her as Mistress of Megeb. From the reign of Hatshepsut Mut was depicted in all the major temples but she was not widely worshipped. This was probably because she was largely a Goddess for royalty. There is one reference to her worship by an ordinary person during the New Kingdom. Zimut-Kiki *"found Mut above all the gods"* and bequeathed her his entire fortune. *"I gave her all my possessions...she alone is effective. She took away my distress; she protected me in difficult times. She came, preceded by her sweet breath, when I called her name."*[143]

Mut and the Cat

Votive offering statues of cats were dedicated to Mut and the cat may have been considered her sacred animal. The similarity between the word *Mwt* and that of cat, *miit*, may have suggested the connection to the Egyptians. Zandee suggests that the cat was associated with Mut before Bastet. The Greeks associated Mut with their Goddess Hera. A votive offering of a bronze cat was found dedicated to Hera of Samos.[144]

A 20th dynasty *stele* depicts the *"cat of the mistress of heaven"* and *"goose of Amun"* and is dedicated to *"give praise to Amun; to kiss the earth before Mut"*. The *Ritual for Mut* from the *Berlin* papyrus of the 3rd Intermediate Period refers to Mut in the form of a cat. *"Let us dance and shout for our Mistress in her form in which she was when she was found at the splitting of the ished-tree together with Re in Heliopolis."*[145] A relief at the Shrine of Mut in a Luxor temple shows two decorated jars. Two cats sit either side of one of the jars while two lions flank the other. Above both jars are papyrus and the Hathor Cow. These jars probably held wine or beer for festivals.

---

[142] *The Cat as a Scared Animal of the Goddess Mut*, te Velde, 1982:135
[143] *The Gods of Ancient Egypt*, Vernus, 1998:181
[144] *The Cat as a Scared Animal of the Goddess Mut*, te Velde, 1982:136
[145] *The Cat as a Scared Animal of the Goddess Mut*, te Velde, 1982:132-134

Is Mut a Feline Goddess?

Although Mut is called the Eye and the *uraeus*, has an association with cats and a relationship with Sekhmet she does not come across as a Feline Goddess. She is very much a Solar Goddess and in character is more like Hathor. Unlike Hathor she is not widespread nor well known.

Satis and Anukis

Anukis (Anuket) is the Goddess of the southern border region of Egypt and of the Cataracts and since the Old Kingdom was considered a Daughter of Ra and an Eye Goddess. Her name may mean *"embracer"* but it is not clear if this refers to a loving embrace or a strangling one. This may be an indication of the dual temperament common in the Eye Goddesses. She is depicted as a woman wearing a headdress with long plumes and she carries the generic *ankh* and papyrus sceptre. Her sacred animal is the gazelle. In some mythologies she was considered a pacified Eye Goddess. She is strongly associated with the inundation and can also be one of the mothers of the king. Her cult was established by the Old Kingdom and centred on the Aswan region especially at Elephantine and Sehel. She was also worshipped in Lower Nubia. In the New Kingdom she became part of a triad as the daughter of Satis and Khnum. At Thebes Anukis was associated with Hathor and at Kawa she appears to have been considered equivalent to Mut. A 25th dynasty Kushite shrine at Kawa is dedicated to Amun-Ra. One king, Aspelta (600-580 BCE), is shown standing before Amun-Ra of Thebes and Mut on the eastern wall and before their Nubian counterparts Amun-Ra of Gematen and Anukis on the western wall. On the walls of this shrine is the only known representation of Anukis as two separate Goddesses; Anukis Nethy and Anukis Ba. The king is shown standing with Sekhmet on the northern wall. Analysis of the paint remains indicates that the dress of Anukis and the hair of Sekhmet were painted blue.[146]

Satis (Satet) is another southern Goddess who guarded the frontier with Nubia and was associated with the inundation through her identification with the star Sirius. The *Pyramid Texts* refer to her as *"the burning one"* who is more powerful than Ra.[147] She is usually depicted

---

[146] *The Two Non-Blue Amuns of the Shrine of Taharqa at Kawa*, Armstrong, 2015:177-195
[147] *The Ancient Egyptian Pyramid Texts*, Faulkner, 2007:146 utterance 439

as a woman wearing the White Crown of Upper Egypt. She is sometimes the consort of the Theban Warrior God Montu but is usually considered the consort of Khnum. Like Anukis she is a daughter of Ra and is considered the angry version of the Eye Goddess, probably due to her more warrior-like aspect.

Although both these Goddesses are sometimes referred to as the Eye of Ra neither of them has feline or solar attributes or associations. It is probable that they took on the role of the Eye Goddesses due to their strong association with the inundation and because they were popular local Goddesses of the southern border regions.

Raet - The Female Sun

The Goddess Raet first appears in the *Pyramid Texts*. Her name is the feminine form of the name Ra which has led some to suggest that she was created to compliment Ra or to show the dual gender of the Creator rather than being an individual Goddess in her own right. She is also called Raettawy, which means Raet of the Two Lands. Her other epithets are those common to most Goddesses; Lady of Heaven and Mistress of the Gods. She was the "*sun-goddess, mistress of cities*". Like Sekhmet she was sometimes associated with Thebes and there is a hymn to "*the goddess Raiyt and Thebes*".[148] One text from Abydos is for "*adoring the goddess four times*" although the king is shown kneeling before Ra-Harakhti. The king recites "*hail to thee, Rait, mistress of the Two Lands, Hathor who resides in Denderah…men rejoice when you shine, the rhyt live and every god is in awe of you*". (The *rhyt* are the ordinary people.) He also addresses her as the "*female falcon*".[149]

There are only a few depictions of Raet and she is shown in a similar form to Hathor as a woman wearing the cow horn sun disc and the *uraeus*. Sometimes there are two feathers above the disc. From the little information we have, Raet seems closest to Hathor and may be an aspect of her or a similar local Goddess. There is nothing to suggest that Raet was an Eye or Feline Goddess. She does not play a part in any of the mythology.

---

[148] *Hymns, Prayers and Songs*, Foster, 1995:69
[149] *Temple Ritual at Abydos*, David, 2016:71

CHAPTER 8

FELINE GODS –
A DIFFERENT ENERGY

"The Great Cat who dwells in Heliopolis."[150]

Introduction

Given all their solar imagery and power it is strange that the lion isn't a major symbol of the Solar Gods. Even the creator Amun-Ra has little lion imagery, there are very few references to Ra and lions, and he is rarely depicted in that form. In one spell in the *Book of the Dead* the deceased says *"I am the Lion, Re"* but is this lion really a manifestation of Ra or one of his aides?[151] In a vignette for spell 62 of the *Book of the Dead* Ra is shown as a lion with a yellow mane. The likely reason for this lack of lion imagery is that the lioness was strongly connected with the original female power in the form of the Eye Goddesses, which was well established before the Solar Gods rose to prominence. It was not appropriate to assign the same symbol to the Solar Gods who frequently

---

[150] *The Gods and Symbols of Ancient Egypt*, Lurker, 1986:39
[151] *The Gods and Symbols of Ancient Egypt*, Lurker, 1986:77

took the form of the falcon. As with the Goddesses there are genuine Lion Gods whose standard form and character is leonine and there are Gods who can take lion form but show little if any feline aspects.

Aker

Aker is an ancient God. The plural of his name is Akeru and these were Pre-dynastic Earth Gods. He, or they, had no independent cult and were more of a cosmic-geographic deity. Aker was originally depicted as a strip of land with a lion or human head at each end, one facing east the other west. Later he was shown as the front parts of two lions then as a double-headed sphinx who provides access to the afterlife for the deceased and guards the body of the Creator. His main role is funerary. Later funerary texts include the *Book of Aker* or the *Book of Earth*. This was inscribed in the tomb Rameses VI (20th dynasty) in the Valley of the Kings. Aker's afterlife role will be covered in chapter 16.

Why would an Earth God be depicted as a lion, given their strong solar symbolism for the Egyptians? One reason may be the guardian aspect of lions. Aker guards the gates of the east and west horizons which are the entrance and exit to the underworld and important places of transition. In effect it is a double horizon; the west where the sun dies and the east where it is reborn, so it needs two guardians. It was often depicted as a pair of trees guarded by a double sphinx or lion. The word *akhet* means horizon. On a purely visual level in a dry, dusty land the coat of a lion will soon match the colour of its surroundings. The monochrome sight of a lion walking in a swirling cloud of dust could be perceived as the earth itself taking animal form. The Double Lion image on amulets and magic wands may represent Aker as a symbol of protection or renewal. He was believed to neutralise poisons in the body if someone was bitten or had eaten poisonous or bad food. Certain types of clay are used medicinally as they are said to prevent the body from absorbing poison.

In this double form Aker is similar to Ruty (see below) and it is not always easy to differentiate between the two of them. The same image, of two lions back to back, is described variously as Aker, Ruty or other Gods such as Ra or Amun.

Mahes (Mihos or Miysis)

The name Mahes means Savage Lion, the word *mahes* appearing in the *Pyramid Texts* to denote a lion. In the Middle Kingdom names incorporating Mahes appear but he is not referenced as a God until the New Kingdom. His other epithets further emphasise his aggressive nature such as "*Savage-faced*" and "*Lord of Slaughter*".[152] He is not depicted as a lion, which is strange given his leonine name, but as a walking man wearing a short kilt and the *atef*-crown. Other headdresses include the sun disc and *uraeus*. During the 22nd dynasty he was associated with Nefertem and sometimes wears Nefertem's lotus headdress. Like Nefertem Mahes can be the son of Bastet or Sekhmet. Mahes often holds a knife and a clump of lotus flowers, a further connection to Nefertem. An amulet from the Late Saite Period depicts Nefertem standing on the back of a lion who represents Mahes. He can also be associated with Horus and Ra.

Mahes is believed to have originated at Leontopolis in the eastern Delta where his main cult centre was. There was a temple here in the 18th dynasty but there is only evidence of his worship from the Late Period. He was locally important in the Delta but doesn't appear in any myths. He was seen as a War God and Guardian of sacred places and helped in the fight against Apophis.

Osorkon III (22nd dynasty) built a temple to Mahes in the northern part of the temple of Bastet at Bubastis. His cult spread south and he is represented in the Greco-Roman temples of Dendera, Edfu, Philae and Diabod, and Dendur in Nubia. His worship was also attested to at Bahariya Oasis and Siwa Oasis. Mahes is mentioned in amuletic papyrus of the late New Kingdom and is frequently depicted in small glazed amulets or bronzes in the Late Period.

Ruty

Ruty is the name of the divine twin lions or Double Lion. The word *ru.ty* translates as a pair of lions and he was associated with the eastern and western horizons. Ruty can be depicted as a single lion or a lion-headed God but is most frequently shown as a pair of lions sitting back to back. In the hieroglyph for the word horizon the image of Ruty can

---

[152] *The Gods and Symbols of Ancient Egypt*, Lurker, 1986:32

replace that of a mountain on either side of the horizon. By the time of the New Kingdom Ruty was a pair of lions and the sun rose over their backs. *"Ruty who comes forth from the sky"* is a cosmic deity.[153] The Double Lion may be an ancient God, in the *Coffin Texts* he is described as being older than Atum. He is a mysterious God who was neither seen nor heard. Despite this Ruty was present in popular religion. The amulet form of Ruty symbolised the daily regeneration of the sun, an important symbol in both life and funerary contexts.

Ruty could be the Creator God Atum just prior to creation where he represents the divine force awakening within himself. *"Atum who goes forth...magically empowered as Ruty."*[154] The Double Lion as a concept can also refer to the first generation of the deities - Shu and Tefnut. The *Leiden* papyrus says of Atum *"his soul is Shu, the air, his heart is Tefnut, the fire"*.[155] This association was present from the earliest times. As an Eye Goddess Tefnut is a Lioness Goddess but a leonine form is not an obvious one for Shu. He is the God of sunlight and air but he isn't solar, in fact he has more lunar aspects (which is discussed in chapter 13). There is no doubt that the Egyptians held him to have lion aspects and the *Coffin Texts* refer specifically to Shu as a lion. Shu and Tefnut have always been siblings and partners so it was easy to depict them as twin lions which then merge into the Double Lion. Shu and Tefnut were venerated in lion form at the Delta town of Leontopolis where they were regarded as lion cubs created by Atum. Shu isn't always equated to the Ruty. One spell in the *Book of Two Ways* refers to *"Shu and Ruty, Shu to the sky, Ruty to earth"*.[156] Or does this mean that the cosmic Shu becomes part of the Double Lion when he manifests on earth?

Shu and Tefnut are the parents of the Sky Goddess Nut and the Earth God Geb. Nut and Geb embraced so closely that there was no space for any life to exist. Shu, on orders from Ra, separated them. In doing so he created space and he and Tefnut become aspects of time. Shu illustrates the concept of eternal recurrence and Tefnut eternal sameness; everything has to change to survive yet all remains fundamentally the same. The Egyptians had two words for eternity, *neheh* meaning always and *djet* meaning persistently. When used

---

[153] *An Ancient Egyptian Book of Hours*, Faulkner, 1958:23
[154] *An Ancient Egyptian Book of the Dead*, O'Rourke, 2016:168 spell 3
[155] *Egyptian Mysteries: New Light on Ancient Knowledge*, Lamy, 1986:79
[156] *The Ancient Egyptian Book of Two Ways*, Lesko, 1977:112 spell 1103

4 – Ruty

together they appear to be the equivalent of our phrase 'forever and ever'. *Neheh* implies eternal cyclical movement, it is a masculine word and is depicted as an image of the sun. *Djet* is a feminine word and is represented by an image of the earth. It implies immovable consistency.[157] This is contradictory to other Egyptian concepts as the earth is often equated with Gods and the female power of *sekhem* is solar and constantly moving. Shu and Tefnut can also have the different temporal meanings of yesterday and tomorrow as they bind together the passing days. On an ivory headrest of Tutankhamun (18th dynasty) the column depicts Shu who supports the head of the king and he is flanked by two small images of lions. Symbolically the king sleeps between the guardians of yesterday and tomorrow, which is a good way of describing sleeping through the night.

The *Naos of the Decades* was commissioned by Nectanebo I (30th dynasty). It was one of many shrines produced in the Late Period which recorded cultic, mythological and astronomical information formerly held on papyrus within the temple libraries. The unsettled times and fear for the future prompted this desire to start preserving sacred knowledge in a more secure and permanent form. The *naos* originally stood in the temple of Shu at Saft el-Hinna then was moved to the Canopus region

---

[157] *The Egyptian Calendar: A Work For Eternity*, Bomhard, 1999:xi

where the various fragments were found. The inner wall depicts Shu as a seated lion and explains that the *"real-life image of the god"* was 30cm high and made of silver covered with gold.[158] The outside surfaces of the *naos* are covered with a calendar which divides the year into *decans* and gives details of the influence which Shu and the *decans* had on life on earth. (*Decans* are covered in chapter 17.)

Tutu (Tithoes)

Tutu is an obscure God and was unknown before the 3rd century BCE and he shows a Greek influence. He was depicted as a walking lion, a human-headed sphinx or as a composite deity with wings and a snake tail. Sometimes he had extra heads of crocodile, ram, falcon or ibis showing that he had incorporated the power of other deities. Given the variety of pre-existing deities it seems strange that people felt the necessity for a new hybrid. Was this 'pick and mix' approach symptomatic of the Greco-Roman Period with the decline of the established religion, changing society, increased superstition and new influences? Were the single deities no longer seen as proactive and benevolent whereas a compound one would be? Was polytheism faltering, with so many deities to choose from was it safer to merge the many into one? Or was it a way of trying to show the all-encompassing power and aspects of a deity?

Tutu was mostly venerated for his apotropaic aspects and was said to be the son of Neith. She has no leonine aspects and was probably deemed to be his mother as she was an important Goddess in the Delta. A late 1st century CE inscription calls him *"the most violent, the valiant lion who strikes whoever opposes him"*. Originally he was seen as one of the Gods fighting Apophis, but in the Roman Period he became popular as the *"Chief of the emissaries of Sekhmet"*.[159] As the leader of Sekhmet's demons he could protect people from them and he had strong magical powers. His gaze was said to have the power to repel maleficent forces. Another epithet was *"the one who keeps enemies at a distance"*[160] and he was often depicted holding knives or axes in his paws to fight these enemies.

---

[158] *Sunken Cities Egypt's Lost Worlds*, Goddio & Masson-Berghoff, 2016:137
[159] *Religion in Roman Egypt*, Frankfurter, 1998:116
[160] *Magic in Ancient Egypt*, Pinch, 2006:36

Tutu was a popular local deity in the Delta. At Deir el-Hagar is a tomb with an astronomical ceiling which shows Tutu standing behind Opet (the hippo). On a similar ceiling at Esna he is shown in a different position with the 3rd month deities, which might be because he had a local festival with Neith in the 3rd month of *Akhet*.[161] Tutu was also one of the Gods of the Dakhla Oasis. He had a mudbrick shrine dating to 2nd century CE at Kellis where he is depicted with Neith and a local Goddess called Tapsais. Paintings on walls in private houses in the Roman town of Karanis include Tutu.

Apedemak of Nubia

Nubia had a close relationship with Egypt during many periods and in the north of Nubia, Meroe, the Egyptian influence is clearly seen. Their Lion God Apedemak was the most leonine of the Gods discussed so far and is an entirely African God despite Egyptian influence. He is normally depicted as a lion-headed man with a lion and he holds a sceptre topped by a seated lion. Other depictions include a lion or a lion-headed snake. He was often accompanied by lions. Apedemak is a War God particularly associated with battles. He was also identified with the inundation. Excavations have uncovered shrines to him in the channels designed to carry water from the Nile.[162]

His principal cult centres were at Musawwarat el Sofa and Naqa. Both of these are in the desert to the east of the Sixth Cataract in Sudan. His largest known temple was at Musawwarat where he was worshipped from 300 BCE to about 450 CE. It was an important place of pilgrimage. There is a long prayer to him inscribed in hieroglyphics. He is described as the "*splendid god at the head of Nubia, lion of the south, strong of arm*".[163] Hieroglyphics might have been seen as more prestigious or sacred than the Meroitic script.

The influence of Egyptian religion is seen in some of these temples. Apedemak might not have lost his Nubian origins but he gained Egyptian deities in his temples. In the Lion temple at Naqa Apedemak is depicted with Hathor and Amun and also as a triad with Isis and Horus. Apedemak was integrated with the Eye Goddesses although he retained

---

[161] *The Astronomical Ceiling of Deir el-Haggar in the Dakhleh Oasis*, Kaper, 1995:175-195
[162] *Lion*, Jackson, 2010:111
[163] *The British Museum Dictionary of Ancient Egypt*, Shaw & Nicholson, 2008:37

his independence. Amenhotep III built temples in Nubia honouring himself and his wife Tiy. At Sedeinga Tiy was identified with Hathor and her Lioness Goddess counterparts Tefnut and Sekhmet. As the Nubians were familiar with lion deities these Goddesses obviously resonated with them. The Eye Goddesses remained favourites in Nubia long after Egyptian rule had ended. One item from King Shabaka's (25th dynasty) tomb is a bronze and gilded silver mirror. The handle is composed of four figures. One is the queen (or possibly the king's sister) the others depict Hathor, Sekhmet and Mut.[164]

Other Gods with Lion Forms

As with the Goddesses, some Gods can be referred to as lions or depicted as such without really being leonine deities. Depicting a God in lion form emphasised their majesty and power. Min is shown with a lion's head on a few occasions, such as in the temple of Khonsu at Karnak. A New Kingdom papyrus refers to Ptah as *"light in the day, lion in the night"*.[165]

Amun

Amun is a Solar Creator God and for many Egyptians was the supreme deity. In the New Kingdom he became Amun-Ra, a manifestation of the Sun God. His sacred animals are the ram and the goose. As a Solar God he can be associated with the lion but he is usually depicted as a man. Amun is described as the *"fierce red-eyed lion"*.[166] He can be the *"Rampant lion with knife-edged claws, in a swallow he drinks the power and blood of pretenders"*.[167] A New Kingdom hymn to Amun-Ra describes him as the *"Hidden Lion with resounding war-cry, who hugs to himself whatever comes under his claws"*.[168] The 18th dynasty temple at Kawa (Nubia) is dedicated to Amun-Ra *"the lion over the south country"*.[169] Here he is a fusion of Amun of Thebes and a local Lion God.

---

[164] *Jewels of Ancient Nubia*, Markowitz & Doxey, 2014:121
[165] *Le Role et le Sens du Lion dans L'Egypte Ancienne*, de Wit, 1951:229 (My Translation)
[166] *The Routledge Dictionary of Egyptian Gods and Goddesses*, Hart, 2005:14
[167] *Ancient Egyptian Literature*, Foster, 2001:167
[168] *Hymns, Prayers and Songs*, Foster, 1995:72
[169] *Between Two Worlds*, Torok, 2009:239

From the start of the Middle Kingdom Amun of Thebes was a very important deity and his name is often inscribed in cryptic form on amulets. One example is on the base of a scarab dating from the Late or Greco-Roman Period. It has the hieroglyphs for the sun disc, a cat and a basket; *aten*, *miu* and *neb*. Reading just the initials gives *amn* which is Amun.[170] The basket looks like the perfume jar hieroglyph used for Bastet's name and she can be represented by a cat and, as a daughter of the Sun God, by the sun disc. Was this writing of Amun's name also a reference to Bastet who was sometimes considered the consort of Amun of Thebes?

Bes

Bes was a popular deity, he was friendly and protective and helped women in childbirth. He is depicted as a dwarf with a lion-like face, which may have originally been a mask, and he sometimes wears the entire skin of a lion. He was a favourite of Hathor and her cult and was often shown dancing and playing music for her or accompanying the Distant Goddess on her return to Egypt. Although connected with the Eye Goddesses he does not have any solar or feline attributes. Bes was often depicted with Bastet and with cats. Both are pleasure-loving and associated with fecundity and birth.

Horus

Horus is usually depicted as hawk-headed or as a hawk but there are a few depictions of him as lion-headed. As a Solar God Horus does have a connection with the solar lion but this is seldom emphasised. During the New Kingdom he could be depicted in leonine form in his aspect of Horem-akhet, the rising sun. He was later identified with the sphinx in this form. Referring to him as a lion was often more a way of emphasising his regal status rather than any lion attributes. At Edfu he was called "*Noble Lion*" while at Dendera he was "*the Great Lion*", "*Living Lion*" and "*Lion King of Punt*".[171]

The Falcon God of Letopolis was Mekhentyirty, a form of Horus, and in the Late Period he was closely associated with Wadjet. There are lion-

---

[170] *The Cat in Ancient Egypt*, Malek, 1993:92
[171] *Le Role et le Sens du Lion dans L'Egypte Ancienne*, de Wit, 1951:242 (My Translation)

headed depictions of Horus of Buto, which was the cult centre of Wadjet.[172] Blocks from a cult building of Ptolemy XII (80-51 BCE) have been found at Tell Maessalem, near Port Said in Sinai. One fragment shows part of a lion-headed God. It has been suggested that this relief is of a lion-headed Horus because at nearby Tell Heboua there is a statue of a seated lion-headed God which is inscribed as Horus Lord of Mesn.[173]

Nefertem

Nefertem was the young God of the Blue Lotus (*Nymphaea cerulean*) which rose out of the primaeval waters and opened to reveal the infant Sun God. Through this he was a God of Perfume. At Memphis he was the son of Sekhmet and Ptah and in the *Coffin Texts* he was the son of Sekhmet, but at Buto he was considered the son of either Wadjet or Bastet. He was usually depicted as a man with a lotus flower headdress but because of his mother and his solar associations he could also be shown as lion-headed or as a lion. There is a statue of him with a seated cat at his feet. Nefertem was a royal deity and wasn't commonly worshipped although there are a reasonable number of Late Period votive offerings to him. As the son of Sekhmet he might have been feared or appealed to for protection from her plagues. An amuletic decree from the 3rd Intermediate Period promises to protect the new-born child from the harmful manifestations of Nefertem.

Thoth

Although normally seen in ibis and baboon form there are a few references to Thoth as a lion. This is probably a result of his association with Shu, who has leonine form, in the myth of the Distant Goddess. Thoth of Pnubs was particularly associated with Shu. Some of his epithets are *"Lion of the south, mighty in strength"* and *"Lion with dreadful growl"*.[174] He was the *"living lion who repels the rebels"*.[175] It is unlikely that he actually took lion form. This might have been a safer option when

---

[172] *A Wooden Figure of Wadjet with Two Painted Representations of Amasis*, James, 1982:156-165

[173] *Searching for Ptolemy XII: Inscriptions from Sinai*, Hussein, 2016:28-29

[174] *Thoth Or The Hermes Of Egypt*, Boylan, 1922:186

[175] *Le Role et le Sens du Lion dans L'Egypte Ancienne*, de Wit, 1951:274 (My Translation)

he was trying to pacify the raging Distant Goddess but then it might have aggravated her further.

In the *Book of Thoth* there is reference to the House of the Lion. "*May his fingers work in the house of the lion...he becomes an apprentice of the Servant of Thoth.*"[176] The significance of the House of the Lion isn't clear but the text infers that the apprentice will have to do a lot of studying. Is the House of the Lion a library of Thoth in his lion form? There is a town in the 7th *nome* of Upper Egypt called the House of the Lion. However Jasnow cautions that this might just be a miswriting of, or a pun on, the House of Maat as the words are similar.[177] Thoth has a very strong connection to Maat and this pun may also have emphasised his identification with the lion.

Ra and the Great Cat

Ra is the only God who is depicted as a cat which reflects the cat's late arrival after the majority of the religious symbolism had been established. Another major factor may be the association of the cat with all things feminine.

Ra is the Sun God of Heliopolis and is most commonly depicted as a falcon wearing the sun disc draped by the *uraeus*. He has strong links with the monarchy and became the supreme Creator God alongside, or merged with, Amun. The solar theology was fused with that of Osiris and the nightly journey of the sun paralleled the deceased's journey through the underworld where they were reborn like the sun. Despite various problems with humans and other deities Ra's nemesis is the Chaos Serpent Apophis. He represents the hostile forces of the pre-creation chaos which forever threaten creation and each night tries to destroy Ra and with him everything. Apophis can never be defeated, only warded off until the next sunset.

By the Middle Kingdom the cat was associated with Ra because of its ability to kill snakes, regardless of any other solar attributes. Lions were not known to kill snakes. A statue of a cat from the Saite Period has the face and breast of a falcon. This might be a depiction of the dual aspects of Ra. Taking the form of the Great Tomcat Ra fights and kills Apophis under the *ished*-tree in Heliopolis. This is referred to in the

---

[176] *The Ancient Egyptian Book of Thoth*, Jasnow & Zauzich, 2005:192
[177] *The Ancient Egyptian Book of Thoth*, Jasnow & Zauzich, 2005:198

Coffin Texts and also in spell 17 of the *Book of the Dead*. "*I am the cat who split the side of the isd-tree in the night when the enemies of the All-lord were destroyed. Who is that male cat? It is Re himself who is called miw because of the speech of Sia. He is like that which he has made, thus his name is cat.*"[178]

The *ished*-tree was a sacred tree and at Heliopolis was sacred to the Sun God. The Greeks called it the persea. Its fruit was said to ripen with the inundation making it very symbolic. It is thought that the persea was a species of *Mimusops*, a fruit-bearing evergreen. This tree was also sacred to Hathor and later to Isis. Its flowers were considered life-giving and called the "*flowers of life*".[179] When Ra split the tree in two it became the Two Trees of the Horizon. This seems to be the first active role of Ra; normally he just gives orders. When in his cat form Ra seems at his most proactive, a reflection perhaps of feline energy. What is the relevance of the tree symbolism? The sun was born at the eastern horizon so it was appropriate that Apophis would wait there in the hope of ambushing the new-born sun. Snakes are often found in or under trees either resting or lying in wait. Was the tree split by the stroke that killed Apophis? The story could have originated when a lightning strike was seen splitting a tree. Originally the sun would have appeared to rise from the tree; now it rose between the two parts.

The *Litany of the Sun* lists Ra's 75 names and 74 forms. In this Ra appears as the Great Cat or Great Tomcat and also as the cat Muity, who is a gatekeeper in the underworld. The funerary monument of Thutmose III (18th dynasty) shows the king being suckled by Hathor the Sycamore Goddess. With him are his six wives and various forms of the Sun God including that of a cat. The golden shrine of Tutankhamun shows a cat-headed Sun God, there is also a depiction of him in a lion-headed form. At Heliopolis there was a cat-headed image of the Sun God. The original Great Cat of Heliopolis was probably a swamp cat which lived in the marshes of the Delta.

A number of *stelae* dedicated by craftsmen in Deir el-Medina show Ra in the form of a seated cat. One from the 19th dynasty shows an unnamed couple shown "*offering prayers to the Two Great Cats*". The one on the right is the "*Cat of the god Re*", that on the left is the "*Great Cat, the peaceful one, in his perfect name of Atum*".[180] This depiction of the two

---

[178] *The Goddesses of the Egyptian Tree Cult*, Buhl, 1947:80-97
[179] *The Goddesses of the Egyptian Tree Cult*, Buhl, 1947:80-97
[180] *Ancient Egypt and Nubia*, Whitehouse, 2009:90-91

aspects of the Sun God is unusual; normally such duality is seen in the Goddesses, especial the Eye Goddesses. The depiction of the couple appears generic; it was probably bought readymade without a personal dedication.

Another *stele* from Deir el-Medina depicts two cats. "*To give praise to the great tom-cat...O peaceful one who is peace. Thou lettest me see darkness through what thou hast done. Make light for me that I may behold thy beauty. Turn unto me, o peaceful one, versed in forgiveness.*"[181] The phrasing about seeing darkness is probably a reference to blindness which was sadly very common in Egypt. It was often viewed as a punishment from a deity as a consequence of a transgression. In the *Litany of Re* there is the phrase "*Homage to thee, Re, supreme power, Great Cat...thou art the bodies of the Great Cat*".[182] This does imply a duality to the Great Cat, possibly the male and female aspects of an androgynous creator.

The Nebre *stele* from Deir el-Medina shows a cat and a swallow being worshipped. They are referred to as "*the good cat*" and "*the good swallow*". The cat is probably Ra and the swallow an unknown local deity.[183] Without inscriptions it is not clear if the cat is Ra or just associated with him. The cats brandishing knives on ivory wands may be Ra in the form of the Great Cat or just his helpers and protectors.

The Character of Lions

The Feline Gods of Egypt differ considerably from the Feline Goddesses and their Nubian counterpart Apedemak. This is because their underlying character and energy are very different. Only Mahes and Tutu give the impression of being true Lion Gods in terms of their aggressive character and appearance. Both are later deities and Tutu in particular shows a strong Greek influence. Ra only takes the form of a cat because it is a solar animal who kills snakes.

Aker and Ruty, the Twin Lions, don't show many characteristics of lions apart from their guardian aspect. Both are Earth Gods and both appear in dual form. While the Lioness Goddesses represent the energising life-giving life-taking power of the sun, the Lion Gods take on

---

181 *The Cat as a Scared Animal of the Goddess Mut*, te Velde, 1982:133
182 *The Litany of Re*, Piankoff, 1964:27
183 *The Animal World of the Pharaohs*, Houlihan, 1996:87

the characteristics of the earth with its solid, reassuring and protective aspects – the safety and comfort of home or dry land and the protective roles of doorway, gate and passage guardians. Lions are most active at twilight and during the night, and this is the time when Aker and Ruty become important, in the dark of the underworld that the Sun God and the deceased have to travel through. The Lion Gods lack the duality of the Lionesses with their angry-pacified aspects although this is present in Ruty as Shu and Tefnut.

CHAPTER 9

CREATION AND THE ORIGINAL POWER

"Sekhmet, Lady of the Original Power."[184]

Why the Preponderance of Lioness Goddesses?

Other countries, such as Nubia, have Lion Gods but none that I am aware of have native Lioness Goddesses. This is something unique to Egypt. Here, most feline deities are Goddesses, the majority associated with the lioness but some can be associated with the cat as well. Why is this? In art depictions of lions are far more common than those of lionesses. This is not surprising as their mane makes them very distinctive and they were well-established symbols for the monarchy and other male heroes. Lions were considered 'worthy' opponents of kings. As Egypt was an absolute monarchy it is all the more significant that Lioness Goddesses dominate. It was the nature of the feline energy which

---

[184] *Sekhmet et la Protection du Monde*, Germond, 1981:109 (My translation)

caused it to be manifested in Goddesses rather than Gods and this energy goes back to the time of creation.

The Creation of the Universe According to the Egyptians

Before creation there were only the primaeval waters of the *nun* which were endless and boundless. The *nun* is a chaotic region (although it is actually the antithesis of a place being both nowhere and everywhere) where *maat* (order) has no sway. Chaos has many negative associations but it also has positive ones. It is fertile because it contains potential which is essential for manifestation.

Although there are a number of creation myths and Creators the basic principle is the same; in the shapeless, formless *nun* something happened, and the seething potential came together to create our universe. The Creator existed as consciousness in an inert form which managed to bring itself together to create everything out of nothing. There were three main creation theories which originated in Hermopolis, Memphis and Heliopolis. The Hermopolis theory was based on Thoth and eight primaeval deities, the Ogdoad, who personified aspects of the *nun*. Of more concern to the feline deities were those of Memphis and Heliopolis. At Memphis the Creator was Ptah who used his powers of thought and speech to manifest the universe while at Heliopolis the Sun God Atum used the less elegant biological means of masturbation or spitting. Goddesses were also Creators. At Esna it was Neith who emerged from the *nun* to create the universe as did the Celestial Cow. Isis and Hathor were also given the role of Creator at times.

The snake was often used as a symbol of the Creator due to its undivided body and the way it sheds its skin symbolising rebirth. With the death of the universe Atum will revert back to snake form and sink back into the *nun*. The negative, destructive elements of chaos were also personified as a snake, the Chaos Serpent Apophis. He dwells in the *nun* as a non-existent form constantly emerging to attack the Sun God and the created world. The powers of chaos were held at bay at the perimeter of creation, hence the recurring battles with Apophis. As the temple was a metaphor of the created world, the enclosure walls were often decorated with the symbol for water which represented the waters of the *nun* surrounding creation

Creation floats like a fragile bubble in the waters of the *nun,* held in existence by the five strands used to create it; *maat, heka,* time, energy, and matter. *Maat* is order; it is the laws of physics and of nature. Without *maat's* control everything would revert to the chaos of the *nun.* The two main deities associated with *maat* are Maat and Thoth. Maat, the Goddess personifying cosmic harmony, is a consort of Thoth and is a Daughter of the Sun God Ra. Thoth is a constant upholder of law and justice. *Heka* is the magical force. It is the mysterious force which we can't yet, or maybe never, explain. It is seen in the effectiveness of correctly spoken words of power, the life-force, the secrets of the magician and the healer, in wisdom and creativity and the miraculous answering of prayers. The God Heka is a personification of this magic power which is heavily manifested in Isis and Thoth.

Time enables growth, change and decay and it produces destiny and the multiple cycles of nature. The main deities associated with time are the first generation of deities in the Heliopolitan theology Shu and his sister and consort Tefnut. These first three strands of creation (*maat, heka* and time) can be represented by, or manifest in, both Gods and Goddesses. The final two strands of energy and matter are treated differently and they are viewed as female and male respectively.

Sekhem is the original power that arose at First Time, the instance of creation, and which drives creation. It is heat, light, fire and especially the life-giving energy of the sun. The Goddess Sekhmet is the divine and visible representation of *sekhem* and she embodies these primaeval energies in both their negative (destructive) and positive (protective) forms. We tend to characterise protective energy as good, but often the outcome depends on your point of view. Are you the one being protected or protected against? In most cases we are not talking about a power of two separate entities which are either good or evil in intent but a range on a continuum of the same power. Heat will keep you alive until it reaches a certain temperature and then it will start to kill you. There is no malicious intent just a biological and physical fact. Two opposites can be complimentary. The Egyptians were fascinated by apparently contradictory forces and how they could be reconciled.

Matter is inert and inanimate. It forms the substance of everything living and otherwise and is acted upon by the other four forces. Unlike most other cultures the Egyptians had Earth Gods; Geb, Aker and Ruty. Gods in other cultures tend to take an active role but the Egyptian Earth

Gods tend to be passive. Osiris can also be considered a Chthonic God and he had very passive aspects.

One element is missing from these strands, the essential one of water. Other cultures viewed the earth herself as fertile but Egyptian theology developed in a dry landscape and water was seen as the generator of fertility with the earth seen as largely inert. Water was believed to originate from the waters of the *nun* appearing on earth either through a subterranean source, such as water seeping into wells, or as rain. The origin of the inundation was said to be from a cavern beneath the First Cataract. The membrane separating creation from the *nun* was permeable and both the beneficial (water) and the dangerous (chaos) could enter. The Egyptians didn't have water deities to any great extent and this might be in part due to the belief that water came from the *nun*. Not even the Nile had a resident deity; the God Hapy presided over the inundation rather than the river itself. It was only in Greco-Roman times that Isis acquired a strong water element. There are Chaos Gods in the form of Apophis and Seth.

As everything created came from the chaotic *nun* then it must contain elements of its birth. The original power will contain chaotic elements too, but this is a chaos which is a part of creation and which plays a critical part in the maintenance of creation. It can be used to fight against the chaos which invades directly from the *nun* and undermines the stability of creation and it also prevents *maat* from becoming too rigid; for in perfect order there is no movement and no growth. The ultimate objective of creation was survival and self-sustaining life; of animals, plants and humans in the created world, of the souls of the deceased in the afterlife and of the deities.

The Egyptians knew that something was controlling creation and causing regular cycles and chaotic events at all levels, from the celestial bodies down to small components of an individual's life. The concepts and natures of the deities arose partly from trying to understand these forces and being able to predict, if not control, them. When a deity was worshipped it was their divine power that was being worshipped. This power manifests as the deity in heaven (or wherever you consider the deity to reside) and in a reduced form on earth in their statue, sacred animal or natural event. This does not mean that a deity is merely a natural force personified. Plutarch (46-119 CE) said that such a concept would *"put into men's minds dangerous and atheistic notions, by transferring names of Gods to natures and to things that have no sense or soul*.[185]

Lioness energy was important in two out of the three creation myths and one of Sekhmet's epithets was *"Mistress of the Beginning"* reflecting her role in creation.[186] In the Heliopolitan theology the Creator was considered to be the Sun God; variously Atum, Ra or Atum-Ra and Sekhmet is his daughter. At Memphis the Creator is Ptah and it is his consort Sekhmet who provides the primaeval energy for Ptah to channel into creation. The God or male principle can't achieve anything alone but needs the Goddess or female principle to activate and energise him. Consciousness needs energy to be active and energy needs consciousness otherwise it is chaotic and aimless. The interplay of male and female energies is very prominent with the feline deities. This leads into the other concept which had long fascinated the Egyptians, that of duality. Duality fed into their beliefs with Dual Goddesses and each living being having a double or shadow of themselves. The dual aspect is particularly prominent in the Feline Goddesses and will be covered in chapter 13.

The third creation myth, of Hermopolis, does not require feline energy. The primaeval deities of the Ogdoad consisted of four frog-headed Gods and four snake-headed Goddesses which already had the necessary balance of male and female energies. The Goddess Neith was considered a Creator who rose from the *nun* as was the Celestial Cow Mehet-Weret. Being Goddesses they apparently had no need of the feline creative powers.

The Representation of Power

The Egyptians used a number of other animals to depict power such as the snake, hawk, crocodile and bull. Power has many forms; the power of the king, physical strength, fertility, magic and so forth. Power depicted by a lioness will have been subtly different to the power suggested by other animals. Sekhmet in particular was associated with *sekhem*, the primaeval power of creation. Her lioness form was considered the visible manifestation of this power. But why was this? The understanding of *sekhem* must have preceded the selection of the

---

[185] *Plutarch: Concerning the Mysteries of Isis and Osiris*, Mead, 2002:241
[186] *Les Statues Thebaines de la Desses Sakhmet*, Gautier, 1920:117-207 (My translation)

lioness to depict it. What does a lioness represent that the other animals can't? It isn't clear if the concept of *sekhem* was recognised in the Pre-dynastic but if it was it didn't appear to be depicted in leonine form. The *uraeus* may have originally incorporated *sekhem* as well as other forms of power and as the Egyptian's understanding of the concept deepened it was separated out and depicted in leonine form.

The Lioness Goddesses

The lion and cat were considered ideal symbols of solar power and came to embody the original power of *sekhem*. This power was considered female which led to the dominance of the Lioness Goddesses. As her name suggests Sekhmet became the ultimate Lioness Goddess. This predominance of the Lioness Goddesses was further reinforced because sun's disc, the Solar Eye, was regarded as female and the Lioness Goddesses were considered the Eye of the Sun.

The nature of *sekhem* is inseparable from the fundamental nature of the Feline and Eye Goddesses. This is illustrated by looking at what happened with Isis. As she rose in importance during the Late and Greco-Roman Periods Isis absorbed Feline Goddesses such as Sekhmet and Bastet but she didn't become a Feline Goddess herself. Similarly, when Isis assimilated Hathor and aligned herself with the Solar Tradition, she never became an Eye Goddess because it is not in keeping with her fundamental character. Unlike the volatile Feline and Eye Goddesses Isis is focused and self-controlled. Her underlying power is that of *heka* not *sekhem*.

CHAPTER 10

THE EYE OF THE SUN AND THE *URAEUS*

"Thy Living Eyes which emit fire, thy Heavenly Eyes which lighten the darkness, awake in peace, so thy awakening is peaceful."[187]

The Importance of Eyes

Eyes are of great importance to all cultures as sight is our most important sense; eyes are the most significant part of the face in terms of identifying a person and in non-verbal communication. The eye is one of the most widespread and complex symbols of Ancient Egypt. As the main providers of light for the eye to see by, the sun and moon were closely linked with the eye, they are also a similar shape. They were considered the eyes of the Creator, the *"Fiery eyes who came forth from Sekhem"*[188] which links them back to Sekhmet and her personification of the original power. The sun and moon were of divine substance but

---

[187] *The Litany of Re*, Piankoff, 1964:47
[188] *An Ancient Egyptian Book of Hours*, Faulkner, 1958:24

were not usually considered deities in their own right. Both had deities who were closely associated with them.

The Solar and Lunar Eyes

The Solar and Lunar Eyes are the visible discs of the sun and moon. The Solar Eye is usually the right eye of the Sun God (Atum or Ra) and is considered to be his daughter who is known as the Eye Goddess. The Lunar Eye is the left eye and is often referred to as the Eye of Horus (this being Horus the son of Isis and Osiris). In addition, Horus the Elder was originally considered the Creator and the sun and moon were his eyes so both can be referred to as the Eye of Horus and both can be the avenging eye. However the symbolism is fluid and one hymn to Horus says *"Thine eyes are thine, Horus, thy right eye is Shu, thy left eye is Tefnut"*.[189]

As the word for eye, *irt*, was feminine the Eye was seen as a Goddess and so the daughter of Ra. The word sounds like one used for 'doing' so the Eye was viewed as the active principle of the divine and associated with divine intervention. She becomes his agent, his striking power. The Creator contains both male and female energies and aspects but our language struggles with this concept. By giving the Sun God an independent Solar Eye Goddess the Egyptians might have been attempting to express the initial androgyny of the Creator. The Solar Eye has two aspects. On the positive side it has creative power and is an agent of life and renewal powering life on earth. It provides the light to see by and which allows the vegetation to flourish. On the other hand there is a dangerous aspect to the sun's heat, and this was an ever-present threat in Egypt. It desiccates vegetation, dries up water sources and turns fertile land into barren desert bringing drought and famine.

If the Eye of the Sun was female then why wasn't the Eye of the Moon? The Egyptians always had a Lunar God either Thoth, Khonsu or Iah. It wasn't until the Greco-Roman Period that the Greeks introduced the concept of the Lunar Goddess. Perhaps the perceived masculine energy of the moon was more significant than the gender of the word for eye. Lunar energy is not as obviously active as solar energy is. Another factor may have been that the cool and male Lunar Eye balanced the hot and female Solar Eye. Eye symbolism is not straightforward though and Tefnut can sometimes be equated to the moon. One of Mehit's epithets

---

[189] *The Litany of Re*, Piankoff, 1964:52

is "*She who has been completed*". Watterston suggests that the word *Mehit* was used to refer to the Healed Lunar Eye and that this got merged with the myths of the Eye Goddesses.[190]

The Element of Fire

As we are dealing with the fiery Eye Goddess it is worth investigating the Egyptians' beliefs about this element. Fire has very important and powerful practical, symbolic, and magical attributes for all cultures. The Egyptians had about 30 words which translate as fire or flame, four being in common usage; *khet, sedjet, nesret* and *neser*. *Khet* is an earthly, practical fire. It is the heat of normal fire or smoke. It has both protective and dangerous qualities. It was relevant in reference to both domestic and magical uses and was also associated with the desert.

Sedjet has a strong connection with water. It is water based and hotter than *khet*, which suggests something like burning oil or a liquid which burns such as acid. In the *Pyramid Texts sedjet* was said to come from the watery *nun* which would give a strong water element. "*O flame which came forth from the Abyss.*"[191] *Sedjet* was sent by Satis and Anukis from the south, both Goddesses are associated with Elephantine and the mythical source of the inundation. It is strongly linked with the power of the sun. In one *Coffin Text* spell it is described as part of the third portal of the underworld. "*The rivers around her are flames of sedjet. One is khet. Two is heat. The third is the blast of the mouth of Sekhmet. The fourth is nun. Four rivers are flames of sedjet fire.*"[192] *Khet* denotes its essential nature, fire, to which is added power from Sekhmet and fluidity from the waters of the *nun*. *Sedjet* predominates in the *Coffin Texts* which emphasises its importance in terms of the journey through the underworld and rebirth. The worthy deceased are protected and given light by *sedjet* but to the undeserving and enemies of Ra it brings destruction, hellfire. For the latter reason it also dominates in the *Book of Overthrowing Apep*.

Nesret and *neser* are usually translated as flame but they appear to be purely conceptual. Their transliteration is *nsr.t* and *nsr*. The addition of the 't' denotes a feminine noun. This may imply that the different types of energy were considered male and female. *Nesret* is directly linked to

---

[190] *Gods of Ancient Egypt*, Watterson, 2003:35
[191] *The Ancient Egyptian Pyramid Texts*, Faulkner, 2007:55 utterance 233
[192] *Playing with Fire*, Smethills, 2014:12-16

the *uraeus* and can refer to both her and her flame. *Nesret* is also an epithet of Sekhmet. Its use was common in the Ramesside Period when clay figurines of cobras were placed in houses to ward off demons and disease. The *Cairo* calendar refers to *"the great nesret which is in your house"*.[193] In medical texts it is used in the context of fevers and the burning sensation of poison.

In the *Pyramid Texts neser* is associated with a fiery blast of air. *"Unas is neser at the head of the wind to the limit of the sky and the limit of the earth."* Air connects it to speech and there is a pun with the word for tongue, *nes*. In the *Coffin Texts* it appears to be a type of inner energy, a force which enables the soul to depart from the body after death. *"The neser of my soul shall not be upon my corpse, my soul will not be restrained."*[194]

The Eye Myths

Eyes are very vulnerable and eye diseases and blindness were unfortunately very common in Egypt. The Eye myths reflect this, with the *Wounding of the Eye of Horus*, as well as illustrating cycles of separation and convergence. Cycles of myths associated with the Eye Goddesses became increasingly prominent during the 3rd Intermediate Period and the Late Kingdom.

Before creation the original state was one of unity, but separation and space were needed for the creation of the universe. The Creator God separated from the *nun*, Shu and Tefnut left their father and then Shu separated Geb and Nut to create space for life. But what has been split will eventually come back together. Energy and nature can't be static and they have a natural oscillating cycle, like snakes winding around a staff. Divergence tends to be initiated through conditions such as isolation and boredom as well as anger and destruction. The original entity splits into two. These tend to polarise as *maat* and mildness versus chaos and anger with like attributes clustering together to generate duality and balance. Convergence comes through pacification, loneliness and restoration of the original unity. On an everyday level convergence brought the inundation and the return of prosperity. On a cosmic scale

---

[193] *Playing with Fire*, Smethills, 2014:12-16
[194] *Playing with Fire*, Smethills, 2014:12-16

convergence will bring the end of creation when it returns to the *nun* and the Creator.

There are three basic themes to the Eye myths two of which will be covered in this and the following chapters. Firstly separation and reunification - the Eye retrieves Shu and Tefnut from the *nun* and Shu (or Onuris or Thoth) brings back the wandering Eye Goddess. Secondly, creation and destruction - humanity is created by the Eye and later destroyed by it. The third, wounding and healing, only applies to the Lunar Eye and is a reflection of the waxing and waning of the moon. The Lunar Eye is injured by Seth and restored by Thoth. The sun will wander north and south over the year but with the exception of the eclipse its disc is always full, hence the journeys of the Solar Eye. The moon does move about the sky but its most noticeable feature is its waxing and waning, hence the injured and restored Lunar Eye. Robbing or damaging the Eye of Horus was a common theme in some Middle Kingdom texts. In the *Book of Two Ways* there is reference to wounds on the face of the Sun God which is comparable to Seth injuring Horus and damaging his Eye. This may have been influenced by the memory of the chaos of the 1st Intermediate Period and the return to order with the Middle Kingdom.

The Protective Eye

The Eye myths give rise to the most important aspect of the Eye, namely its protective function. Much of this role of the Eye is either as the *uraeus* or in the symbol of the *wedjat* eye. The *wedjat* eye is the most important Eye symbol. It combines the human eye with the facial markings of a falcon and represents the healed Lunar Eye of Horus. Through that, it represents healing and wholeness. The *wedjat* eye could also represent the Solar Eye and symbolised power and protection. A *wedjat* eye made of a red material, topped by the *uraeus* or facing right could represent the Solar Eye. *Wedjat* eye amulets were placed on mummies and the *wedjat* eye was frequently offered to deities. Having healed the Lunar Eye Thoth offered it to Ra or Horus and this became the precedent for offering the symbol to all deities. The *wedjat* eye is associated with wings (as is the solar disc as wings symbolise protection), the *uraeus* and felines.

Another element of protection is that of the pupil. As the iris surrounds the pupil, so the power of the Eye Goddess surrounds the protected person or deity. One spell in the *Book of the Dead* describes two *wedjat* eye amulets with figures, such as Bes or Neith, where the pupil would be. Amulets from the Late Period echo this with combinations of dwarves and Feline Goddesses. On one *stele* it says "*May you set your iris-and-pupil as my protector*". The word used is *dfd* which alludes to the Goddess in the Eye.[195] At the eastern end of underworld is the place of the *dfdy.w* "*those relating to the pupil*". These are the blessed dead whose heads mingle with the face of the sun. In this context *dfd* is the Eye of the Sun and the defender of the Solar Barque, namely Sekhmet or Bastet.

In some depictions of the Eye a child or dwarf is present inside the Eye. Here the pupil is comparable to the womb in which the divine child, or sun, is formed. The child inside the Eye represents the sun which will be born at dawn. In one of the funerary texts of the Netherworld Hathor is referred to as she who "*clothes her lord with her light, she hiding him within her pupil*".[196]

The Angry Eye

The first Eye myth is that of the Angry Eye which results in the creation of the *uraeus* and humanity as a by-product. After Shu and Tefnut had been created they did not remain with Ra but drifted away into the *nun*. Ra then sends his Sole Eye to look after them and bring them back. "*By my father Nun, the Primordial Waters, were they brought up, my Eye watching after them since the aeons when they were distant from me.*" At this early point in creation his Eye appears to have been a separate active force. Shu and Tefnut evolved in the *nun* rather than in the newly created world. Ra said "*I came into being in this earth, but Shu and Tefnut rejoiced in Nun*".[197] They contain the elements of the *nun* within themselves but don't appear to have absorbed its chaotic element. Not everything which comes from chaos is bad and Shu and Tefnut portray the good aspects of the *nun* in terms of its fertility, regenerative ability and life-giving water. Tefnut will have acquired her watery aspect from her time in the *nun*.

We do not know why they wandered away from Ra. Perhaps the created universe wasn't yet strong enough to nurture or hold them or maybe they needed to be separate to develop on their own. Lamy

---

[195] *The Apotropaic Goddess in the Eye.* Darnell, 1997:35-48
[196] *The Enigmatic Netherworld Books of the Solar-Osiran Unity,* Darnell, 2004:134
[197] *The Wisdom of Ancient Egypt,* Kaster, 1968:56

suggests that the story of Shu and Tefnut wandering off and the Eye searching for them explains the beginning of movement in creation with the introduction of space and time which is essential for the development of life. Physical space is needed to move into and time is needed to allow this movement.[198] The Eye *"gave light to the darkness"* of the *nun* which may have been the first sunrise or the light which marked the start of creation.[199] In the early versions of the myth the Eye can be Venus, the Morning Star which heralds the sunrise.

Whilst his Eye was away Ra replaced her, maybe he was unable to function without an eye or thought that she was lost forever, or possibly he just didn't think about the consequences of this action. The act had major repercussions and proved to be a turning point in the evolution of creation. It is no surprise that the Eye *"was wroth with me when it returned and found that I had made another in its place"*. Here was the first act of separation, betrayal and anger. The Eye can now never be totally pacified and reassured or completely reconciled with Ra. The Eye wept in anger and distress and this is *"how men came into being from the tears which came forth from mine Eye"*.[200] The Eye can be viewed as the Mother Goddess creating humans from her tears. Given the circumstances of their creation it is not surprising that humans reflect the anger and distress of their creation. The tears of the Eye contrast with its alter-ego the fire-spitting *uraeus*.

In some versions of the myth Thoth placates the Eye then places it upon Ra's forehead in a place of honour, in others Ra does this himself. *"I advanced its place onto my brow, and when it was exercising rule over this entire land, its wrath fell away completely, for I had replaced that which had been taken from it."*[201] The Eye was now the *uraeus*, the most powerful of the deities. Ra says to her *"Great will be your power and mighty your majesty over the bodies of your enemies...all mankind will cringe beneath you and your might, they will respect you when they behold you in that vigorous form"*.[202] In the *Book of the Dead* it was Thoth who *"returned the sacred eye, he has pacified it after being sent out by Re...it was enraged, but it was Thoth who satisfied the eye after it had*

---

[198] *Egyptian Mysteries: New Light on Ancient Knowledge*, Lamy, 1986:79
[199] *Egyptian Mythology*, Pinch, 2002:129
[200] *The Bremner-Rhind Papyrus III*, Faulkner, 1938:166-185
[201] *The Wisdom of Ancient Egypt*, Kaster, 1968:56
[202] *Myth and Symbol in Ancient Egypt*, Clark, 1978:221

given vent to its wrath".[203] In another spell it "*became enraged against him after he had sent it forth. But it was Thoth who raised the hair from it*". There is a pun between rage, *neshen*, and hair, *shen*. *Neshen* is the hair which hides the eye, similar to rage which blinds common sense, as well as the clouds which obscure the sun and hide its light.[204]

Tefnut is one of the main Eye Goddesses which is strange given that she was one of the pair of deities whom the Eye went looking for. The myths we have are silent on this transition. Does this suggest that Tefnut was originally two Goddesses who have been merged into one?

The *Uraeus*

The *uraeus* is the cobra on the forehead or crown of all deities and kings. She is the emanation of the sun and their protector. Her body is raised and her hood is always extended, the position a cobra assumes when threatened. The word is a Latinised version of the Greek translation of *iaret* which translates as "*risen one*".[205] The cobra is one of the most impressive of all snakes. One of the species native to Egypt, the black-necked spitting cobra, can grow up to 1.5 meters in length and project venom up to 2 meters. It is both intimidating and instantly recognisable. There are many venomous snakes in Egypt but the cobra was selected as a symbol for the *uraeus* for three reasons; its impressive hood, its ability to attack by spraying venom so it doesn't have to leave its position and thirdly the fact that it will aim for the victims' eyes. As a symbol for the Eye Goddess the latter was significant. The burning sensation caused by snake venom also linked it to the burning Eye of the Sun. The *uraeus*' means of attack is fire, an appropriate method of attack for such a solar creature. "*The uraeus, which is on your head, punishes them...it burns by its flame.*" She is referred to as "*Mistress of the Flame*" and "*Mistress of the Fire*".[206]

---

[203] *Hathor and Thoth: Two Key Figures of the Ancient Egyptian Religion*, Bleeker, 1973:121
[204] *Myth and Symbol in Ancient Egypt*, Clark, 1978:224
[205] *The Cobra Goddesses of Ancient Egypt*, Johnson, 1990:33
[206] *Death as an Enemy*, Zandee, 1960:133 & 137

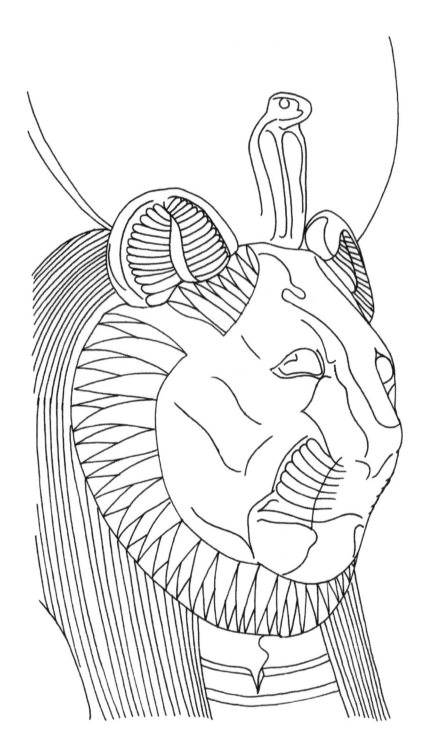

5 - The Uraeus Serpent

The *uraeus* has been an important symbol from the start of the Dynastic Period and is Egypt's oldest snake symbol. *"Most ancient female of the world."*[207] The earliest depiction of a royal *uraeus* is on an ivory label showing Den (1st dynasty) smiting his enemies, although there is some doubt about its authenticity. The earliest confirmed *uraeus* occurs in a rock-cut scene of Djoser (3rd dynasty) in Wadi Maghara, Sinai[208] whilst the earliest known *uraei* on sculpture dates to the 4th dynasty. It is a ubiquitous symbol in Egypt and appears on all forms of art from jewellery to monumental architecture. The *uraeus* is the ultimate protector. She protects the king against his enemies and the deities against theirs, especially the annihilating chaos of the *nun* in the form of Apophis. She is the personification of the original feminine energy of *sekhem* and is often shown in a dual form which doubles her protective power as well as alluding to her duality. *"Sekhmet is on your head, Wadjet is on your forehead."*[209]

The Cobra Goddesses

There are many snake deities in Egypt but the Snake Goddesses were all cobras. The determinative for the word 'goddess' is a cobra and all Goddesses can be depicted as either a cobra or a *uraeus*. It is not clear why the cobra was considered female. It might just be because it was a symbol of the *Uraeus* Goddess. A rearing cobra with its hood extended is both recognisable and intimidating. They were said to be good mothers and perhaps the hood suggested the more curving form of the female body. Life means movement, especially upward, and a rearing snake could be used to depict the vital life forces. The deceased are frequently exhorted to *"raise yourself"*.

The three main Cobra Goddesses are Wadjet, Renenutet and Meretseger and only Wadjet is an Eye or Lioness Goddess. Renenutet was the Goddess of fertility and harvest presiding over cultivated land, granaries and kitchens. She was considered a beautiful and bountiful Goddess with no dangerous aspects despite her Cobra form. In contrast was Meretseger who was not malevolent but could be dangerous if disturbed. A local Goddess she was the guardian Goddess of the Peak of the West, a pyramid-shaped mountain that overlooked the Theban

---

[207] *Myth and Symbol in Ancient Egypt*, Clark, 1978:224
[208] *Early Dynastic Egypt*, Wilkinson, 1999:300
[209] *Sekhmet et la Protection du Monde*, Germond, 1981:214 (My translation)

necropolis. Both Renenutet and Meretseger can be depicted as lioness-headed but this seems to be just a different way of depicting their power or aspects. For example, on the *stele* of Neferabu from Deir el-Medina it says of Meretseger "*a lion exists within her. The Peak strikes with the stroke of a fierce lion*".[210] This is a strange method of attack for a Cobra Goddess. At Dendera Renenutet is shown as lioness-headed. The *Fayum* papyrus depicts a lioness-headed *uraeus* named as Renenutet. In theory any deity could be depicted as feline or partly feline as a way of emphasising their power or particular aspect.

Wadjet (Edjo)

Wadjet is the tutelary Goddess of Lower Egypt. Her name means the Green One, possibly a reference to the snake's colour or to the green and fertile Delta region. Her main cult centre was at Buto in the Delta. She is linked with the Vulture Goddess Nekhbet, the tutelary Goddess of Upper Egypt, but there is also reference to "*Edjo of the South*".[211] Wadjet is normally depicted as a cobra. During the Late Period she was increasingly associated with Sekhmet and so was often depicted as an enthroned lioness-headed Goddess rather than as a cobra or *uraeus*. This may have been a consequence of the increase in popularity of the Lioness Goddesses at this time. Purification ceremonies depicted in some of the Greco-Roman temples invoke "*Sekhmet of yesterday...Wadjet of today...protect the King with that papyrus of life which is in your hand, in this your name of Wadjet*".[212] Standing statues of Sekhmet often hold a papyrus sceptre. A bronze throne (now in the Louvre, Paris) depicts women adoring a lioness-headed Goddess described as Wadjet. A similar throne (now in *the Civic Archaeological Museum, Bologna*) depicts Apries (26th dynasty) offering a papyrus sceptre to a lioness-headed Wadjet.

Weret-Hekau

Weret-Hekau personified the magic of the royal crown and the *uraeus* and her name means Great of Magic. This was also a common epithet of Isis, Mut, Hathor, Sekhmet and Pakhet. She can be depicted as a Cobra Goddess, a Lioness Goddess or a combination of lion and

[210] *The Literature of Ancient Egypt*, Simpson et al, 2003:287
[211] *An Ancient Egyptian Book of Hours*, Faulkner, 1958:2
[212] *A Wooden Figure of Wadjet with Two Painted Representations of Amasis*, James, 1982:156-165

cobra. Her main role is to guard the king and she is depicted doing this in many New Kingdom reliefs. On the eighth pylon of the temple of Amun at Karnak a lioness-headed Weret-Hekau accompanies Thutmose III (18th dynasty) in the procession of the sacred barque. A fine representation of a lioness-headed Weret-Hekau is found on the interior northern wall of the Great Hypostyle Hall at Karnak. Here she presents Sety I with the symbol of his jubilee festival.

On the golden shrine of Tutankhamun (18th dynasty) the king is called *"beloved of the goddess Werethekau"*.[213] He and his queen Ankhesenamun are often linked to Weret-Hekau who is sometimes called Mistress of the Palace. One scene on the shrine shows Tutankhamun being nursed by Weret-Hekau depicted as a human-headed cobra with arms. On a statue of Horemheb (18th dynasty) and his queen Mutnodjmet an inscription tells how Weret-Hekau embraced the king at his coronation and then established herself on his brow as his *uraeus*.

Snakes on the Throne

The Snake God Nehebu-Kau and other snakes often adorn the thrones of Bastet and Sekhmet. Two statues of an enthroned Sekhmet-Bastet from the 22nd dynasty have extensive snake symbolism on the throne decorations. One includes a four-coiled snake, a snake in the form of a *djed* symbol, Nehebu-Kau and two double-headed snakes. One has both heads looking inwards the other both looking outwards. The second statue has more ornate decorations and shows other deities as well as snakes and no doubt has a great deal to tell us if we could find the key. Nehebu-Kau is depicted five times and there is Wadjet as a *uraeus* and Hathor. Snakes are shown standing on their tails, with human arms and heads, with wings and on a sledge.[214]

Nehebu-Kau is a Protector God of Egypt and the underworld. One tradition says he is the son of the Earth God Geb and the Harvest Goddess Renenutet. He has a dual aspect which reflects that of the Earth as a source of life and fertility but also of death and the dark underworld. The deceased associated themselves with Nehebu-Kau when they feared danger from him. His strong chthonic powers will complement those of Sekhmet and the other Feline and Eye Goddesses. He and the other

---

[213] *Hieroglyphs & the Afterlife in Ancient Egypt*, Foreman & Quirke, 1996:22
[214] *Two Statuettes of the Goddess Sekhmet-Ubastet*, Shorter, 1932:121-124

snakes may be present on the throne as protection or to balance the fire of Sekhmet with that of earth or to ground her power. Are the snakes a reference to the enemies of Ra which have been subdued by the Goddess? Are they her messengers? What does the double-headed snake mean? Snake symbolism generates endless questions.

Some depictions of Sekhmet show her standing on the back of a double-headed snake holding each head in her hands. Is Sekhmet controlling it, subduing it or working with it? Or does it represent her power? The undulating snake is a good way to depict the flow of energy. Perhaps it depicts her energy which creates a circle around her, her aura formed by her power manifesting from the enclosing *nun*. The double-headed snake might have a similar meaning to the *ouroboros* illustrating the cyclical nature of creation and the continuum of life and death and infinity. In the *Book of Gates* time is shown as a meandering snake out of whom the Hour Goddesses are born. Could the snakes held by Sekhmet have similar allusions to time and her control over time and hence fate? But there is so much symbolism with snakes and we need to return to the Lioness.

From Cobra to Lioness

Female solar power is represented as the *uraeus* cobra and the transition of the Eye Goddess into the *uraeus* cobra is explained in the myths but how did the Eye Goddess become a Lioness Goddess? What was the original connection between a cobra and a lion? We shall probably never know. Both had strong solar associations from the beginning and were important symbols, and it is probable that their combined symbolism was needed in an attempt to portray the essence of the Eye Goddess. A more detailed study of the snake in Egypt might clarify the link. One reason might be that while the *uraeus* represents the focused power of the sun, aimed from one point in the sky, the lioness represents a more defused power free to spread out over the land. Whatever the reason it is as a Lioness that we encounter Sekhmet in the myth that describes her 'coming into being'.

CHAPTER 11

DIVINE RETRIBUTION

"I have prevailed over mankind and satisfaction was in my heart...thus came into existence Sekhmet."[215]

The *Destruction of Mankind*

The myth of the *Destruction of Mankind* shows the wrath of the divine turned against humanity. It attempts to explain the reason for personal and national tragedy and suffering and also tells us how Sekhmet came into being. Our version of this myth comes from the *Book of the Heavenly Cow*, a collection of spells from the royal tombs of the New Kingdom. A study of the linguistics suggests that it was written in the Middle Kingdom. Translations are given in a number of books including Simpson (2003), Kaster (1968) and Lichtheim Volume II (2006).

The story takes place at a time when there was no separation between humans and deities and Ra rules Egypt. As he grows old people start to lose their respect for him and a group of rebels start to plot against him. *"Men who have come into existence from my eye – they have*

---

[215] *The Destruction of Mankind: A Transitional Literary Text,* Spalinger, 2000:257-282

plotted against me."[216] His creation is turning against him. Exactly what humans could do to a God, apart from ignore him, isn't clear. Ra appears in the guise of a human king so this myth may incorporate what a king once did or could do. As Ra's power wanes people don't respect him anymore. The concerns of the elite and kings are reflected here. Fear enforced by power is the way through which the people, the state and neighbouring countries are kept under control. Take away this fear and authority diminishes. In contrast to the other solar myths the enemy is not the Chaos Serpent Apophis but humans. We may not be able to damage the sun directly but humans can cause chaos and through that threaten *maat* on earth. What happens on one level of creation will impact on the others.

A number of other cultures have myths in which the Creator God decides he hasn't made a very good job of humanity and tries either to eradicate all of them so he can start afresh or to remove the worst elements. As early as the Middle Kingdom there is a reference to the Creator working to destroy humanity. One difference to those myths is that Ra calls together his Ennead to discuss the problem with them. Either he is not a dictator or he doesn't know what to do and needs advice. A closer reading of the texts suggests that the decision is not his alone.

Ra invokes the primordial deities which existed before he came into being, here he is not seen as the original Creator. He addresses Nun as "*O thou Eldest God in whom I originated*"[217] and his words imply that he is not the sole creator of humanity and so cannot destroy them without permission. "*I cannot kill them until I hear what you will declare against them.*" The other deities, perhaps fearing that the insurrection could spread, agree with Ra's plan. "*Let your eye go out so that it might smite them for you, those who have planned evil...there is no eye which is more prominent than it in order to smite them for you. It will go down as Hathor.*"[218] The phrase 'go down' refers both to the descent of Hathor from the sky and the descent of the *uraeus* from Ra's brow, there is also a pun with 'descend' and 'destroy'. There is symmetry in the tale as humans were created from the Eye and threatened with destruction by the Eye.

---

[216] *The Destruction of Mankind: A Transitional Literary Text*, Spalinger, 2000:257-282
[217] *The Literature of Ancient Egypt*, Simpson et al, 2003:290
[218] *The Destruction of Mankind: A Transitional Literary Text*, Spalinger, 2000:257-282

The rebellious humans must have known that they were in trouble and they fled to the desert or to the south depending upon the source. Perhaps this is where this particular group came from, like the foreign invaders or groups of bandits who raided Egypt periodically and then retreated back into the safety of their domain. The desert was seen as a chaotic realm. If the rebels fled to the south does this imply that it was the Nubians who had rebelled against the Sun God? It would please the somewhat xenophobic Egyptians if it hadn't been their race who had rebelled. The south is also where the sun goes in winter when its power declines.

Ra sends his Eye down as Hathor but at some stage she turns into Sekhmet the furious destructive aspect of the Solar Eye. The fact that Sekhmet drinks and wades in the blood of her victims is significant. Spilt blood represents the life-force flowing away. Flowing blood can also be considered a medium of creation. In the *Jumilhac* papyrus it says that the Creator's blood falls to earth as red minerals.[219] Ra may have only wanted the rebels killed but he has unleashed a destructive force which is going to carry on until all of humanity has been slain. Having tasted blood the avenging Eye will not be satisfied. Perhaps Ra has had time to think of the consequences of his action. Does he take pity on the innocent or has he realised that without people there would be no adoration and no offerings?

Ra sends his messengers to Elephantine to get red ochre. These messengers are probably associated with the seven messengers of Sekhmet. The ochre is ground by the priests in Heliopolis and added to beer brewed by the maid-servants to make it look like blood. 7,000 jars of beer were poured onto the fields before dawn, to a depth of 3 palms (about 23 cm). The first slaughter takes place in the realm of chaos, the desert, but the chaos unleashed by the Eye is now heading towards civilisation. This is emphasised because it was the fields which were flooded with beer rather than the uncultivated land. Sekhmet is starting to penetrate the realm of order and civilisation and is threatening creation with the disruption of *maat*. It will need guile to deflect Sekhmet as she is more powerful than all the Gods.

Sekhmet arrives at dawn, an appropriate time for a Solar Eye. Sunrise on flooded fields will have turned them red at certain times. Sekhmet sees her beautiful reflection in the flooded fields. Thinking it is

---

[219] *The Cannibal Hymn*, Eyre, 2002:100

blood Sekhmet drinks the beer until she becomes drunk and happy and forgets about killing humans. *"She came back drunk, without having even perceived mankind."*[220] A relieved Ra greets her *"How well you have arrived, O Gracious One"*. The text then adds *"the Beautiful One came to pass in Imau"*.[221] Sekhmet has reverted back to the peaceful Hathor. Ra doesn't appear angry with his daughter, or perhaps he is scared of her and worried about upsetting her in case she resumes her carnage. His words are reconciliatory. Is this because the anger of the sun has been completely split off leaving the remaining parts, the Sun God and Hathor, with no anger left?

The choice of Elephantine as the source of the ochre is important. It is an island in the Nile at the First Cataract which was considered the source of the inundation. The border between Egypt and Nubia lay in the vicinity, although the actual border did vary over time. This area is close to the Tropic of Cancer. The word tropic is derived from a Greek word meaning to turn or change direction and refers to the fact that the sun appears to change direction at the solstices. This made Elephantine a very significant location for a magical substance which is being used to turn the path of the Eye of the Sun.

The positive outcome of the story is that Sekhmet and the other Eye Goddesses can be placated and reunited with Ra and *maat* can be restored. What happens on the divine level is thus echoed by the need, and potential, for pacification at all levels of society. It also introduces the concept of divine forgiveness. One hymn to Ra calls him *"the merciful, who changes his mind and forgives"*.[222] In celebration of this lucky escape Ra institutes a festival for Hathor and says *"make for them intoxicating drinks on the yearly feasts"*.[223] This explains the prevalence of the various *Festivals of Intoxication*, an important ritual to pacify the volatile Eye Goddesses. Sekhmet didn't recognise people when she was drunk. Was that part of the reason why intoxication was used as a method of getting closer to the divine? Alcohol blurs the distinction between us and the deities making it safer for us to approach them.

It is fair to ask why the usually benevolent Hathor turned into a savage murderer. The Egyptians would say that she hadn't. She was angry and had to protect her father and as this powerful energy was

---

[220] *The Wisdom of Ancient Egypt*, Kaster, 1993:70
[221] *The Destruction of Mankind: A Transitional Literary Text*, Spalinger, 2000:257-282
[222] *The Gods of Ancient Egypt*, Vernus, 1998:168
[223] *The Wisdom of Ancient Egypt*, Kaster, 1993:70

focused it transformed into a separate entity which became Sekhmet. As Sekhmet was formed from angry energy she has to be constantly placated. It is important to remember that Hathor was a Solar and Eye Goddess who was present in the rays of the sun which in Egypt could easily become life-threatening.

The Issue of Divine Retribution

Ra does not come over very well in this myth, he is fed up with people's behaviour but can't think of any way to deal with the problem other than killing them all. Why do the deities agree so readily to kill people? It is a reflection of human mentality that the easiest solution to a problem is to remove the cause, and with humans that means to kill them. Unwilling to do the deed himself, he uses the Eye Goddess and Sekhmet becomes an expression of the willingness of Creator to destroy humanity. Ra then changes his mind and resolves the situation with some thinking but then decides he is fed up with the whole affair and retreats to the heavens. Egypt is then ruled by the next generation of Gods and eventually kings as the Golden Age slips away. The myth explains the loss of the Golden Age and the distance between people and deities. The biggest test of any theology is to explain a world full of injustice, violence and evil whilst claiming a benevolent Creator. The *Book of the Heavenly Cow* may have been an attempt to do this with one section about the inherently evil nature of people. Does it also remind us that it is not weak to change tactics when circumstances change or if mistakes have been made? It also contains the moral of the consequences of acting without thinking.

Sekhmet has now changed from the protector of the Sun God to his avenger and is invoked by people to save them from herself. Sekhmet's role as protector is most often seen in her healing aspect which is discussed in chapter 15. The Egyptians were no different to any other culture in viewing the traumas of life as divine punishment. People could suffer through no fault of their own and for no apparent reason whether it was through the action of the king or another person or through the natural environment. The myth of the *Destruction of Mankind* attempts to explain this suffering.

The myth could also have a basis in celestial events with the retreat of the sun at the winter solstice reflecting Ra's withdrawal to the heavens. The destructive heat of the sun after the summer solstice is seen as Sekhmet's raging anger. A period of very hot, dry summers and unusually cool, cloudy winters could also have been instrumental in the development of the myth.

Doing Another's Dirty Work

Like Ra the kings will rarely, if ever, have killed their enemies themselves: they merely issued instructions. An echo of this is seen in the Ptolemaic Period *Book of Thoth*. One entry says "*A vulture will embrace them...the lion sits by her throne...she speaks, while he makes a slaughter of the ones whom he will slay*".[224] We don't know who the lion is but he is obviously a servant of the enthroned Vulture Goddess who is probably Mut or Nekhbet. The lion, like Sekhmet, is given orders to slaughter the king's enemies.

The *Uraeus* becomes a Lioness

In this myth Hathor was the protective *uraeus* cobra on Ra's forehead. When she leaves Ra's forehead and descends to earth she is transformed into a lioness in the form of Sekhmet. Why did this additional transformation take place? One explanation is that the *uraeus* attacks from afar and with fire. A cobra will attack in a single strike and spray venom. Other snakes, apart from the constrictors, will leave only one small puncture wound. A lioness, on the other hand, rips open her victim's body and causes blood to flow and may well devour the flesh. Whilst neither fate is desirable, death as a consequence of a snake attack will leave the body intact and the Egyptians had a great fear of the corpse being mutilated because a complete body was essential for rebirth. An attack by a lioness was thus more terrifying. Whilst there are a number of Lioness Goddesses it is always Sekhmet who takes on this avenging role in the *Destruction of Mankind*.

---

[224] *The Ancient Egyptian Book of Thoth*, Jasnow & Zauzich, 2005:334

CHAPTER 12

THE RETURN OF THE DISTANT GODDESS

"Welcome! Come back upon the head of him whom you have protected, that head from which you went forth."[225]

Introduction

The myths of the Distant Goddess have been recreated from scattered passages in the Ptolemaic Temples of Philae, Esna, Edfu, Kom Ombo and Dendera and some Nubian temples as well as from the *Leiden* papyrus. It is considered a very old myth. All myths try to answer the fundamental questions of what happens and why and they would have been a constant presence in daily life. Each area had variations on the basic myth and the deities involved, and it would have been altered to suit local conditions and situations. The literary versions were probably put together from a number of oral sources and may have been designed to be read aloud.

---

[225] *The Apotropaic Goddess in the Eye.* Darnell, 1997:35-48

The underlying theme of the Distant Goddess is the conflict between order and chaos and the savage versus the civilised life. It is also a reflection of how Egypt descended into chaos during the Intermediate Periods, as if the Goddess has turned her back on Egypt, until order is reasserted in the following period when the king and Goddess return. The Distant Goddess is usually Hathor or Tefnut although at Esna Sekhmet takes on the role. Its calendar refers to the *"feast of the distant Eye, meaning Sekhmet"*.[226]

Alienation and Exile

For some reason Ra and the Eye Goddess quarrel and she leaves him, taking up residence in a distant land where she rages in her lioness form. We are never told what the quarrel was about. In human terms this is a comment on the father-daughter relationship which often turns from affection in childhood to ambivalence and rebellion in teenage years where the father has to adjust to the daughter's growing sexual development and desire for independence. Alienation over turbulent teenage years is not unexpected and only as both partners mature, accept and readjust can there be reconciliation. Ra himself seems difficult to live with as seen in the *Destruction of Mankind*.

Whatever the source of the problem Ra misses his daughter and wants her back. The texts state that the *uraeus* is firmly joined to Ra's forehead hence any separation is a crisis. He is crippled and powerless without his striking power. It appears that the Eye Goddess is the only one who can protect him from human rebels and the ever-threatening chaos personified by Apophis. The power of the Eye is stronger than all the other deities. Moreover his daughter is dangerous when separated and becomes allied with chaotic forces.

The Goddess goes to the deserts of Nubia, or occasionally Libya. These regions of chaos increase the anger of the estranged Goddess. Unable to lose her anger she rampages across the country as a lioness, a danger to all life. She terrorises both humans and animals. That she drinks blood and eats flesh is not unexpected from a lioness but, true to her elemental nature, she also emits fire from her eyes and nostrils. A relief from the temple of Dakka, in Nubia, shows her with a full mane and swollen teats. As a nursing lioness she is at her most ferocious. This

---

[226] *Sekhmet et la Protection du Monde*, Germond, 1981:133 (My translation)

seems to be purely to demonstrate how dangerous she was. There is no mention of who the father was or what happened to her cubs. Was the pregnancy was the source of the quarrel with Ra? This is probably unlikely.

In one version of the myth the Goddess takes the form of the Ethiopian or Nubian Cat. A number of Ramesside *ostraca* show Thoth with the Ethiopian Cat. It isn't clear which species of feline this is, possibly the serval. Why the myth should have a serval rather than the more dangerous lioness is not clear. Perhaps it was because the serval was seen as more foreign or it was part of a similar myth which was merged with that of *the Return of the Distant Goddess.*

The Peacemakers

Ra needs his daughter and sends a peacemaker to pacify her and bring her back home to him. Three Gods are mentioned in the variations of the story; Onuris, Shu and Thoth. The earliest versions of the myth involve Onuris (Anhur). He was a War and Hunting God with a cult based in This, a district near Abydos. His name means "*he who brought back the Distant One*".[227] He also had the epithet the Son of Ra. The name Onuris can also be written (as can that of Thoth) as a God carrying the *wedjat* eye. He is depicted as a man with a beard, wearing a short wig and *uraeus* topped by two or four tall feathers. His right hand is raised as if to throw a spear and he often wears a long kilt decorated with a featherlike pattern. He uses his hunting skills to track down the Goddess and is often depicted with a length of rope in his hand. He subdues her and brings her home and as a reward marries the Goddess. This is a nice change from the European fairy tales where it is a weak, passive princess who needs rescuing but both Goddess and princess are still considered trophies handed out as a reward to the hero. The principle mythical role of Onuris is his return from Nubia with the Distant Goddess Mehit who becomes his consort. A number of commentators have suggested that the myth of the alienated Eye Goddess became merged with that of a foreign Goddess brought to Egypt from Nubia. To the Egyptians Mehit may have personified the deserts of Nubia before she was identified with Hathor or Tefnut as the wandering Eye of Ra.

---

[227] *Myth and Symbol in Ancient Egypt*, Clark, 1978:227

Shu *"brought back his beautiful sister to her father"*.[228] As the sister-consort of Tefnut, Shu is an obvious choice to be sent to make peace when Tefnut is the Distant Goddess. The original myth of the Angry Eye, where she goes in search of Shu and Tefnut, may have been merged with the later myth of the Distant Goddess where Shu searches for Tefnut. Unlike Onuris who takes the brute force approach, Shu prefers diplomacy and talks to the Goddess and eventually *"pacified her who is in the middle of her rage"*.[229] Thoth is a Lunar God and also viewed as the son of Ra. Sometimes Thoth accompanies Shu but in other versions he goes on his own. *Ostraca* dating to the New Kingdom show Thoth with the Distant Goddess Tefnut. Thoth may not have been in the original myth but as the God who restored the lost and wounded Eye of Horus he is the ideal God to bring back the Solar Eye and adds symmetry to the series of myths. Peacemaking is one of his attributes. *"I am Thoth who wanders abroad to seek the Eye for its owner (Re), I come and I have found it."*[230] Like Shu, Thoth uses his eloquence to pacify the Goddess. Does this show the development of Egyptian culture from a warrior based hero to a more intellectual one where the emphasis is on the importance of words of power over brute force?

Pacification

Thoth disguises himself as a baboon, which is one of his normal forms, when he approaches the Goddess. We are not told why he adopts a disguise; perhaps he reasoned that it would upset her less or maybe he is just hiding his power for when he needs it. An obviously armed peacemaker would be perceived as a threat. When Shu is involved he too disguises himself as a baboon. He doesn't normally have this form so it may be a way of aligning himself with Thoth. When the peacemakers arrive they find the Goddess as an Ethiopian Cat. *"Her heart was burning, her lips were hot, the blasts of her mouth were the fiery breath of a flame like the horned viper, her eyes were evil and her looks were diverted, her body was in a state of disturbance."*[231]

---

[228] *Egyptian Mythology*, Pinch, 2002:177
[229] *Egyptian Mythology*, Pinch, 2002:72
[230] *Hathor and Thoth: Two Key Figures of the Ancient Egyptian Religion*, Bleeker, 1973:120
[231] *Emphasizing and Non-Emphasizing Second Tenses in the "Myth of the Sun's Eye"*, Widmer, 1999:165-188

Despite the threat to his life Thoth alternately lectures the Goddess and entices her with tales about Egypt. He reminds her about her duty and tells her that fate punishes every crime. In between the lectures, he entertains her with a series of animal fables about justice. The main moral to these stories is that the wise work to maintain the common peace and the strong mustn't despise the weak as they may need their help or friendship. The best-known of these is *the Lion in Search of a Man* in which the lion is saved by a mouse who gnaws through the ropes which bind him.[232] The plot is the same as the one used by Aesop in the 6th century BCE in his fables. Egypt had a long tradition of animal fables, incidents from some of the other fables included in the *Return of the Distant Goddess* can be seen in drawings from the Middle Kingdom.

It takes a while for the Goddess to calm down and listen to Thoth. Reference is made to his perseverance in the *Book of Thoth*. *"Call out to her 120 times. She hears...he calls out to her seven thousand times seventy-seven times and she does not come at his voice."*[233] The text was to encourage the students, reminding them that even Thoth sometimes has a hard time getting a response from the Goddess but that he continued calling until he got a response. The numbers quoted are significant. In *the Destruction of Mankind Ra* orders 7,000 jars of beer. 77 is associated with Ra and multiples of seven indicate an infinite number.

The Goddess was not immediately pacified. In one version she gets angry with Thoth and transforms from the Ethiopian Cat into a Lioness with fire shooting from her eyes and nostrils, which sounds much like the *uraeus* with her fiery glance and breathing fire. *"Thoth jumped like a frog, he quivered like a grasshopper."*[234] Thoth explains how desolate Egypt is without her and tells her of the dancing, music and offerings which await her return. *"Joy is in the woodlands and amusement among the Ethiopians. My Lady, Egypt is in trouble before you."*[235] The absence of the Solar Eye plunges Egypt into fear and gloom. This is echoed in other tales of a departed deity, such as Demeter and Persephone and Ishtar and Tammuz. The life of the land dies when the deity departs. *"The*

---

[232] *Ancient Egyptian Literature Volume III*, Lichtheim, 2006:157-159
[233] *The Ancient Egyptian Book of Thoth*, Jasnow & Zauzich, 2005:204
[234] *Egyptian Mythology*, Pinch, 2002:71
[235] *Emphasizing and Non-Emphasizing Second Tenses in the "Myth of the Sun's Eye"*, Widmer, 1999:165-188

time of the absence of the Goddess – whether the Eye or another – is the season of fear and lifelessness."[236]

The place where the Goddess was found can be Nubia but it is also given as *Knst, Bwgm* or "*Gods' Land*". *Bwgm* is translated as the Place of Finding and *Knst* alludes to a country in another world. This infers that the Goddess is brought to Egypt from a mythical and divine land. The Goddess descends from her world into ours but has to shed some of her divine power as it will be too powerful and dangerous for the capacity of humans, and probably the created universe, to handle. She cannot shed any part of her underlying power for long, hence the need for continual pacification. Daily pacification rituals were carried out in the major temples. This raw chaotic solar energy must be balanced by *maat* to make it safe for the created world. The pacification and application of *maat* is carried out by Thoth, the Lord of Maat.

Regardless of the variation of names of the principal characters, when the Goddess is estranged from her father she is a raging lioness or wild cat. When she is reunited with him she assumes the character of a peaceful cat. Thus the cat becomes a symbol for the reconciled Eye. The myth also parallels the domestication of the cat from a wild animal into a pet.

The Return

Eventually the Goddess is persuaded to return to Egypt, thanks to Thoth's persuasive skills. She was "*amazed while listening to his voice and being full of desire for the land (of Egypt) thanks to him, he being a source of great wonder in her heart*".[237] One passage tells of an attack by the forces of chaos on the Goddess whilst she was sleeping. Thoth manages to wake her in time and she defeats them. For all his magical powers Thoth, like the other deities, needs the formidable power of the Eye to defend against the power of chaos. This seems similar to the final assault on the sun by Apophis just before dawn in the funerary texts.

The Goddess is soothed by the sound of the First Cataract. She bathes in the Nile which turns red as it washes away her anger. Ochre from here coloured the beer used to pacify Sekhmet in *the Destruction of*

---

[236] *Myth and Symbol in Ancient Egypt*, Clark, 1978:229
[237] *Emphasizing and Non-Emphasizing Second Tenses in the "Myth of the Sun's Eye"*, Widmer, 1999:165-188

Mankind. It seems to have had important pacifying qualities despite being a border area, or maybe the border was there for that very reason. At the border the Goddess is greeted by music and dancing and this also helps transform her into the *"beautiful of face"*.[238] As soon as she touches the sacred Egyptian soil the Angry Goddess transforms into her benevolent form. Often this is Mut the Lady of Asheru or Hathor the Lady of the Southern Sycamore. The Goddess returns to Memphis accompanied by musicians, monkeys and dwarfs. On reliefs at Philae the God Bes is depicted celebrating her return. At each city she was greeted by musicians and dancers, and feasts and festivals were held in her honour. Her return was particularly celebrated at el-Kab, Philae, Edfu, Esna and Dendera.

At Memphis, or Heliopolis in some texts, she is reunited with her father Ra. Sometimes she becomes his consort and mother of a divine child, the new Sun God. It is said that Ra arranged a festival of Tefnut, in honour of her return, in the Mansion of Lady of Sycamore (Hathor's chapel). She then recounts to Ra all the tales told to her by Thoth.

Additional Symbolism

The vulture, the symbol of Nekhbet the Goddess of Upper Egypt, appears in the tale. Thoth finds the Goddess under a tree on which a vulture perches. A 19th dynasty *ostracon* shows Thoth as a seated baboon persuading the Goddess, in the form of a seated lioness, to return to Egypt. Above them a vulture is depicted on a nest with eggs. The setting is in the south but is this the only reason for the vulture? The word for mother is written with the vulture sign so it may allude to her pregnancy, as may the eggs. Like many symbols the vulture was ambivalent. It was seen as protective and is shown hovering over the king but it was also a carrion eater associated with battlefields and the destruction of the corpse, another link to the dangerous destructive Goddess. In some ways the vulture is comparable to the dangerous yet protective *uraeus*. They are symbols of the Two Ladies, Wadjet and Nekhbet, who show the same contradictory duality as the Distant Goddess does. We are also told that the Goddess took vulture form. While he was speaking to her Thoth *"caused the goddess to appear in the form of a vulture"*.[239] This

---

[238] *Egyptian Mythology*, Pinch, 2002:71
[239] *Emphasizing and Non-Emphasizing Second Tenses in the "Myth of the Sun's Eye"*, Widmer, 1999:165-188

transformation into a vulture could be an indication of her pacification and her return to a more responsible and friendly form. The vulture may suggest Mut as the pacified Goddess.

The sycamore tree is also a motif. There are depictions of Thoth resting under a sycamore tree and the temple in Dakka is called the "*the house of the nbs-tree*".[240] The temple is dedicated to Thoth of Pnubs and in the Roman side chapel is a depiction of him worshipping Tefnut in lion form. Hathor has a strong link to the sycamore and it can be a manifestation of her, so this may allude to the Distant Goddess returned to her pacified state this time as Hathor.

Baboons and monkeys play a major role in the story, which may be another reason why Shu assumes the form of a baboon. The baboon was a sacred animal associated with the Sun God as well as the Lunar Gods Thoth and Khonsu. They are often depicted greeting the rising sun. Wild baboons become active at first light and this was interpreted as praising Ra. This close association with Ra aligned them with the Eye Goddesses as well. One version in the *Berlin* papyrus tells how the Goddess went to the land of Punt, itself a liminal and mysterious land. The word it uses to describe her rage has the determinative of an angry baboon. While she was in Punt the monkeys and baboons danced for her and then accompanied her as she returned to Egypt.

The Inundation

The annual inundation, which arrives from the south of Egypt, is usually seen as the underlying basis for the myth of the Distant Goddess. The inundation was also connected with Isis, through her tears of grief at the murder of Osiris. Isis was closely connected with Sirius, the star considered responsible for the inundation. The heliacal rising of Sirius coincided with the start of the inundation. One of Hathor's epithets was Ruler Over Sirius. An Esna text describes Mehit as Sothis who brings the inundation. The inundation brought the return of the Nile waters, and the promise of stability and plenty, after the dangers of the end of the year. The flood, itself a chaotic event, was often seen as the return of Hathor or Sekhmet. Initially angry and dangerous the flood subsided, and the Nile returned to its benevolent, peaceful form.

---

[240] *The Goddesses of the Egyptian Tree Cult*, Buhl, 1947:80-97

The calendar of the temple of Edfu alludes to the myth of the Distant Goddess. The annual return of the flood to Egypt was much anticipated but not guaranteed. There was always the very real fear that it might not return or be too high, with catastrophic results for everyone. The Angry Goddess (Tefnut or Sekhmet) transformed into the benevolent Goddess (Hathor, Mut or Bastet) represents the periodic return of positive, favourable elements of nature. Every year the Goddess has to be persuaded to return home, bringing the floodwaters, but if she is not fully pacified the waters will be too high and too destructive. One interpretation of the above-mentioned relief at Dakka is that the vulture is the symbol of the south, the source of the inundation, and the lioness as Hathor or Tefnut is the inundation. Thoth is present as the God of the Calendar trying to avoid a delay in the flood.

Kiosk shrines (small open temples) were built along the edges of the Nile. These were decorated with dwarves and animals who danced and made music to pacify and welcome both the Goddess and the inundation. The Medamud hymn describes the welcome procession accompanying the Goddess back to Egypt and the inundation is greeted in the same way. The inundation took a few weeks to travel north so temples along the route greeted them in turn.

Other Interpretations of the Myth

Over the year the sun wanders between the north and south, losing much of its ferocity as it moves south, so this too could be an element in the myth. The transformation of the Eye Goddess from an aggressive to benevolent form could be seen as the hot, desiccating summer sun of Sekhmet as opposed to the warming, gentle sun of Bastet. There are myths to explain the sun's daily journey through the sky during the day and the underworld at night so it would be expected that another would explain its north-south movement over the year.

Bleeker says the myth is not about the north-south wandering of the sun but an explanation of a solar eclipse. The moon is invisible during an eclipse which can be explained as the Moon God gone searching for the missing Eye of the Sun. Or could the myth have been influenced by a one-off natural event? A volcanic eruption blanketing out the sun for a period of time or a series of unusually cloudy seasons which were interpreted as the Solar Eye leaving Egypt?

Conclusion

Whatever the details, this third Solar Eye myth tells how the angry and estranged can be pacified and reunited and emphasises the contrast between the savage Other lands and the civilised Egypt. The Angry Goddess returns to her gentle and peaceful form as Hathor, Mut or Bastet. The myth introduces the elements of cyclical change and duality. This is seen with Bastet in particular as she transforms from Lioness to Cat Goddess, in parallel with the domestication of the cat, as well as being the pacified aspect of the Feline Goddess.

CHAPTER 13

DUALITY AND BALANCE

"She rages like Sekhmet and is peaceful like Bastet."[241]

Introduction

The Egyptians were fascinated with duality and opposites, a fascination which dates from the Pre-dynastic Period and remained a constant theme in Egyptian religion. The geography of Egypt gave a particular emphasis to duality with its very distinctive divisions; the south-north flowing Nile split the country east and west, the country itself consisted of the Upper and Lower Kingdoms of Egypt and there was a very clear contrast between the desert and the cultivated land. This gave additional focus to the normal dualities of life and death, day and night, hot and cold and so forth. This duality is seen very clearly in the Feline Goddesses and is expressed by changes of form. The Eye myths abound with duality and pairs. The need for balance is also present and seen in the characters of the deities in the myths and the Two Lions of the Horizon. This chapter reviews all the dualities associated with the

---

[241] *Soulful Creatures. Animal Mummies in Ancient Egypt*, Bleiberg, Barbash & Bruno, 2013:41

feline deities before their specific aspects are discussed in the following chapters.

The Dual Power of the Goddess

Sekhmet in particular demonstrates duality and is an expression of the nature of the original power of *sekhem*. Although her aspects of healer and destroyer appear contradictory, they are in reality complementary and essential for the protection and maintenance of creation. The myths tell of the struggle between the negative and positive elements of the universe which need to be reconciled so that order can be imposed on chaos and life can arise from the inanimate. Her dual power acts at all levels; creation, the king and state of Egypt and on individuals. An inscription from Abydos makes reference to her duality *"radiant are her souls"*[242] and one of her statues gives her the epithet *"Mistress of the Doubles"*.[243]

A number of the funerary texts refer to deceased being conceived by Sekhmet but carried and birthed by another. *"The King was conceived by Sakhmet, and it was Shezmetet who bore the King."*[244] This role is usually taken by Shesmetet but in one spell in the *Book of the Dead* it refers to Satis who gives birth, while in the later *Books of Breathing* it is Nut. Life occurs between the two poles of conception and birth and having Sekhmet conceive but Shesmetet give birth may be a way of emphasising this. Many Goddesses are referred to as the mother of the deceased but this split role only appears to occur with Sekhmet. Is this because Sekhmet's energy is more suited to the act of creation? Or was Shesmetet originally seen as a manifestation of Sekhmet in a gentler role?

Sekhmet is the Original Power which drives creation. In an echo of creation, each individual is created at conception by that same power. Sekhmet is not the agent of physical manifestation, namely development and birth, that role is allotted to another Goddess. This concept is important in the afterlife. If a person was conceived by the Original Power they carry it within themselves, what we would term a 'spark of the divine'. Like energy, this divine aspect can never be destroyed only

---

[242] *Temple Ritual at Abydos*, David, 2016:220
[243] *Les Statues Thebaines de la Desses Sakhmet*, Gautier, 1920:117-207 (My translation)
[244] *The Ancient Egyptian Pyramid Texts*, Faulkner, 2007:60 utterance 248

changed from one form to another making it an important component of rebirth.

Sekhmet contains duality but she is also paired with other Goddesses to emphasise their complementary but opposing aspects. The *Return of the Distant Goddess* myth emphasised the pairing of Goddesses as the Angry Goddess returned to her gentler form. Sekhmet was viewed as the angry aspect of Hathor or Mut. Sekhmet and Bastet were paired as complementary opposites as early as the 12th Dynasty, if not before, despite the fact that both originally manifested as Lioness Goddesses. Are Bastet and Sekhmet Dual Goddesses, the dual nature of a single Goddess, or two individual Goddesses? The same question can also be asked of Hathor and Sekhmet and Mut and Sekhmet. There is no definitive answer as the ancient texts support all views. Goddesses are not to be tied down for our convenience. The depiction of a pair of animals facing each other was seen on decorations referencing the Distant Goddess myth. Temple reliefs show vessels, probably used for wine or beer offerings, decorated with Hathor Heads flanked by two cats. They reflect both aspects of the Goddess and her ultimate absorption of the two.

In some places another pair of Goddesses were worshipped as the angry and pacified Eye; at Aswan this was Satis and Anukis and at Herakleopolis it was Ayet and Nehemtawy.[245] Little is known about Nehemtawy; she is cited as a consort of Thoth in the New Kingdom. A Late Period *stele* of Nectanebo I (30th dynasty) refers to her as the Eye of Ra.[246] I can find no information about Ayet.

Twins and the Union of Opposites

Nature doesn't tolerate one-sidedness for long and always tries to find a balance. The Egyptians were aware that for any process to occur there is the need for polarity, water for example needing a height differential for it to flow. Polarity also creates duality and the potential for conflict. Their awareness of this fundamental law was shown in the symbol of Ruty. He is the Double Lion, Shu and Tefnut, who unite opposites as well as symbolising male and female, yesterday and

---

[245] *Egyptian Mythology*, Pinch, 2002:130
[246] *Two Overlooked Oracles*, Klotz, 2010:247-254

tomorrow and the continuity of time. The sun rising over the back of Ruty illustrates how it rises between two opposing elements.

The Contrasting Sisters

Maat has no solar aspects. She is the cool, level-headed and reliable daughter of the Sun God and is a complete contrast to her volatile, fiery feline sisters. She is an essential part of creation and because of that is closely allied with Ra. Maat is the Goddess of truth, justice and balance. She is cosmic harmony and order which enables creation to exist and is present at all levels down to the acts of an individual. Without her constant presence creation would be overwhelmed by chaos and to prevent this destruction the kings made daily offerings of *maat* to the deities. She is an ancient Goddess who was present at the start of the Old Kingdom if not before. She is depicted as a woman wearing an ostrich feather on her head and the single feather can represent the Goddess herself. It is this feather against which the deceased's heart will be weighed. Maat is most definitely not a Lioness Goddess but she does have some association with cats. It may be based on a pun between the word for cat and that of Maat. On some bronze cat statues her ostrich feather symbol is used to imitate the pattern of the fur inside the cat's ears.

Ra is dependent upon Maat, she is frequently seen in the Solar Barque, and she sustains him. She is as essential as the protection provided by the Eye Goddess and the *uraeus* but in a different way. Maat protects Ra, and creation, by ensuring creation retains its harmony and by constantly returning disorder to order and imbalance to balance. The Eye Goddess protects Ra and creation by fighting off the forces of chaos. Each role is essential but neither Goddess could perform the roles of the other as it is outside their fundamental natures.

When Tefnut is paired with Maat they form the contrasting yet essential roles of the daughters of the Sun God. Creation cannot be sustained without Maat's order yet it needs the power of the Feline Goddess to provide it with energy and protection. In the *Coffin Texts* Tefnut is sometimes equated to Maat rather than just being partnered with her. Pairing Hathor or Sekhmet with Thoth, in the Distant Goddess, provides the same balance as Thoth is the consort of Maat and a tireless defender of *maat*. On one of her statues Sekhmet is described as *"Maat the Great"*.[247]

The Cat and the Lion

Once domesticated the cat became the opposite of the wild, fierce lion. It could represent the gentle and protective side of the Goddess whilst the lion represented her unpredictable and dangerous side. The two animals thus embodied the opposing and complementary aspects of the Feline Goddesses in particular. As Bastet transformed from a Lioness Goddess into a Cat Goddess her nature softened and she became gentle and approachable. By the Late Period Sekhmet and Bastet embody two different moods. *"Sekhmet yesterday...Bastet today."*[248] As well as being a reference to the pacified Goddess this saying reminds people that bad times will eventually pass. Given the strong association of the cat with women it did not take long for the stereotyping to emerge. *"A man who smells of myrrh, his wife is a cat in his presence. A man who is in distress, his wife is a lioness in his presence."*[249]

The Egyptians were not alone in both fearing and celebrating women's sexuality. For many reasons humanity seems unable to cope with women's sexuality as a single entity hence the duality of Goddess pairs; Hathor-Sekhmet, Bastet-Sekhmet, Mut-Sekhmet. Women's emotions and passions were considered to veer from one extreme to the other. *"The work of Mut and Hathor is what acts among women. It is in women that the good demon and the bad demon are active on earth."*[250] Men's sexuality is never treated this way despite ranging from compassionate lover to rapist. The Feline Goddesses were those associated with love and sex, Hathor and Bastet in particular, and their inherent duality might be one reason for this association.

The cat and lion pairing also emphasises the dual nature of the Feline Goddesses as the safe and the dangerous. Like all natural forces, such as fire and water, divine power varies in intensity and can both kill and nurture. It demands respect. This is most focused in the Eye Goddesses with their inflammable temperament. Their anger can be

---

[247] *Les Statues Thebaines de la Desses Sakhmet*, Gautier, 1920:117-207 (My translation)
[248] *Ancient Egyptian Bestiary*, Germond, 2001:157
[249] *The Literature of Ancient Egypt*, Simpson et al, 2003:515
[250] *Dancing for Hathor: Women in Ancient Egypt*, Graves-Brown, 2010:37

soothed and at heart they are benevolent and friendly. They love life and its pleasures but will always intervene to protect the Sun God and Creation. The Feline Goddesses may be deadly but they were never considered evil in the way Seth and Apophis were. Likewise the lion was a dangerous and deadly animal but was never aligned with Seth or vilified.

The Female Cat and the Two Cats

Cats are often depicted on *stelae*. The tomcat represented Ra as the Great Cat but some of these cats are referred to, or depicted, as female cats. It is thought that they represent the Eye of the Sun but it is possible that they are the female form of Ra. The gender of the cats is rarely clear and the grammar is often contradictory. The difference between male and female cats is not easily seen, when it was important to specify a female cat she was shown with visible teats. One depiction of the Great Cat defeating Apophis is definitely a female cat. Possibly it didn't matter in many contexts or perhaps it is our understanding which is at fault.

6 - The Great Cat slays Apophis

On a two-cat *stele* of Ra and Atum the name of the Great Cat of Ra is given as *miit nufer* and that of Atum as *miit oa*. *Miit* translates as female cat. Is this an early reference to the Eye of the Sun as a cat or could it be the Great Female Cat of Raet? The accompanying inscription reads *"Giving praise to the great cat, kissing the earth before Pra, the great god...lighten me that I may perceive your beauty...o beautiful one when at peace, the peaceful one who knows a return to peace"*.[251] The latter portion sounds very much like an address to the Distant Goddess. The word for 'beautiful' can also mean 'to return' giving a punning allusion to the Distant Goddess. We may also have a problem because we have to use gender-specific words to describe a deity which is both male and female.

Not all of the *stelae* decorated with cats make it clear which deity is being addressed. One was dedicated by a lady called Hemetnetjer to the *"good and peaceful (female) cat"* asking for life, prosperity and health.[252] On it are two cats who face each other. Many of the *stelae* show two cats. Do these represent the two eyes of the Sun God or Ra and the Eye Goddess? Or is the cat shown twice for symmetry or to indicate the dual aspects of the Goddess? And if so which Goddess? Bastet is an obvious choice but Malek suggests this could represent Mut or Hathor.

The Lunar and Solar Balance

The Egyptians regarded the moon very differently to the Europeans who viewed it as unstable and somewhat sinister. To them it was a regulator and time-keeper and the full moon was the time when the sun and moon united to form the healed eye. Thoth, one of the Gods sent to pacify and retrieve the Distant Goddess, is a Lunar God. He is sometimes referred to as the Son of Ra. Shu is another of the peacemakers who goes in search of his sister Tefnut. He isn't considered a Lunar God but he is often linked to Thoth and Khonsu and can take on the role of the Lunar Eye. It is not by chance that a Lunar God is sent to persuade a Solar Goddess to return to Egypt, here we see the symmetry of siblings. Given the fact that a face has two eyes and heaven has its two eyes of the sun and moon this emphasis of the lunar-solar balance is almost inevitable.

---

[251] *The Cat in Ancient Egypt*, Malek, 1993:89
[252] *The Cat in Ancient Egypt*, Malek, 1993:91

With Greek influence, all the Goddesses were seen as lunar rather than solar, but Tefnut always had a suggestion of lunar influence for some reason. Perhaps it was her water aspect. In later periods Bastet could assume the role of the Lunar Eye as well. The significance of the moon is seen in this comment from a temple calendar. On the 18th day of the 1st month of the Inundation is the Feast of Shu and Tefnut. *"If it is a day of full moon when the sister (Tefnut) comes, then this lunar feast becomes a full festival day."*[253] In the Greco-Roman Period the cat was seen as lunar, another Greek influence, but the lion always retained its solar imagery and association. Plutarch records some beliefs about cats. He reports that the cat has first one, then two kittens increasing at each birth until the seventh which gives a total of 28 *"the number of lights of the moon"*. He does add *"this, however, is probably somewhat too mythical"*. When describing the *sistrum* he said *"at the top, they put the metal figure of a cat with a human face...and by the cat the moon, on account of the variable nature, night habits, and fecundity of the beast"*.[254]

Amenhotep III (18th dynasty) was sometimes given the attributes of a Lunar God while Queen Tiy (his principal wife) was identified with the Solar Eye Goddess. He built a temple at Soleb, in the Third Cataract region of Nubia. It was dedicated to Amun-Ra, a deified form of Amenhotep as Lord of Nubia and Nebmaatra a local version of the Lunar God Khonsu. One ritual which was held here was *"joining the dais"* where Nebmaatra was invoked to ensure the regular appearance of the full moon by healing the Eye of Horus.[255] Queen Tiy was deified at the nearby temple of Sedeinga. She is depicted as a prowling sphinx and took the form of Tefnut or Hathor as the Distant Goddess. Both temples held rites for the *Pacification of the Goddess*. The Eye of Ra (in the person of Tiy) *"joined the deity Nebmaatra to return to Egypt and restore order to the world"*.[256] Did this lunar emphasis in the far south of the country balance the solar emphasis in the north? This far south the temperatures might have been considered hot enough without the additional emphasis on the Solar powers. In a similar theme Amenhotep IV (18th dynasty) and his queen Nefertiti were allied with Shu and Tefnut at one of their shrines at Karnak.

---

[253] *Temple Festival Calendars of Ancient Egypt*, el-Sabban, 2000:173
[254] *Plutarch: Concerning the Mysteries of Isis and Osiris*, Mead, 2002:239-240
[255] *The British Museum Dictionary of Ancient Egypt*, Shaw & Nicholson, 2008:310
[256] *Between Two Worlds*, Torok, 2009:232

It is possible that the pair of red granite lions referred to as the Prudhoe Lions, now in the British Museum (London), may have represented Tefnut-Mehit as the full moon. Mehit had the epithet *"She who has been filled"* which is thought by some to refer to the fullness of the moon, as the healed Eye of Horus rather than the Solar Eye.[257] One inscription from the Temple of Mut associates Mut with both the sun and moon as the Eyes of Atum. *"Mother of his Right and his Left Eye...Mother of the Two discs."* A king is shown offering *"two mirrors before your beautiful face, Mut, Eye of Re"*[258] which may allude to this. Her son, Khonsu, was a Lunar God which adds another element of balance to the Solar and Lunar Eyes. In Khonsu we see a parallel with the transition of the Angry Goddess into the benevolent Bastet. He was originally a bloodthirsty God but becomes increasingly benevolent in later periods. His mother can be Bastet or Mut, and at Kom Ombo it is Hathor.

Fire and Water

The underlying aspect of the Eye Goddess is solar, her element being fire and heat; the warming and burning rays of the sun and the flames of the fire, fever and the effects of venom and the burning anger of rage. Yet Tefnut is an Eye Goddess who is also the Goddess of moisture, an apparent contradiction. Eyes do have a connection with moisture via tears. Humanity was created when the Eye wept and Bastet is said to represent the moisture present in the Eye. Tefnut can be viewed as the moist, tear-filled Eye of the Sun. She brings pure water for the purification of the deceased. Tefnut and Shu *"will come to you bearing nemset-vessels...they outpour pure water...they will refresh you with their own hands"*.[259]

The *Return of the Distant Goddess* coincided with the inundation and the pacified Goddess brought the life-giving waters to Egypt when she returned. A cool benevolent contrast to her fire-spitting aspect in the desert. Sekhmet is the least likely of the Feline Goddesses to have an association with water, but nevertheless it is still present. A love song from the New Kingdom says *"Look at the River...Ptah himself is the life of those reed shoots. Lady Sakhmet of the lilies – yes, our Lady of Dew*

---

[257] *Myth and Symbol in Ancient Egypt*, Clark, 1978:227
[258] *The First Pylon of the Mut Temple, South Karnak: Architecture, Decorations, Inscriptions*, Fazzini & van Dijk, 2015:21&24
[259] *Traversing Eternity*, Smith, 2009:187

dwells among lily pads...Nefertem...blossoms newborn in the blue lotus. Twilight is heavy with gods."[260]

Some Thoughts on Triads

Triads, a grouping of three deities who may or may not be related, became an important part of Egyptian theology from the New Kingdom. Some are family groups such as Ptah, Sekhmet and their son Nefertem whilst others have no perceivable relationship. Another form is that of the three aspects of the same deity such as Khepri, Ra and Atum being the Sun God at dawn, noon and evening.

On reliefs from some temples there is evidence for another triad that of Ptah, Shu and Tefnut. A relief above the doorway of the sanctuary entrance in the temple at Hibis shows Ptah with two *ba*-birds named as Shu and Tefnut. In the Ptah temple of Sety I (19th dynasty) at Abydos there are two depictions of Ptah with the two *ba*-birds. It is not clear if Shu and Tefnut are shown as independent deities or as the souls of Ptah.[261]

The Daughters of Ra were often given compound names or treated as a grouping. When Hathor is angry she is Sekhmet, when she is happy she is Bastet. A New Kingdom Theban tomb refers to *"Mut, the mistress of heaven – Sekhmet, Ptah's beloved – Bastet, Re's eye"*. A Roman Period inscription at Dendera refers to *"Sekhmet, Ptah's beloved, the glorious one, who is at the head of Dendera – Tefnut – Maat, the great mistress at Memphis"*.[262] This is never viewed as a triad because it is emphasising specific aspects of the Goddess rather than connecting three individual Goddesses. They were not referring to a triple Goddess as modern Pagans understand it with the Maiden-Mother-Crone aspect, this concept was not present in Egyptian religion.

Conclusion

Everywhere you look in Egyptian symbolism and religion there are examples of duality, polarity and the union of opposites. The feline deities tend to predominate, especially the Goddesses, but they do not have the monopoly of this symbolism. Isis and Nephthys are a prime

---

[260] *Ancient Egyptian Literature*, Foster, 2001:47
[261] *A Memphite Triad*, Kakosy, 1980:48-53
[262] *The God Ptah*, Holmberg, 1946:190

example of Dual Goddesses who are not feline neither are the eternally battling Gods Horus and Seth. The Egyptians may not have viewed the fundamental elements as we do, but it is interesting to note that in the feline deities there is a balance of elements. Bastet and Sekhmet (and the other Feline Goddesses) represent fire. The Double Lion and Aker represent earth. Shu brings the element of air and Tefnut (and the Distant Goddesses) water.

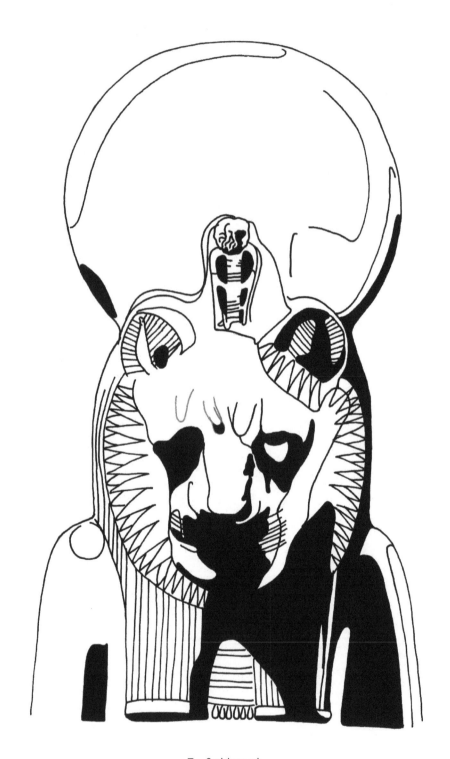

7 - Sekhmet

CHAPTER 14

THE DANGEROUS AND THE PROTECTIVE

"The Eye of Re has power over thee…the executioners of Sekhmet slay thee…thou art condemned to this fire of the Eye of Re; it sends forth its fiery blast against thee in this its name of Wadjet…it has power over thee in this its name of Sakhmet."[263]

Introduction

The Eye of Ra as the *uraeus* becomes the fierce protector of deities and kings, the ultimate power directed against their enemies. Sekhmet's role in the *Destruction of Mankind* makes her an instrument of divine retribution and thus very dangerous. All the Feline Goddesses were dangerous and this made them excellent protectors. Sekhmet and the other Goddesses defend the Sun God, creation, the king and Egypt and the individual. Along with other deities they protect Osiris and the deceased as well as providing protection against disease and the various

---

[263] *The Bremner-Rhind Papyrus IV*, Faulkner, 1938:41-53

dangers at the end of the year, these aspects are covered in chapters 15 and 16.

The Protection of Creation

Sekhmet, once appeased, becomes in effect the guardian spirit of the universe. The created universe is very vulnerable as it is surrounded by the chaotic waters of the *nun*. There are two main ways in which it is protected; by the repulsion and control of the chaotic entities which try and break through and by continual application of *maat* within creation.

An 11th dynasty hymn to Ra ends *"My protection is the (angry) red glow of your eye"*. The word used for angry-red differs from that for the colour red. This is the protective red glow of the Eye Goddess who sends death and sickness and causes the destruction of the enemies of Ra and of creation. It is the unnerving glow of feline eyes in the darkness. The Eye Goddess as the *uraeus* *"Preeminent on the head of her lord"* is the protector of the Sun God.[264] Rather than being the *uraeus* on his brow the Goddess can sometimes be described more as the Solar Eye encircling Ra with her protective flame and concealing him within her pupil.

Apophis

Why does the Sun God need so much protection? The answer is because he represents creation. Life cannot exist without the sun which is subject to constant attack from the surrounding chaos. The protection of the Sun God on his nightly journey through the underworld is covered in chapter 16. He is mainly at risk from Apophis whose evil eye will destroy the Solar Barque if his gaze is not constantly averted. The destruction of the Solar Barque will annihilate creation. This fear of Apophis was particularly prominent from the time of the New Kingdom and daily rituals were carried out in temples to deflect the evil power of Apophis. The Solar Eye has power over Apophis and can annihilate his soul and form according to the inscriptions. However this is only temporary. Apophis can never be destroyed; because he is from the *nun* he dissolves back into the nothingness from which he can endlessly emerge.

---

[264] *The Apotropaic Goddess in the Eye*, Darnell, 1997:35-48

The Greco-Roman *Bremner-Rhind* papyrus contains the *Book of Overthrowing Apophis* which gives details of these rituals. In this spell a number of Lioness Goddesses attack him with their fiery power. *"Sakhmet cuts out his heart...her flame is on him in this her name of fire...Wadjet parches him...Pakhet has put him in her fire."* A similar version says *"the Eye of Re shall appear against you...it shall consume you and chastise you in its name of Devouring Flame; it shall have power over you in this its name of Sakhmet; ye shall fall to its blast and fierce is the flame of fire which comes forth from its blast."*[265] In these spells it is usually the Goddesses who attack Apophis though sometimes there is the threat of Mahes. *"See, thou art (committed) to the fierce lion, the son of Bastet, lady of terror."*[266]

Belief in the power of the evil eye was widespread in Egypt and it is attested to in deities, demons and people. Deities invoked for protection against the evil eye tend to be those such as Thoth and Sekhmet who have an association with the Eye myths. One important ritual was *Hitting the Eye of Apophis.* In this the king hits a ball which equates to the eye of Apophis. As it is his evil glance which will destroy the Solar Barque it is Apophis' eye in particular which needs to be destroyed. The ritual was carried out in front of one of the Eye Goddesses, usually Hathor. Bourghouts studied 21 depictions of this ritual. In 13 the Goddess was Hathor, three depicted Sekhmet and one Tefnut. The other four reliefs were too damaged to accurately identify the Goddess. By playing a game with his eye in front of the Eye Goddess Apophis is humiliated as well as defeated. The club used to hit the ball was made of *bzk*-wood from the *moringa*-tree. This was believed to have sprung from the Eye of Ra so it had divine power. Using a substance which came from the Eye of Ra to attack the eye of his enemy was in effect fighting like with like.

There are depictions of this ritual in various temples at Deir el-Bahri, Luxor, Edfu, Dendera and Philae with the earliest dating to the 18th dynasty. At Luxor Amenhotep III (18th dynasty) is shown before Sekhmet. He says *"I have bent down the pupil of the rebel...I have hit it in order to make your heart rejoice"*. In one inscription at Edfu Hathor is addressed. *"He-whose-character-is-evil has been driven away, his pupil has been hit. Rejoice you, O Eye of Re."* She is referred to as *"the uraeus...the Eye of Re...the daughter of Re, who came forth from his body, the Eye which bestows brightness, as the iris of the Sound Eye"*. At Philae Augustus (27

---

[265] *The Bremner-Rhind Papyrus III*, Faulkner, 1938:166-185
[266] *The Bremner-Rhind Papyrus IV*, Faulkner, 1938:41-53

BCE – 14 CE) appears before Sekhmet in a relief entitled *"hitting the ball"* and also before a lioness-headed Tefnut who is described as *"the daughter of Re, lady of the Abaton, who slays Apophis through her flame".*[267]

Texts from Edfu refer to the *Book of Protecting the King*. The ritual is designed to protect the king during the twelve hours of the night. In a ritual which echoed that directed against Apophis four balls were identified with Sekhmet, Bastet, Wadjet and Shesmetet. These were thrown towards the four cardinal directions.

The War Goddess – Protector of the King and Egypt

Sekhmet might have been the protector of the king but she still needed to be treated with caution. In a relief from the temple of Edfu a king is shown offering to Sekhmet but he has his head turned away from her. Her power is too great for even a king to confront directly.

Her strength and anger make Sekhmet an excellent War Goddess and her role as the *uraeus* ensures that her wrath is put to good service protecting the king and Egypt by guarding the borders and expanding Egyptian territory. Sekhmet rode into battle with the king and is sometimes depicted in his chariot. The destructive rage of Sekhmet was transmitted to the king when he was in battle. Sekhmet's weapon was the bow and arrow. Was this because it was a high-status weapon or because it is used to attack from afar? The rays of the sun could be viewed as arrows shot by a divine archer, illustrated by rays of sunlight shining through clouds. *"When shooting an arrow as Sekhmet does, you fell thousands."*[268] The bow and arrow is not her only weapon; she is the *"One who wields the knife"* during the nightly battle between order and chaos.[269]

A hymn to Senusret III (12th dynasty) says *"How great is the lord of his city: Lo, he is a Sekhmet against his enemies who have trodden on his boundaries".*[270] Kings also claimed to be *"the fierce lion, son of*

---

[267] *The Evil Eye of Apophis*, Bourghouts, 1972:114-150
[268] *The Literature of Ancient Egypt*, Simpson et al, 2003:303
[269] *Egyptian Mythology*, Pinch, 2002:188
[270] *Voices from Ancient Egypt*, Parkinson, 1991:47

Sekhmet.[271] Rameses II (19th dynasty) recorded that his enemies at the battle of Kadesh said *"Don't approach him. Sakhmet the Great is she who is with him...anyone who goes to approach him, fire's breath comes to burn his body"*.[272] Rameses III (20th dynasty) said that Sekhmet made him invincible. Sekhmet also protected the king against insurrection within the country. A *stele* from Dakhla states *"As for anyone who shall disregard it* [his authority]...*he shall fall to the blaze of Sekhmet"*.[273]

On the walls of the temple of Horus at Edfu Ptolemy XI (88-80 BCE) is shown offering meat to the sacred falcon of Efdu as he invokes the Feline Goddess to protect him. *"O Sakhmet of yesterday, Edjo of today...shoot thine arrow at all the victuals of those who shall speak any malicious word against the Living Falcon. Let a slaughter be made of them like when thou didst prevail over the enemies of Re in the primordial age in that thy name of Sakhmet...O Bastet, mayest thou draw out their hearts...mine arrow shall not miss them. I am Sakhmet who prevaileth over a million...the papyrus-wand of Sakmeht is about the flesh of the Living Falcon, whole for life."*[274]

The Nubian king Tanutamani (25th Dynasty) left a record of his victories including his triumphant entry into Memphis. Mindful of the power of the resident deities he went to the temple of Ptah and *"gave offerings to Ptah-Sokaris. He made Sekhmet satisfied, as much as she desired"*.[275] Nectanebo I (30th dynasty) was particularly concerned about a new Persian invasion. He is depicted at Philae offering unguents to Sekhmet and *sistra* to Tefnut asking for protection. He probably made similar offerings and requests at temples in the north as this is where the Persian army would have invaded. The *Triumph of Horus of Behdet* is a drama from the New Kingdom. In it Horus fights Seth with the help of the other deities. *"Sakhmet abideth in front of him and Thoth protecteth him."* Horus makes *"the river to flow blood-stained, like Sakhmet in a blighted year"*.[276]

---

[271] *The Legend of the Capture of Joppa and the Story of the Foredoomed Prince. Being a Translation of the Verso of Papyrus Harris 500*, Peet, 1925:225-229

[272] *Ancient Egyptian Literature Volume II*, Lichtheim, 2006:70

[273] *The Smaller Dakhla Stele (Ashmolean Museum No. 1894. 107 b)*, Janssen, 1968:165-172

[274] *The King of Egypt's Grace before Meat*, Blackman, 1945:57-73

[275] *The God Ptah*, Holmberg, 1946:135

[276] *The Myth of Horus at Edfu: II. C. The Triumph of Horus over His Enemies a Sacred Drama (Concluded)*, Blackman & Fairman, 1944:5-22

The Protection of the Individual

People viewed Sekhmet as a very effective protector. She "*will keep you safe. She will assure your protection*".[277] One man, talking about a magistrate, said "*however powerful he may be, he cannot cause injury, for the matter is in the hands of Sekhmet the Great. The scope of her actions cannot be measured*".[278] Statuettes of Sekhmet in bronze or enamelled clay started to appear in the Middle Kingdom and became increasingly popular with large volumes being found from the Late Period.

Amulets of the Feline Goddesses, as well as of felines, were very desirable as they provided protection for both the living and the deceased against all misfortunes, natural and man-made. An amulet could protect the wearer or endow then with particular capabilities through its substance, colour, shape and decoration. There are four words used for amulets and three are derived from words meaning 'to protect'. The other sounds the same as the word used for 'wellbeing'. Lion claws were used as protective amulets giving the wearer both the protection of the lion and of the Feline Goddesses. These have been found dating to the Naqada II Period. Amulets with lioness-headed Goddesses first appear in the 3rd Intermediate Period and they were very popular. The volume of these type of amulets found dating to this period is a reflection of how unsafe people felt during this turbulent time.

Sekhmet's amulets repelled ghosts and demons as well as protecting the wearer from the terrors of the end of the year. Many jewels, amulets and scarabs were carved with her head for protection. Towards the end of the New Kingdom the *aegis* was a popular form. Often made of bronze or enamelled clay the head of Sekhmet was depicted on a broad collar. One scarab is decorated with a scene of the king offering wine or beer to Sekhmet under a winged solar disc. This is a reference to the *Destruction of Mankind* and Sekhmet's pacification. It may have been worn or carried over the end of the year or all the time.

The amulets of Lioness Goddesses vary in quality but there are some finely modelled ones. They are usually glazed but can also be worked in metal or precious stone and the Goddess is depicted walking or enthroned. They are not always inscribed so it isn't always clear which

---

[277] *Traversing Eternity*, Smith, 2009:148
[278] *The Gods of Ancient Egypt*, Vernus, 1998:184

Goddess is depicted. When the Goddess wears the double crown and carries a papyrus sceptre it is thought to represent Sekhmet-Mut. If the Goddess stands on prostrate captives she is probably Pakhet. If she wears the sun disc and *uraeus* she is usually interpreted as Sekhmet but some amulets of this form have been inscribed for Wadjet or Bastet. Perhaps it didn't matter which Goddess was being portrayed as all the Feline Goddesses are protective. It was the essence of the Goddess which was critical not what name we like to ascribe to her. The Egyptians tended to view them as interchangeable at certain times.

Other Protector Goddesses

Bastet also takes on the role of War Goddess. *"O Bastet, mayest thou draw out their hearts."*[279] At Karnak Rameses II is shown in war scenes with *"His bow being with him like Bastet"*.[280] Both Bastet and Sekhmet were invoked on a Middle Kingdom *stele*. *"He is Bastet who guards the Two Lands...he is Sakhmet to him who defies his command."*[281] Like Sekhmet she strengthened the heart of the king and his army and was often invoked as a War Goddess in the New Kingdom.

The aggressive aspect of Mut was harnessed to protect Egypt and the king. On temple walls she is often shown with Amun as Mistress of the Nine Bows, symbolic of the enemies of Egypt, as Amun hands the king the scimitar of war. She was Mistress of the *"war cry...Cobra of dread. The vigilant mistress of Karnak"*.[282] A 2nd Intermediate Period text calls Mut *"the Akhet-cobra who protects her father"*.[283] As the Lady of the *uraeus* *"there is no form who escapes her flame"*.[284] The *uraeus* was sometimes called The Flame of Mut. In recognition of this divine weapon traitors were burned alive on braziers in her temple.

Neith, the Creator Goddess of Sais, has a warrior aspect and other Goddesses are drafted in as necessary but the main War Goddesses are the Feline ones. The Feline Gods are not War Gods, largely due to their more passive and less aggressive nature. As with the Goddesses any God could be called upon when divine assistance was required but specific War Gods were not a prominent feature of Egyptian religion. The main

---

[279] *The King of Egypt's Grace before Meat*, Blackman, 1945:57-73
[280] *Minor War Scenes of Ramesses II at Karnak*, Gaballa, 1969:82-88
[281] *Ancient Egyptian Literature Volume I*, Lichtheim, 2006:128
[282] *Excavating the Temple of Mut*, Fazzini & Peck, 1983:16-23
[283] *Mut Enthroned*, Troy, 1996:307
[284] *A Crossword Hymn to Mut*, Stewart, 1971:87-104

War God was Montu, the falcon-headed God from Thebes. Horus, another Falcon God, did his fair share of fighting.

Feline Protection

Any deity can be called on for protection but a strong, fierce one had a more reassuring presence, hence the popularity of the Feline Goddesses. Other Goddesses such as Isis, Nephthys, Maat and Nut have very protective aspects. Theirs is a more gentle protection than that offered by the Feline Goddesses, which is why they are often depicted with wings which protect by sheltering. When the sun disc and *wedjat* eye are shown with wings it demonstrates that they are being protected in this way. The Feline Goddesses are not shown with wings, the aggressive *uraeus* being a better symbol of the nature of feline protection.

CHAPTER 15

SEKHMET THE HEALER

"To save a man from the plague of the year."[285]

Introduction

Of all the feline deities Sekhmet is the only one seriously associated with healing. All deities can be invoked in healing spells and prayers but Sekhmet was considered particularly effective, especially in the treatment of plagues and other epidemics. As she was considered responsible for inflicting them she was the best deity to invoke to prevent and cure them. The Egyptians used the word *sunu* as a title for physicians and healers and applied it to some deities. Isis, Thoth and Horus are referred to as *sunu* but not Sekhmet for some reason. Was this because she controlled her demons, withdrawing them from the body, rather than using healing magic to expel them?

---

[285] *Charms for Protection During the Epagomenal Days*, Raven, 1997:276

The Dangers of the Year

Liminal times are the passage from one phase to the next; nightfall, the end of the month, the end of the year or even the succession of a new monarch. They were considered dangerous because at these times the veil thinned and chaos could enter. The end of the year was particularly fraught as it consisted of the five *epagomenal* days, days out of time which Thoth had created to allow the Sky Goddess Nut to give birth. Normal, cyclical time had been suspended and there was the fear that it wouldn't restart again.

The Plague of the Year

The hot summer months were an unpleasant time in Egypt. The New Year brought the inundation and the days before it arrived were a worrying time, if it failed there would be famine but if it was too high it brought destruction. The Nile and other water sources ran dangerously low and food supplies were running out. Pests and insects flourished in the dry conditions and people were weakened by the lack of food and water making them vulnerable to a wide range of contagious diseases and infections. Sekhmet, as the Eye of the Sun, scorched the vegetation and dried up the water and so she was seen as bringing the Plague of the Year. With all this misfortune and worry it is not surprising that the deities appeared to be punishing people. There are many references to the diseases brought by Sekhmet. In the *Tale of Sinuhe* the king is described and *"Respect for him pervades the world like fear of our Great Lady in a year of plague"*.[286] Similarly in the *Tale of the Eloquent Peasant* an official is told *"you surpass the Lady of Plague"*.[287]

Plagues and epidemics were described as an evil wind, the breath of the emissaries of Sekhmet. Some epidemics are caused by airborne infection but this was not the reasoning behind the description. The suffocating, scorching wind was instinctively seen as unhealthy and a lot of spells were to repel these bad winds. *"The wind will not reach me."*[288] Flies were also correctly blamed with spells *"against all of the year's noxious flies"*.[289] Plagues and epidemics might have become more

---

[286] *Ancient Egyptian Literature*, Foster, 2001:129
[287] *The Tale of Sinuhe and Other Ancient Egyptian Poems*, Parkinson, 1998:64
[288] *Sekhmet et la Protection du Monde*, Germond, 1981:293 (My translation)
[289] *Daily Life of Egyptian Gods*, Meeks, 1999:131

common at certain periods due to prolonged and widespread contact with neighbouring countries.

Sekhmet's Messengers

Seven was an important number and is thought to have represented wholeness and perfection and had magical properties. Spells are often recited seven times. Hathor and Sekhmet both have a seven-fold aspect, which is not surprising given their relationship. They are the only deities to have this form and it is not clear why. It could be that their association with fate prompted it and seven because it is a magical number, but they are not the only deities associated with fate. The benevolent Seven Hathors foretell fate and have a strong magical aspect especially with regard to fate, unlike Hathor who has little *heka*. In symmetry with this Sekhmet has a seven-fold aspect in the form of the seven demons or messengers. Unlike the Seven Hathors these always bring misfortune and the messengers were known as *"the slaughters of Sekhmet"* and held responsible for the *"breath of the plague of the year"* and divine retribution in general.[290] In particular they symbolised the dangers of liminal times and represented all the misfortunes that could arise. From the 3rd century BCE they were believed to be led by the Lion God Tutu. The number of messengers can vary, with seven or twelve being the most common. Sekhmet could also conscript the 36 gods of the *decans*. (See chapter 17 for more details about *decans*.) Her messengers were also referred to as those *"who shoot their arrows from their mouths"*.[291] The words 'arrows' and 'messengers' hint at the force and mobility of the troubles of year. They allude to active chaotic forces rushing in, as well as targeted attacks on individuals. The words used for messengers, demons and so on are all used slightly differently so they probably refer to slightly different effects.

Appeasing Sekhmet

All temples held formal rites to appease Sekhmet and combat the epidemics she brought. The spells were documented in the *Book of the Last Day of the Year*. The purpose was to transform Sekhmet back into her benevolent form and persuade her to fight the plague and pestilence

---

[290] *Magic in Ancient Egypt*, Pinch, 2006:38
[291] *Egyptian Magic*, Raven, 2012:79

she brought. No one was immune from the arrows of Sekhmet. Complicated and lengthy rituals were held to protect the king from the Evils of the Year. The temple of Horus at Edfu contains many of these inscribed upon the walls. Sekhmet is addressed by her numerous epithets, the *"Eye of Re in each of her names"*.[292] She is praised and asked to protect the king, the Living Falcon, against these arrows and not to release her plague or contagion. She reassures the petitioners that she will protect the king against a wide range of misfortunes.

The terminology is deliberately vague. Terms include evil contagions, all fever, all pestilence, all bitterness, all impurities, all ills, setbacks, troubles and bad things. It asks that flies be not attracted to him, nor that he step in the path of the arrows and asks that he may pass through a gap in the contagion and the evil.

The Litany ends with seven couplets designed to protect the king against the *"seven arrows of the year"*. The nature of each arrow is not specified as it was a widely cast spell to catch everything that might possibly occur. *"Oh Sekhmet, you who love justice and abhor injustice...save him...guard him, protect him from the 6th arrow of the year! O Sakhmet-Uraeus, you who open the circle...protect him from the 7th arrow of the year."*[293] The rituals also ask for protection against those who might plot against king and for the protection of the king's family, friends and the people.

The ordinary people also wanted protection and there are many spells against Sekhmet's anger and her messengers and their arrows. One spell was recited over a piece of cloth which was worn around the neck as protection. Another involved walking around the house holding a club while reciting the spell.

Magicians often claim to be the son of Sekhmet, or to seek his protection, in order to divert the anger of Sekhmet, on the assumption that she wouldn't harm her son. *"I am Horus...sprout of Sekhmet! I am the unique one, the son of Bastet – I will not die on account of you."*[294] They also align themselves with Sekhmet and other Eye Goddesses, as in this spell against the plague of the year. *"Murderers who stand in waiting upon Sekhmet who have come forth from the Eye of Re...who bring slaughtering about, who create uproar...who shoot their arrows through*

---

[292] *Sekhmet et la Protection du Monde*, Germond, 1981:19 (My translation)
[293] *Daily Life of Egyptian Gods*, Meeks & Favard-Meeks, 1999:131
[294] *Ancient Egyptian Magical Texts*, Bourghouts, 1978:15

their mouths...be on your way...you shall have no power over me...I have arisen as Sekhmet, I have arisen as Wadjet...I will not fall for your slaughtering."[295]

The *epagomenal days* at the end of the year were the most feared, especially the last day of the year. The *Leiden* papyrus contains a *Book of the Last Day of the Year* giving spells designed for this frightening time. It includes a charm against the twelve *"murderers who stand in wait upon Sekhmet, who have come forth from the Eye of Re, messengers everywhere present in the districts, who bring slaughtering about, who create uproar, who hurry through the land, who shoot their arrows from their mouths, who see from afar."* These were the *"words to be said over a piece of fine linen"*.[296] Twelve deities were drawn on the linen and twelve knots were tied. The spell stresses that the fabric must be new and fine, similar to that used for mummy wrappings. Knotting is very common in charms and one of the words used for amulet is written with the sign for a knotted cord. With this spell the knots will have immobilised the demons. It is thought that the offerings of bread, beer and incense made during the recitation were to mollify the demons for the duration of their captivity. The linen was worn around the throat, examples of such bandages have been found and they look like a modern choker. The spell was to be recited from the last day of the old year until the start of the New Year.

There are many similar spells. One vignette shows the twelve deities to be drawn on the linen which includes four enthroned lioness-headed Goddess named as; *"Sekhmet the Great, Mistress of Asheru. Shesemtet, Mistress of Punt. The Eye of Asheru. The brilliant Eye of Horus, Mistress of Wine."* There is also one human-headed Goddess described as the *"Eye of Re, Mistress of the Two Lands who rules over Ill-neserser"*. In other examples the deities are different but there are always twelve. One has Sekhmet, Wadjet (human-headed), Shesmetet, Mistress of Asheru, the Eye of Ra and the Eye of Horus. Depicting the Eye Goddess is not unexpected. Another example shows Shu and Tefnut but no other Feline deities.[297] The *Edwin Smith* papyrus included similar spells to be recited over linen bandages and *"incantations against pest"*.[298] One involves drawing Sekhmet, Bastet, Osiris and Nehebu-Kau.

---

[295] *Religion and Ritual in Ancient Egypt*, Teeter, 2011:166
[296] *Charms for Protection During the Epagomenal Days*, Raven, 1997:276
[297] *Charms for Protection During the Epagomenal Days*, Raven, 1997:277
[298] *Charms for Protection During the Epagomenal Days*, Raven, 1997:284

Bastet was also implicated in the *Plague of the Year*. One spell for purifying something during a plague includes *"Let your murderers retreat, Bastet...your breeze will not reach me"* and another *"the fire-spewing of Bastet will fail against the house of a man"*.[299] New Year's Day was a return to the proper order and a time of celebration where gifts of amulets, depicting Bastet or Sekhmet, were exchanged. Although Sekhmet was viewed as bringing the seven arrows of misfortune each year, she was never seen as evil just dangerous.

The Priests of Sekhmet

The Greeks said *"in Egypt men are more skilled in medicine than any of mankind"*. Medicine was closely entwined with magic, an alien practice to modern professionals. The *Ebers* papyrus states that *"magic is effective together with medicine; medicine is effective together with magic"*.[300] A recent study of the medical papyri concluded that 50 percent of the drug sources referenced were still in use today; these included opium, henna, garlic, coriander and juniper. No doubt some of the practices were ineffective and others dangerous but the Egyptians were serious in their study and application. A number of recipes for medicine include cat and lion dung, as well as that of other creatures. Much debate has been held over this. Did they really use dung or was it just the folk name of a herb or a name of an ingredient they wished to keep secret?

Through her healing attributes Sekhmet became the patron Goddess of physicians.[301] Professionals tended to hold priesthoods, or at least be associated, with their patron deities hence most physicians were priests of Sekhmet. Contagious diseases were dealt with by the *"pure priest of Sekhmet"*.[302] The *Edwin Smith* papyrus lists medical practitioners as *"any priest of Sekhmet or physician"* whilst the *Ebers* papyrus refers to *"any physician, any priest of Sekhmet, or any magician"*.[303] Priesthood may have been part of the requirements for training at a certain level. There were at least three levels of medical practitioners; magicians, doctors who weren't priests and the priests of Sekhmet who had the

---

[299] *Ancient Egyptian Magical Texts*, Bourghouts, 1978:16&17
[300] *Egyptian Medicine: Science and Superstition in the Ancient World*. David, 2013:38-40
[301] *Religion and Magic in Ancient Egypt*, David, 2002:200
[302] *Daily Life in Ancient Egypt*, Szpakowska, 2008:174
[303] *A Note of the Edwin Smith Surgical Papyrus*, Wilson, 1952:76-80

highest status. The priests of Sekhmet appear equivalent to modern consultants and they worked in temples healing, teaching and compiling texts. As to be expected there was a hierarchy of priest-physicians. In the reign of Nectanebo II (30th dynasty) there is reference to an official who was the Director of all the Priests of Sekhmet in the country. Other titles include Chief of Priests of Sekhmet, Chief of Physicians, Chief of Magicians, High Priest of Sekhmet and the King's Physician.[304] Graffiti from the 12th dynasty quarries of Hatnub includes one from the *"priest of Sekhmet Herishefnakht says 'I used to be overseer of the pure priests of Sekhmet, overseer of magicians, and chief physician of the King...who lays his hand on the patient and thereby acquires knowledge about him"*.[305] At this level the physicians were mostly men but there is a 4th dynasty *stele* from Giza which refers to Peseshet who was *"overseer of female physicians"*.[306] I have not found any references to Priestesses of Sekhmet. It is not known if the ordinary people had much access to the highly skilled, and one assumes expensive, priests of Sekhmet. They may have had to rely on local wise women and magicians.

In Bubastis there are references to *wab*-priests of Sekhmet connected with the *per-ankh*, the *House of Life*. These institutions were attached to temples and they functioned as a combination of centre of learning, scriptorium, library and archive. One of these *wab*-priests, Iuny, *"knew the secrets of the chest (of books) of Bubastis"*. There is reference to Sekhmet as *"Mistress of the House of Books"*.[307]

Veterinary Practice

Livestock, especially cattle, were of great importance both for the economy and as religious offerings so a lot of care was taken over their welfare, although this might have been more for practical reasons than compassionate ones. There is evidence to suggest that some of Sekhmet's priests specialised in veterinary medicine. A papyrus of veterinary medicine was found at Lahun. In one of the above-mentioned graffiti at Hatnub a man describes himself as *rekh-kau* *"one who knows oxen"* which some have interpreted as being a vet. From the Ptolemaic Period comes the comment *"your herds are numerous in the stable, thanks to the*

---

[304] *Magic and Medical Science in Ancient Egypt*, Ghalioungui, 1963:14
[305] *Egyptian Magic*, Raven, 2012:29
[306] *Egyptian Medicine: Science and Superstition in the Ancient World*, David, 2013:38-40
[307] *Magic and Medical Science in Ancient Egypt*, Ghalioungui, 1963:68

science of the priest of Sekhmet.[308] An Old Kingdom tomb relief shows three priests of Sekhmet supervising the butchery of offering cattle. It is thought that they may be vets responsible for checking the health of the animals to ensure that they were suitable for offering.

Healing *Stele*

Healing *stele*, known as Horus *cippi*, originated in the 18th dynasty and became very popular by the Late Period. They depicted Horus as the vanquisher of dangerous animals and are covered in inscriptions, depictions of deities and protective symbols. Texts on the back refer to the healing of Horus by Isis. Water was poured over the *cippi*, dissolving some of its healing powers, and used as a medicine. Decorations on many healing statues show an interesting array of lion and snake symbolism. There are snakes, lion-headed snakes and lion-headed winged snakes. Lionesses and cubs and cats are also present. Most of the lioness-headed Goddesses are Sekhmet or the composite Sekhmet-Bastet-Tefnut while others are anonymous. The lion-headed Gods are usually anonymous.

The statue of Psamtik-Seneb dates to the end of the Late Period. The first register depicts Hathor the Mistress of Hotepet, Shu, a lioness-headed Tefnut and a falcon-headed Ra. The third register shows a cat on a pedestal, Horus, Thoth as a baboon and an unidentified God with a spear (this could be Onuris). Other registers show Sekhmet as a reclining lioness and a large *sistrum* on a pole flanked by two cats each one with the inscription "*Mistress of Beauty*".[309] Hathor is also present, grasping a snake, as Mistress of the Sycamore Tree. The fourth register depicts Thoth as an enthroned baboon wearing a lunar disc. He presents a *wedjat* eye to a cobra who sits on the top of a platform with stairs. This summarises the myth of the Distant Goddess; healing spells frequently refer to myths and the patient and physician aligned themselves with the various protagonists in the story.

Another *cippi* from the 4th century BCE is the statue of Hor. On one register Isis is shown nursing Horus in the marshes, facing her is a lioness-headed Goddess. She is unnamed but given the context is likely to be Wadjet as she was a protector of the Horus child in the marshes.

---

[308] *How Now Sick Cow*, Lord, 2010:20-34
[309] *Egyptian Healing Statues in Three Museums in Italy (Turin, Florence, Naples)*, Kakosy, 1697:65

The third register is unusual in that it depicts Sekhmet as a pregnant woman which suggests that the *cippi* was used to protect and help women during pregnancy and childbirth. The other registers depict lioness and lion-headed deities with various snakes, two lioness-headed cobras and a cat seated on a pedestal. One of the lion-headed deities has the hieroglyph for fire on its head, the other a sun-disc.[310] In some of the illustrations it is not clear if the image is of a god or goddess. One *cippi* shows the baboon Thoth holding a *wedjat* eye to Sekhmet-Bastet-Tefnut who is depicted as a lioness-headed snake. The text says *"I did not give this heart of mine...on the brazier of the Two Gods, to the charcoal of Sakhmet...raise yourself...I am the Lion who went round the netherworld and rose in the wedjat eye. Fear the Lion born to the Godhead which rests in Djeme."*[311] The myth that this alludes to is unknown.

Another *cippi* has a huge *sistrum* decorated with six *uraeus* cobras and Sekhmet who grasps a huge snake with both hands. She is Sekhmet *"who subdues the rebels"* alluding to her role in the *Destruction of Mankind* and *"Mistress of Flame who defeats all the reptiles which are in the sky, in the earth and in the water"*.[312] Other registers are filled with lioness-headed Goddesses, lion-headed Gods, Sekhmet as a recumbent lioness and a double-headed lion deity. On the back Isis nurses Horus in the marshes, who had many misadventures with snakes and scorpions, flanked by the ibis-headed Thoth and a lioness-headed Goddess, probably Sekhmet.

One *stele* for protection against scorpion stings, or their healing, shows Tefnut as a lioness-headed winged cobra. Another register depicts a lion-headed deity wearing a scorpion as a crown and holding a snake. A scorpion headdress is the symbol of Serket, the Scorpion Goddess who is invoked for protection against and healing from scorpion stings. A cat seated on a pedestal is described as she who *"permits to breathe that which is short of breath"*.[313] One of the effects of scorpion poison is difficulty in breathing.

---

[310] *Egyptian Healing Statues in Three Museums in Italy (Turin, Florence, Naples)*, Kakosy, 1697:83-8

[311] *Egyptian Healing Statues in Three Museums in Italy (Turin, Florence, Naples)*, Kakosy, 1697:106

[312] *Egyptian Healing Statues in Three Museums in Italy (Turin, Florence, Naples)*, Kakosy, 1697:134

[313] *Egyptian Healing Statues in Three Museums in Italy (Turin, Florence, Naples)*, Kakosy, 1697:151

The number of anonymous lion-headed Gods on these *cippi* is interesting given the general lack of Lion Gods elsewhere. The reason for this is not clear - obviously there is a gap in our knowledge and understanding. Is there a Lion God who has a strong healing aspect like Sekhmet? If there is we haven't yet discovered him. Mut is depicted as an ithyphallic androgynous deity on a healing statue from Hibis as is an unnamed lioness-headed Goddess in the chambers of Khonsu at Karnak. On another register of this healing statue a lioness-headed Goddess sits on a throne and holds the *wedjat* eye. A bird's tail protrudes from her back and she has two tall plumes on her crown. No doubt this references an unknown myth.

It has been suggested that the large numbers of Amenhotep III's Sekhmet statues were intended to contain the power of Sekhmet and transform it into a force protecting the country against these regular epidemics. The statue of Sekhmet of Sahure was also famed for its healing miracles (see chapter 19).

Other Healing Spells

Any deity could be invoked for healing spells but the Feline deities are not commonly petitioned for healing other than for their speciality of plagues and fevers. They may be alluded to indirectly when cats or lions are mentioned. One charm for a headache says "*Flee, headache, lion flees beneath a rock*".[314] More useful medical advice is given in one spell for a bone stuck in the throat. The patient is to swallow a little oil while the physician massages their throat. "*Spit out this bone for me...for I am a lion's forepart...I am a panther's tooth.*"[315] One spell against poison includes reference to Ruty. "*I am the lion, I am the Lion Pair.*"[316]

There are a number of spells specifically for cats who have been poisoned by snakes or scorpions. Their hunting and generally inquisitive nature would have put cats at considerable risk from attack by these two creatures. One spell to conjure poison from a cat refers to Bastet herself being stung in the hope of getting a swift response from her father. "*O Re, come to your daughter, whom the scorpion has stung on a lonely road. Her cries reach heaven; harken on your way. The poison which has*

---

[314] *The Greek Magical Papyri in Translation. Volume I*, Betz, 1996:259
[315] *The Greek Magical Papyri in Translation. Volume I*, Betz, 1996:227
[316] *Ancient Egyptian Magical Texts*, Bourghouts, 1978:55

entered into her limbs flows through her flesh."[317] One invokes Shu asking him "*come to your wife...save her from that bad poison*". Another spell for a scorpion sting includes making a wax cat. There is a spell against snake bite which is recited to a real cat. "*Don't fear, Bastet, powerful of mind at the fore of the sacred marsh...Come out after my speech, you bad poison that is in any limb of the cat who is suffering.*"[318]

Conclusion

Sekhmet is a healer because she can control the diseases and plagues she unleashes. The other Feline Goddesses do not have a strong healing aspect although lion imagery is common on healing statues and *cippi*. There were specialist deities for pregnancy and childbirth. Bastet was associated with childbirth and motherhood but I cannot find any specific references in the medical texts to her for use during pregnancy or childbirth.

---

[317] *The Metternich Stele*, Scott, 1951:201-217
[318] *The Art of Medicine in Ancient Egypt*, Allen, 2005:54

CHAPTER 16

IN THE BEYOND

"My heart is Bastet, I will ascend and rise up to the sky."[319]

Introduction

The journey through the underworld was hazardous and the process of rebirth required strong magic. Despite the changing details one thing is constant: rebirth could be considered a parallel process to that of creation and as such required the interplay of all the different powers and aspects. The main emphasis was on the resurrection of Osiris by Isis and the daily rebirth of the Sun God. The feline deities have a role to play but they are never the most dominant.

The Funerary Texts

The oldest of these texts are the *Pyramid Texts* which were designed solely for use by the king although by the end of the Old Kingdom they started to appear in other royal tombs. The main emphasis is on the king being reborn as a star. The Middle Kingdom saw the development of the

---

[319] *The Ancient Egyptian Pyramid Texts*, Faulkner, 2007:207 utterance 539

Coffin Texts which could be used by anyone who could afford them. A new introduction is the ferry boat, which will transport the deceased across the Winding Waterway (the Milky Way) into the afterlife. The deceased also have to face the dangers of the fishing net which catches the souls of the deceased. The *Book of the Dead* appeared in the New Kingdom and the spells were written on papyrus and on tomb walls. It introduced the concept of the judgement of the deceased and cats feature in this funerary text reflecting their domestication and popularity.

The New Kingdom also saw the development of various books of the afterlife often referred to as the *Books of the Netherworld* which focus on the night time journey of the Sun God. The best studied of these are the *Book of the Amduat* because the text and vignettes combine to form a coherent text. Some scholars who have studied this text in detail suggest that it is also intended as a guide for the living. Because of this I will deal with the feline deities of this text in a separate section as it will give a more coherent description of the process. Other Netherworld books include the *Book of Gates*, the *Book of Caverns*, the *Book of Earth* as well as the *Books of the Sky*. The *Books of Breathing* are short funerary texts dating from the Greco-Roman Period and were said to have been written by Isis for Osiris and by Thoth for everyone else. As their name suggests, they focus on the importance of breathing and the survival of the deceased's name in the afterlife. Sekhmet and Bastet are the only feline deities in these short texts.

Throughout these texts all deities are invoked for assistance and a number of spells align parts of the deceased's body, the ferry boat and the fishing net to various deities. These include the feline deities but there doesn't appear to be any obvious connection between the item and the assigned deity. The Egyptian priests and priestesses would no doubt would tell us differently.

Mummification

The main deity associated with mummification is Anubis. Tayet is the Goddess of Weaving and her most important role is the provision of bandages for the mummy. Sekhmet does not have any connection with textiles but she is invoked in some embalming rituals because of her great protective powers. One mummy bandage was discovered which contains a string of epithets of Sekhmet taken from spell 164 of the *Book of the Dead*. "*Uraeus-serpent on the brow of the sun god...Great of Magic in the bark of millions of years."*[320] Another fragment of funerary cloth, dating to the 1st century BCE, shows Thoth, Maat and Sekhmet walking. One embalming ritual refers to the *"cloth of Sekhmet the Great"* for binding the head. *"A piece of precious cloth belonging to the Mistress of the Uraeus. She gives you her roll of cloth, she binds your head with this strip of magical cloth...she has power over those who would harm you."*[321] Her protection is that of the *uraeus*, the deceased are assured that Sekhmet will direct her flame against their enemies and burn their corpses. Invoking Sekhmet whilst bandaging the head may transfer the power of the *uraeus* onto the deceased's forehead. One mummification spell refers to the fine Nubian ochre which is the ochre used to dye the beer used to pacify Sekhmet in the *Destruction of Mankind*.

Guarding the Body and the Tomb

The solar symbolism of felines associated them with light, life and the rebirth of the sun at dawn and thus the rebirth of the deceased. They were also good guardians. It was essential that the mummy was protected as the body would be needed in the afterlife. Small cat amulets were sometimes placed in mummy wrappings for added feline protection. Tiny amulets, including three of Sekhmet, were found on bodies in the 26th dynasty necropolis of Khawaled. Lion and cat figurines and other objects were also placed in the tomb to protect the deceased. In the 1st Intermediate Period these included faience figurines of crouching cats. Two tombs from the reigns of Amenhotep II and III (18th dynasty) have paintings over the doorway replicating the grilles used on high windows, a cat is shown sitting at the window. This was probably a common sight as cats like high observation platforms as well as being symbolic of the cat guarding the tomb and mummy.

Funerary furniture is often decorated with lions, the bier on which the mummy rested was often in leonine form or had feline feet. More elaborate, and expensive, biers had lion shaped legs and the head and tail of a lion at the foot and the head. The funerary throne of Tutankhamun has legs in the shape of lion legs, including the paws, topped by carved lion heads. Seated on this throne Tutankhamun was identified as the sun rising between the Double Lion. The inscription on his funerary couch references Mehit. The couch has the head of a lion

---

[320] *The Rendells Mummy Bandages*, Caminos, 1982:145-155
[321] *Sekhmet et la Protection du Monde*, Germond, 1981:352 (My translation)

and is inlaid with bright blue glass for the nose, tear-drops and the darker eye rim. The eyes themselves are crystal with the iris and pupil painted black. The 18th dynasty Tomb KV-63 in the Valley of the Kings contained sealed storage jars. On investigation one contained a dismantled wooden bed and two carved lion heads which fitted at the corner of the foot of the bed, another contained the bed's cross supports. It was too fragile to have been used and was intended for the afterlife. Comfort in the afterlife had also been considered as another jar contained linen pillows.[322]

One temple ritual says that body of Osiris was guarded by four Lioness Goddesses; Wadjet, Sekhmet, Bastet and Shesmetet. A vignette in the *Salt* papyrus depicts this as four lion heads set on the roof of a cage. Four clay lioness heads were found in shallow pits in the desert forming a protective circle around an image of Osiris as a mummy. These four Goddesses appear to be connected to the four directions. At Abydos, and some other temples of Osiris, there was a ritual where priests threw four clay balls, inscribed with the names of these Goddesses, to the sky in the four directions as a symbolic defence against Seth.

The theme of the Great Cat killing the serpent Apophis, from the *Book of the Dead*, was popular in the Ramesside tombs at Deir el-Medina. These cats are not modelled on the domestic cat, they look wild and powerful and have long legs and ears reminiscent of a serval. One has a long banded tailed and a coat marked with rows of dark crescents. Some have a very leonine face. Do we have the change from lion to cat being depicted here? Was the artist just not very good at cats or did the creature have a significance we don't know of? It could be illustrating a local cat myth or just his imagination.

Demons and Dangers

The underworld was a very dangerous place, hence the need for divine protectors and guides and some strong magical spells. Some of the dangers would have been familiar, such as snakes, but others were the demons and fearful inhabitants of the underworld. Snakes were a serious threat during life and this continued after death. They are animals of the earth, and a symbol of it, as they move so close upon it and most live and hide in burrows or crevasses. As the Egyptians largely

---

[322] *KV-63 Update: the 2009 Season*, Wilson, 2009:30-38

believed that the underworld was below ground this fear of the earth as a habitat of snakes became entwined with fear of it as a habitat of the deceased and otherworldly creatures. The underworld seems to have been infested with snakes and there are a large number of spells to repel snakes in all of the funerary texts. Animals who attacked snakes, such as the cat and mongoose, were much-valued protectors. Duality is always close in the Egyptian mind and the earthbound snakes of the underworld were matched by the protective solar powers of the *uraeus* snake.

The demons of the underworld were varied and imaginative and included cat and lion demons. Some of these were gatekeepers whose role it was to prevent the unworthy deceased and other enemies from passing. Others acted as tormentors and punishers. They are more prevalent from the New Kingdom and as the cat rises in prominence so demons and gatekeepers start to appear in cat form. The tomb of an official at Saqqara is decorated with vignettes from the *Book of the Dead*. At the eighth gate are a pair of gatekeepers, one lion-headed the other cat-headed. Both wear two tall plumes on their head and carry a knife in both hands. The lion-headed demon carries a snake-shaped wand or sceptre. "*Backwards, lion, white of mouth with flat-squeezed head. Recede for my power.*"[323] In other New Kingdom funerary texts a cat-demon is shown decapitating bound captives. The twelfth gate in the *Book of the Dead* has a lion-headed guardian but the spell says "*the name of the god who guards you is Cat*".[324]

The later funerary texts continue this theme. In the *Book of the Amduat* a demon who is either cat-headed or has cat ears is shown decapitating the enemies of the Sun God. In the *Book of Caverns* a cat-headed demon called Miuty watches over the bound enemies of the Sun God. A demon of the same name guards the final gate in the *Book of Gates*. He is cat-headed and holds two sceptres, one of which is serpent-shaped. "*I make you to be counted out to the miwty, from whose guarding one does not escape.*"[325] Was this image suggested by the sight of a cat patiently waiting for the prey to emerge from its hole? During the Late Period the cat-headed gate-keeper Miuty was painted on the interior of coffins. In the *Coffin Texts* Horus goes to visit Osiris in the underworld

---

[323] *Death as an Enemy*, Zandee, 1960:195
[324] *The Cat in Ancient Egypt*, Malek, 1993:83
[325] *Death as an Enemy*, Zandee, 1960:194

and is challenged by a number of guardians including *"the Leonine One, the dweller in his cavern"*.[326]

Like other cultures, the Egyptians envisaged a fiery underworld. Fire was a great threat as it meant total destruction reducing everything to ash. In the *Coffin Texts* three portals are described as fire from Sekhmet. The first portal has blue fire which stretches for 50 cubits. The third portal is *"the fiery blast of the mouth of Sekhmet"*. This gate is described in detail *"the border with ornaments consists of uraei...who knows his protection against Sekhmet, he is safe from you, basin of these snakes"*.[327]

Despite the descriptions of fire, the underworld is dark and the deceased will need a light to guide them. *"This torch will flourish... just as the name of Tefnut flourishes."*[328] In one tomb is an image of a *wedjat* eye with arms holding a double tapered torch. The accompanying text refers to lighting a torch for Osiris.

The Roles of Sekhmet

Sekhmet is present in the *Book of the Dead* as the guardian and protector of the deceased. They take on her aspect so that they can destroy their enemies as easily as she does. *"O Sekhmet, great of magic... save the Osiris N...guard him, protect him from the power of the dead."*[329] Sekhmet was also invoked in an *Opening of the Mouth* ceremony as the Eye of Re. This critical ritual enabled the deceased to breathe in the Afterlife. *"My mouth is forced apart by Shu...I am Sekhmet, I sit beside her – she who dwells in the sky's storm-wind."*[330] Sekhmet takes on a more active and familiar role in the *Coffin Texts* fighting the enemies of the deceased and the Gods. Often the deceased align themselves with her arrows and her power.

In one section of the *Books of Breathing* Sekhmet is referenced for access to flowing water. This alludes to her role as the Distant Goddess bringing the inundation as well as the lioness coming out of the desert to drink. *"May you refresh my heart in the form of flowing water. May you permit me to have access to water like Sekhmet."* There is also a pun on

---

[326] *Myth and Symbol in Ancient Egypt*, Clark, 1978:145
[327] *Death as an Enemy*, Zandee, 1960:137 & 193
[328] *Traversing Eternity*, Smith, 2009:492
[329] *Sekhmet et la Protection du Monde*, Germond, 1981:345 (My translation)
[330] *Writings from Ancient Egypt*, Wilkinson, 2016:169

shm 'to have access to' and her name *shm.t.*[331] In the *Book of Gates* the fifth gate is illustrated by four people who represent the races to which the Egyptians assigned people; Egyptian, Asiatic, Nubian and Libyan. This infers that rebirth and the afterlife will be available for all people providing that they are deemed worthy, and all will be in the care of Horus and Sekhmet. Foreign lands and foreigners were considered to be under the jurisdiction of Hathor, as Sky and Solar Goddess she was universal and constant over all lands, and Sekhmet has taken on this role.

The Roles of Bastet

In the *Pyramid Texts* Bastet acts as mother to the deceased king but apart from that has no other role. *"My mother Bastet has nursed me."*[332] There is an interesting statement in one of the ascension texts which references Bastet. *"I have not opposed the King; I have not succoured Bastet."* The deceased king recites a brief negative confession to a *"local god of mine"*.[333] The phrasing shows that at least part of it has been taken from a non-royal ritual as the king would not need to say this. Faulkner's translation 'succoured' depicts Bastet in a negative way as one who should not be encouraged or assisted. Zabkar quotes another translation as *"I have not sinned against Bastet"* which is more in line with her role as a royal protector.[334]

Bastet is invoked in one snake spell in the *Coffin Texts* and is mentioned as a general protector of the deceased. *"She is your protection until day dawns, until you go down to the realm of the dead."*[335] In the *Coffin Texts* it is Bastet who provides light as well as protection. *"Bastet...the Eye of Horus is she who sheds light for you, she is with you in the necropolis."*[336] The word used for light in this passage alludes to lighting a torch. The Eye of Horus can refer to the moon so could this refer to the moon lighting the way through the underworld as it does at night? Is this an early connection of Bastet to the moon?

Despite the rise in popularity of the cat during the New Kingdom there is little reference to Bastet in the *Book of the Dead*. She is addressed

---

[331] *Traversing Eternity*, Smith, 2009:509
[332] *The Ancient Egyptian Pyramid Texts*, Faulkner, 2007:183 utterance 508
[333] *The Ancient Egyptian Pyramid Texts*, Faulkner, 2007:156 utterance 467
[334] *Hymns to Isis in Her Temple at Philae*, Zabkar, 1988:124
[335] *The Ancient Egyptian Coffin Texts Volume I*, Faulkner, 2007:55 spell 60
[336] *The Apotropaic Goddess in the Eye*, Darnell, 1997:35-48

as one of the deities in the negative confession and her angry aspect is mentioned in another spell. As Bastet grew in popularity in the Late and Greco-Roman Period she appears in their funerary texts in the role of guide and protector of the deceased. *"She will magnify your strength against your foes."*[337]

The Roles of Mafdet

Mafdet's roles in the underworld are in line with her character; killing snakes and acting as executioner. In the *Pyramid Texts* she protects the king from the numerous snakes in the underworld, as she does in life, and her teeth and claws are likened to knives, barbs or harpoons. *"Mafdet, pre-eminent in the Mansion of Life, she strikes you on your face, she scratches you on your eyes...Lie down! Crawl away."*[338] She continues this role in the *Coffin Texts*, extending her protection to all the deceased. Similarly in the *Book of the Dead* the deceased either assume the role of Mafdet or use her name to threaten the snake with. In one spell she beheads the venomous snakes in the seventh mound of underworld. Mafdet is not present in any of the later funerary texts.

Aker in the Underworld

Aker and the Akeru appears in several spells in the *Pyramid Texts* all of which reflect very clearly the expected role of an Earth God. There are apotropaic spells especially against snakes *"Leap up, O Earth-god and grasp him"*[339] and *"The flame goes out against the Earth-god"*.[340] The snake's poison falls to the ground where it is neutralised. Aker also opened the gates of the earth to let the deceased king pass. *"The doors of the Earth-god are opened for you"*[341] which enabled him to be resurrected and ascend out of the grasp of the earth. *"The Earth-gods shall not lay hold of you."*[342] Their role is taken over by the Double Lion in the other funerary texts but Aker is mentioned in the *Amduat*.

---

[337] *Traversing Eternity*, Smith, 2009:149
[338] *The Ancient Egyptian Pyramid Texts*, Faulkner, 2007:88 utterance 297
[339] *The Ancient Egyptian Pyramid Texts*, Faulkner, 2007:127 utterance 385
[340] *The Ancient Egyptian Pyramid Texts*, Faulkner, 2007:313 utterance 727
[341] *The Ancient Egyptian Pyramid Texts*, Faulkner, 2007:144 utterance 437
[342] *The Ancient Egyptian Pyramid Texts*, Faulkner, 2007:306 utterance 703

The Double Lion, Tefnut and Shu

The Double Lion plays an important role in the funerary texts as do Shu and Tefnut. Sometimes he takes roles similar to the other deities, such as protection and the provision of food and water. In the *Pyramid Texts* he is threatened in a food spell. "*If the King be hungry, the Double Lion will be hungry.*"[343] Other roles are more relevant to his aspects. "*Lift up this King's double to the god, lead him to the Double Lion-god...The King's rank is high in the Mansion of the Double Lion-god.*"[344] This is an expected role of the Double Lion who guards the horizon and the rising sun. Other ascension and resurrection texts refer to Shu and Tefnut in a similar role. "*You are raised aloft on the hands of Shu and Tefenet.*"[345]

The Double Lion is present in a large number of spells from the *Coffin Texts* and the *Book of the Dead*. There is reference to the House of the Double Lion which appears to be the caverns of the underworld and the secret and dangerous paths of the Double Lion. As a personification of the underworld the Double Lion will contain everything including places where even the deities are not safe. He is invoked whilst erecting a bier for the deceased and appears in spells for breathing, for being transformed into a falcon and for going out from the tomb. Allowing the deceased to leave the tomb reflects his Earth God aspect and the Double Lion's power over the horizon. Not surprisingly, the deceased ally themselves with both the Lion (probably Shu) and the Double Lion. He also acts as a gatekeeper, questioning the deceased to ensure that they are worthy for rebirth. Vignettes from the *Book of the Dead* show the deceased adoring the Double Lion as Yesterday and Tomorrow which symbolises eternity.[346]

In the *Pyramid* and *Coffin Texts* Tefnut is referred to as the *uraeus*. "*The Serpent of Praise on her sceptre is my Tefenet.*"[347] In a spell for *Entering into the Sun-disk* from the *Coffin Texts* there is reference to that "*mysterious Eye of yours...which is behind the Double Lion*" which is probably Tefnut [348]. A lioness-headed Tefnut is depicted in a vignette of the *Weighing of the Heart* ceremony from the *Book of the Dead* papyrus

---

[343] *The Ancient Egyptian Pyramid Texts*, Faulkner, 2007:131 utterance 400
[344] *The Ancient Egyptian Pyramid Texts*, Faulkner, 2007:297 utterance 688
[345] *The Ancient Egyptian Pyramid Texts*, Faulkner, 2007:213 utterance 553
[346] *The Animal World of the Pharaohs*, Houlihan, 1996:93
[347] *The Ancient Egyptian Pyramid Texts*, Faulkner, 2007:64 utterance 254
[348] *The Ancient Egyptian Coffin Texts Volume III*, Faulkner, 2007:106 spell 1000

of Hunefer.[349] She is also invoked in food spells in the role of general provider in the afterlife. *"I will not be hungry by reason of Tefenet."*[350] Her association with water makes her important in purification rituals. *"Your purity is the purity of Tefenet."*[351]

Both Shu and Tefnut appear in the *Pyramid* and *Coffin Texts* as protectors. Mirroring their role as the Double Lion guarding both horizons one *Coffin Text* spell refers to Shu as the Lion on the east side of the deceased and Tefnut on the west. In the Late and Greco-Roman Period funerary texts the deceased say they are the child of Shu and Tefnut and it is they who raise up the deceased. By combining their specific aspects they become formidable protectors. *"The god Shu is there as north wind…together with Tefnut as flame in order to burn the enemies of Osiris"*.[352] A strong wind enabling the fire to spread rapidly.

The Great Cat of Ra

Ra appears in all the funerary texts but the *Book of the Dead* introduces Ra as the Great Cat fighting Apophis and this became very popular as a vignette. The Cat usually holds the snake down with one paw while he decapitates it with a knife. As the Cat represents Ra it is normally shown as male. The deceased aligned themselves with the Great Cat and when the deceased is female there is logic in depicting the cat as female. In one such depiction the cat is shown with teats to emphasise this. It is described as *"the killing of the snake Apophis by the living cat who has come out of the underworld and who makes one prosperous in the necropolis"*.[353]

The *Amduat*

This funerary text describes the journey through the twelve hours of darkness, beginning with the setting of the sun at the first hour and ending with its triumphant rebirth and escape from Apophis at the twelfth hour. As in the other funerary texts there is a demon who is cat-headed, or has cat's ears, who decapitates the enemies of Ra. In one section the cry of the tomcat is compared to the voices of the inhabitants

---

[349] *Atum: Creating the World*, Tyldesley, 2012:25-27
[350] *The Ancient Egyptian Pyramid Texts*, Faulkner, 2007:109 utterance 338
[351] *The Ancient Egyptian Pyramid Texts*, Faulkner, 2007:150 utterance 452
[352] *The Temple of Edfu*, Kurth, 2004:58
[353] *The Cat in Ancient Egypt*, Malek, 1993:84

of the underworld which doesn't give a very comforting image. The Sun God and his entourage have entered the underworld at the second hour and pass through fertile lands which grow food for the deceased. Five Goddesses are shown holding the *was*-sceptre and *ankh*, the signs of life and dominion. One of these is "*Sekhmet of the was-sceptre*". Behind them are a variety of figures which include a kneeling lioness-headed figure who is called "*She who imposes respect to the Akh-spirits*". There is a tribunal made up of six mummified deities. All are enthroned and hold knives, the one who is lioness-headed is referred to as "*She of the fireplace who cuts up Ba-souls*".[354]

The third hour is in a watery region dominated by Osiris. Here we have the only appearance of Pakhet in funerary texts. The *Amduat* first appears during the reign of Hatshepsut (18th dynasty) and she was a devotee of Pakhet, as was the succeeding Thutmose III (18th dynasty), which may be the reason for her inclusion. The barque of the Sun God's entourage is called Pakhet and at her prow is the head of a lioness. The barren desert of Sokar forms the setting for the fourth hour. Sokar is the God of the Memphis necropolis and is often combined as Ptah-Sokar. There is a group of five deities including a lioness-headed Goddess "*She who has teeth*" who may be the Distant Goddess given the presence of Onuris as well as the desert environment.[355] The travellers may be in the dangerous and barren desert but the life-bringing deities are approaching. In terms of the psyche this shows that just as the natural world is self-regulating, so is the unconscious. The apparent bias of the moment will eventually be compensated for by its opposite. Unpleasant and confusing periods of drought won't last forever. A helpful force, in this case Onuris, will tame the raging Goddess and bring her back to her rightful position and the good times, symbolised by the inundation, will return.

The fifth hour introduces Aker, or the Double Lion, in the form of a double sphinx who represents the underworld. In the mysterious Cavern of Sokar he guards the corpse of the Sun God as it regenerates. "*Aker guarding the secret flesh*."[356] In many cultures the regenerative power of the underworld is depicted as a return to the womb of the Mother Earth Goddess but not in Egypt. Everything that enters the western horizon is swallowed by Aker and he regenerates them as they pass through his

---

[354] *The Egyptian Amduat* Abt & Hornung, 2007:53-55
[355] *The Egyptian Amduat* Abt & Hornung, 2007:130
[356] *The Egyptian Amduat* Abt & Hornung, 2007:168

body emerging reborn through the eastern horizon. The sixth hour is the deepest part of the *Amduat*, closest to the waters of the *nun*. Here is the union of the *ba* of Ra with his corpse, or the union of Ra with Osiris, and the beginning of his regeneration.

Apophis attacks during the seventh hour in an attempt to extinguish the newly kindled light. A lioness-headed Goddess called the "*Praising One*" carries the *was*-sceptre and *ankh*.[357] She stands with a human-headed *uraeus* cobra behind Osiris who is protected by the *Mehen* snake (a coiled Snake God who protects the Solar Barque). The eighth and ninth hours contain no feline deities. They deal with the provision of new clothing, a symbol of renewal, and the towing of the Solar Barque. Sekhmet has two roles in the tenth hour, both in line with her aspects. With Thoth she heals the Solar Eye making it whole and perfect in anticipation of sunrise at the twelfth hour. In the *Amduat* Thoth is usually responsible for the protection and healing of the Eye but at this hour Sekhmet assists him, which is a fitting role for an Eye Goddess and a Healer. Her presence also embodies the paradox and ambivalence of the forces of nature which are both life-giving and life-taking. Eight Goddesses are shown, four are lioness-headed the others have a woman's head and all carry the *was*-sceptre and *ankh*. They are an eight-fold form of Sekhmet. The four lioness-headed Goddesses are named as "*Sekhmet the Powerful, Menkeret, Maiden, She of the sceptre*".[358] An enthroned Thoth sits facing them holding the restored Eye. Sekhmet also provides additional protection to the Sun God. The eleventh hour deals with the mysteries of time and the birth of the hours and at the twelfth hour the sun is reborn at dawn. There are no feline deities present, their work being completed in the tenth hour.

Conclusion

Apart from their protective aspects the Feline Goddesses are not a major presence in the underworld. Rebirth is driven more by the power of *heka* than *sekhem*. Isis and Nephthys dominate the Osiris myths and Hathor, in her Cow aspect, takes on the protective and nurturing roles of the Goddess of the West. The dominance of Aker and the Double Lion owes more to their earth aspects than any feline ones. The afterworld

---

[357] *The Egyptian Amduat* Abt & Hornung, 2007:220
[358] *The Egyptian Amduat* Abt & Hornung, 2007:306

was underground as are tombs and the deceased have to be reborn from the womb of earth, despite its male attributes.

CHAPTER 17

FATE AND MAGIC

"You are the great one, the great of magic, the Ethiopian Cat, daughter of Ra, the mistress of the uraeus. You are Sakhmet the great, mistress of Ast."[359]

Egyptian Magic

For the Egyptians magic was a normal part of everyday life. It was used in very formal religious rituals, was considered an integral part of medicine at all levels and was used by ordinary people for protection and basic healing. Magic was just one of the ways that people could look after themselves. It worked because it utilised *heka*, one of the forces used in creation. The feline deities do not feature prominently in magic, with the exception of Sekhmet in her healing aspect, but they were called upon and feline symbolism was important.

---

[359] *The Greek Magical Papyri in Translation. Volume I*, Betz, 1996:216

Magicians

The complex at Saqqara was extended during the reign of Rameses II (19th dynasty) by the Crown Prince Khaemwaset who was also the High Priest of Ptah. He was renowned as a skilled magician and it is possible that some of the magical and medical papyri come from his tomb but there is no clear provenance. Khaemwaset constructed a hilltop shrine for Sekhmet.

A lion mask was found during excavation of a house at Lahun and has been dated to the Middle Kingdom. It is made of linen, painted black with a green inverted triangle on the forehead and red cheek spots. Holes for the wearer to see through are cut into the eyes like a pupil. A Middle Kingdom tomb at Thebes contained a wooden figure of a woman wearing such a lion mask. Because she has a mask rather than a lioness-head it is clear that the woman doesn't represent a Goddess, perhaps she is the magician assuming the identity of a Lioness Goddess. She holds two bronze snake staffs or wands. The tomb appears to have been that of a magician as it also contained a bronze snake staff and a chest of medical papyri.

Magicians were popular heroes in stories. In the *Tale of King Cheops and the Magicians* is a magician who *"knows how to make a lion follow after him with its leash trailing on the ground"*.[360] In the *Story of Petese* a magician-priest animates wax figurines of a hawk and a cat which he sends to destroy the house of an enemy.[361]

Wands

Unlike the straight wand that we are familiar with in the west Egyptian wands come in two forms. Some were snake shaped as mentioned above, others were ivory wands in the shape of a throw-stick used for hunting. These are curved, flat, usually made of hippo ivory and were apotropaic in function. Hippo ivory was readily available and the hippo was considered a fierce protector. It is thought that they were used to draw circles of protection around a person or their sleeping and living areas because they are often worn on one side.

---

[360] *The Wisdom of Ancient Egypt*, Kaster, 1968:262
[361] *Magic in Ancient Egypt*, Pinch, 2006:95

The wands are decorated with protective creatures, both real and fantastic. These include snakes, hippos, Bes figures, cats, lions, leopards and griffins. Some of the earliest representations of cats in religious contexts are on ivory wands from the Middle Kingdom. On one a wild cat bites a snake, as does a lion who is depicted standing upright like a human. The creatures depicted tend to be linked to solar rebirth, such as the lions of the horizon, the double sphinx and Bes. The decorations illustrate myths which will have been part of an oral tradition and so are lost to us unless they happened to be written down at some stage. Many of the beings illustrated are identified with the deities of Middle Egypt who are mentioned in the *Coffin Texts*. Inscriptions on these wands reference deities fighting on behalf of a divine child who is in danger. Other wands make reference to the Great Cat beheading Apophis or to the Distant Goddess.

Ingredients

The *Ebers* papyrus recommends cat fat to deter mice. *"To prevent mice from coming near things – put cat grease on everything."*[362] This, along with cat fur and faeces was used in magic and medicine and may have had a mythological link. One spell for an oracle includes an offering of horse manure and the heart of a cat.

Love Spells

Love spells were widespread and popular and many called upon Hathor as the Goddess of Love and Sexuality. The love spells often invoke the Eye Goddesses under their various names; such as Great of Magic, Golden Mirror and Ethiopian Cat. The Ethiopian Cat is a popular reference, perhaps there was a short myth that was relevant. One spell refers to Tefnut as the Eye of Ethiopia. Modern practitioners are often warned against love spells as they interfere with free will. The Egyptians had no such qualms and the spells range from the more innocent, asking that their lover will meet them, to the malicious which forces women to be bewitched for sex. For one love spell, *to Call a Woman,* a gold ring had to be made and decorated with two open-mouthed lions facing each other. One Greco-Roman spell calls upon the Eye Goddess to cause a married couple to separate. This spell is said over oil used to anoint the

---

[362] *Gods of Ancient Egypt,* Watterson, 2003:188

hopeful party. "*Thou art Thoueris, the great of sorcery, cat of Ethiopia, daughter of Re, lady of the uraeus; thou art Sochmet the great, lady of Ast, who has seized every impious person...eye of the sun.*"[363]

Dangerous Creatures

There are numerous spells against snakes, scorpions and crocodiles reflecting the dangers associated with these creatures. Virtually all the deities are invoked especially those who have some mythical connection to the creatures. Lions have no connection with killing snakes either in myth or in reality but they do appear in anti-snake spells. One spell to "*close the mouth*" of a snake is recited over a faience lion amulet which is bound with red linen. The amulet is worn on the hand whilst sleeping. "*He is the Lion who protects himself, he is the great god who fights on behalf of his brother...he is a lion who wards off gods and spirits.*"[364] One spell against a crocodile calls upon Sekhmet. "*Oh you water-dwellers... your throats are stopped up by Sakhmet.*"[365] Another calls on Sekhmet, Thoth, Heka and Ra. "*May these four great gods who guard Osiris protect everyone who is on the waters.*"[366]

Demons and the Evil Eye

Supernatural attacks were widely feared. The Arrows of Sekhmet were powerful weapons and the magician could harness them to work on their behalf, especially against the evil eye. One spell against the evil eye asks, amongst other threats, that the aggressor be struck with the Arrow of Sekhmet.

Malicious Magic

It takes little to turn superstition into aggression against a perceived enemy. There were also plenty of people who wished to do harm and turned to magic. There is a charm to induce insomnia; this included writing the names of Bastet and six other deities on the wing of a live bat. It is much safer to get someone else to do your dirty and dangerous work and so demons were conjured for this purpose. One Greco-Roman

---

[363] *The Leyden Papyrus*, Griffith & Thompson, 1974:91
[364] *Ancient Egyptian Magical Texts*, Bourghouts, 1978:93
[365] *Ancient Egyptian Magical Texts*, Bourghouts, 1978:86
[366] *The Metternich Stele*, Scott, 1951:201-217

spell included drawing a fire-breathing lion-headed man wearing a sash and holding a serpent-entwined staff. Are some of the Greek composers of these spells looking at reliefs of deities and assuming that these were demons? One unpleasant spell starts by drowning a cat which is then mummified and buried in a graveyard facing east. The water used to drown the cat was sprinkled where the rite was to be held. An invocation to the "*cat-faced god*", thought to be Sekhmet-Bastet, compels the cat's spirit to act on behalf of the magician.[367]

Oracles and Divination

Judging by the volume of spells, divination was a lucrative business for the magician. They are usually titled *Enquiry of the Vessel* or *Enquiry of the Lamp*. They start out greeting spirits such as the "*souls of Aker*" or the "*lion of the abyss*".[368] The magician will sometimes assume the role of a deity to give them more protection, stating "*I am Bastet*" or "*I am Sekhmet*". One addresses Mahes who "*shall send out a lion of the sons of Mihos under compulsion to fetch them to me the souls of god...the spirits, the dead, so that they tell me the truth today concerning that after which I am enquiring*".[369] Threats are often needed if the conjured spirit remains mute. "*The fury of Sekhmet thy mother and of Heke thy father is cast at thee.*"[370] Sculls were sometimes used and proved harder to control. A restraining seal for one involved making a ring from a leg fetter. A headless lion and an "*owl-eyed cat with paws on a gorgon's head*" was then carved on it.[371]

A charm to produce a vision included the words "*Hail, serpent and stout lion, natural sources of fire*".[372] Another involved walking towards the sun at the fifth hour, crowned with the tail of a cat. After saying a charm you would see a shadow in the sun which could be asked a question.

---

[367] *The Greek Magical Papyri in Translation. Volume I*, Betz, 1996:18
[368] *The Leyden Papyrus*, Griffith & Thompson, 1974:59 & 79
[369] *The Leyden Papyrus*, Griffith & Thompson, 1974:71
[370] *The Leyden Papyrus*, Griffith & Thompson, 1974:57
[371] *The Greek Magical Papyri in Translation. Volume I*, Betz, 1996:75
[372] *The Greek Magical Papyri in Translation. Volume I*, Betz, 1996:56

Miscellaneous Spells

In a spell asking for a prophetic dream the person assumes the roles of a number of deities including "*I am the lion*".[373] Instead of relying on prayers and offerings there is a spell to "*establish a relationship with Helios*" (the Sun God) namely to ask him for a favour. The Sun God is associated with an animal, bird, tree and stone at each hour. At the third hour "*you have the form of a cat*" and at the fifth hour he has the form of a lion.[374] A similar spell places the lion at the sixth hour and the cat at the first.

Fate

Most magic, healing or otherwise, is an attempt to alter a person's fate. Traces of an ancient stellar religion are seen in the Egyptians' interest in astronomy. Stars were regarded as deities or the souls of the blessed dead. In the *Pyramid Texts* the king becomes a "*star brilliant and far travelling*".[375] During the Pharaonic Period there wasn't the concept of the influence of planets on human affairs. The zodiac was only introduced to Egypt in the Ptolemaic Period. Egyptian interest focused on the *decans* which were believed to control the fate of individuals and the country. The *decans* are 36 groups of stars which divide the year into ten days. For ten days the *decan* indicates the same hour of the night, either by its rising or setting. A new *decan* appears every ten days due to the orbit of the Earth. The first *decan* occurs at New Year and coincides with the rising of Sirius. The funerary chamber of Sety I (19th dynasty) has a ceiling decorated with the *decans* and the constellations of the northern hemisphere, including that of the constellation of Leo. A text at Esna equates the *decans* to the fates and also to the messengers of Sekhmet. "*Who announce what happens, who keep people alive and kill sinners as they please...who bombard the lands with fire, at whose approach everyone trembles...they rove around as the Eye of Re...who shoot arrows from their mouths.*"[376] In the tomb of Osorkon II (22nd dynasty), at Tanis, were two armbands designed to protect the deceased king. They show the *decans* with snake bodies and lion heads.

---

[373] *The Greek Magical Papyri in Translation. Volume I*, Betz, 1996:325
[374] *The Greek Magical Papyri in Translation. Volume I*, Betz, 1996:31
[375] *The Ancient Egyptian Pyramid Texts*, Faulkner, 2007:60, utterance 248
[376] *The Secret Lore of Egypt: Its Impact on the West*, Hornung, 2001:29

Each *decan* had an associated deity and Sekhmet was the Mistress of the *Decans*, controlling fate and administering divine retribution. She determined good and bad luck and could guarantee a good year with an excellent harvest by controlling the inundation. Statues were dedicated to her by individuals requesting health and prosperity. Numerous Sekhmet figurines were given as votive offerings to her at the Serapeum (the burial place of the Apis Bull who was seen as the living embodiment of Ptah) and Saqqara in general.

Conclusion

The deities with the most *heka* are Isis and Thoth and so they dominate the magic of Egypt. The feline deities are less prominent in magic excluding that of healing and control of fate. One exception is the androgynous Mut-Min who was depicted with one or three lion heads. In this form Mut was dangerous, powerful and the "*Great Magician of the North*".[377] There are two reasons for this lesser role in magic. In a polytheist religion the deities are not expected to fulfil all roles and tend to specialise. The main reason is the underlying character of the feline deities. The Feline Goddesses represent the power of *sekhem* which differs from that of *heka* whilst the Feline Gods tend towards the element of earth. Feline symbolism is present because of its inherent protective aspects.

---

[377] *Mut Enthroned*, Troy, 1996:307

CHAPTER 18

FESTIVALS AND RITUALS

"I have passed by Tefnut, Tefnut having purified me...I shall not linger, I shall not turn back...I have come to perform the ritual. Indeed I have not come to do that which is not to be done."[378]

Introduction

The king acted as the High Priest and worshipped the state deities as part of his duties as king. Having taken on the mantle of Horus son of Osiris the king was partly divine himself and as such he was a conduit between the people of Egypt and the deities and his involvement was essential to ensure the continuation of Egypt and creation. The queens also played an important role taking the part of the High Priestess and the embodiment of the Goddesses. Individual monarchs and their families would have had specific deities whom they were personally attached to and the power of the priesthood of various cults would also have an influence on the deities promoted. The majority of information we have about rituals and festivals comes from Late and Greco-Roman Period temples where some of them were inscribed on the walls. Many of

---

[378] *Temple Ritual at Abydos*, David, 2016:63

the rituals would have been performed in secret for the benefit of the deities, the king and Egypt, rather than something the ordinary people could get involved in. Rituals specific to Hathor in her non-Solar aspects have been omitted.

The Turning of the Year

As mentioned previously, the turning of the year was a critical time. For the Egyptians the New Year started on 1st of *Thoth* in the season of *Akhet* (Inundation) hopefully coinciding with the inundation which brought the water back and with it the prosperity of the coming year. By our calendar this is about the 21st August. The old year ended with the five *epagomenal* days, dangerous days out of normal time which brought their own liminal dangers. Sekhmet and her emissaries were ever present. Because of this the ritual calendar was particularly full at this frightening and worrying time and the Feline Goddesses played an important role.

The rituals were considered essential as the continuation of life in Egypt depended upon them and they are recorded in all the major temples. It is thought that the pivotal New Year rituals developed before or at the start of the Pharaonic Period marking the two simultaneous events of the heliacal rising of Sirius and the arrival of the inundation. The first day of the year is mentioned in a 5th dynasty inscription in the temple of Nyuserra but the most detailed information comes from the Greco-Roman temples. New Year also brought a return to the natural equilibrium after the *epagomenal* days as the annual cycle recommenced. The rituals were merged with ceremonies to confirm the king's legal right to rule.

The End of the Year - the *Litany of Sekhmet*

This was a hymn sung to Sekhmet at the New Year to provide the king with protection against the dangers of the coming year. Germond (1981) gives the entire Litany (in French). Details of the Litany have been given in chapter 16. Litanies to Sekhmet are found on reliefs in the temples at Edfu, Dendera and Kom Ombo. They all show variations but the underlying concept remains the same. The fact that such an important ritual could vary illustrates the lack of absolute doctrine on worship even for the major temples. On reliefs in the temple of Edfu

Hathor is depicted with a vulture cap and the white crown representing Upper Egypt while Sekhmet represents Lower Egypt. The king wears the red crown of Lower Egypt. The text specifies that it had to be recited in secret over the king, presumably to ensure that it was not disclosed to his enemies. The king offers *sistra*, bouquets of flowers and incense to Hathor and Sekhmet.

Purification of the Temples

Reliefs from Karnak and Medinet Habu suggest that a ritual purification and rededication of the temples was carried out at the New Year. One refers to the process as *"giving houses to their owners"*. The temple, cleansed of the impurities of the old year, was consecrated and rededicated. Lit torches were paraded around the temple, illuminating the building as the rising sun illuminated the earth. *"Spell for illuminating the house...when it inaugurates a good year."* (It being the torch.) *"This house is illuminated by Amen-Re Kamutef when it inaugurates a good year; likewise by...Mut, Lady of Isheru, mistress of the gods, who is in Ipet-Esut."*[379]

Anointing the King

During the *Reign of the Gods* Geb tried to seize the throne from his father Shu but when Geb put the crown on he was attacked by the *uraeus* who did not recognise his authority. Each year the king was anointed in a special ritual which gave him immunity from the powerful forces which resided in the crown and more specifically the *uraeus*. The ointment rendered them harmless towards the king so the crown could be safely placed upon his head for another year. It also put the powers of the *uraeus* under his command. Sekhmet and the *uraeus* were invoked during the ritual.

Celebrating the New Year

It was traditional to give gifts at New Year and these were often inscribed. After the New Kingdom water was often given in decorated

---

[379] *Certain Reliefs at Karnak and Medinet Habu and the Ritual of Amenophis I*, Nelson, 1949:310-345

bowls or jars. *"May Sekhmet open a good New Year for its owner."*[380] Sekhmet was particularly associated with the inundation from the New Kingdom to the Late Period. Statues of cats were also given as presents or votive offerings.

Union with the Sun Disc

At New Year Hathor, as the Solar Eye, was reunited with Ra so that both Ra and the annual cycles were re-energised. This was a conclusion to *the Return of the Distant Goddess*, the *"Eye of Re that has come to Edfu to see her father"*.[381] Not only does the Goddess have to be brought back to Egypt, she has to be reconciled and reunited with her father and the *uraeus* must return to her place of honour upon his forehead. This ritual wasn't confined to New Year's Day and was also held on the 20th of *Thoth*, the 11th and 15th of *Pashons* (1st month of *Shemu*, Harvest) and on the new moon of *Epep* (the 3rd month of *Shemu*).[382] Texts from the temple of Edfu describe the ceremony. The king, taking the role of Horus, *"will ascend via the eastern staircase, together with his Uraeus-snake, the Great One, in order to see his sun-disc (in the sky)...in order to unite with his Ba (the sun) on the day of the New Year Festival...accompanied by his great Uraeus-snake, the Mistress of Dendera"*.[383]

Texts from Dendera tell how the cult statue of Hathor was carried in her sacred barque to the roof of the temple. Here, in the *Chapel of the Union with the Sun's Disc*, the first rays of the sun on New Year's Day shone on her statue and *"she unites her rays with those of her father in the horizon"*.[384] The walls of the stairways are illustrated with scenes depicting the ritual. It was carried out in secret alongside the public rituals. The merging of the female principle (represented by Hathor) with the male principle (represented by Horus or Ra) was fundamental to the renewal of the annual cycles. *"The eye of the sun is whole when Hathor of Dendera, who resides in Edfu, touches it; for they meet in the horizon and the soul of Re is present in their images."*[385]

---

[380] *Sekhmet et la Protection du Monde*, Germond, 1981:329 (My translation)
[381] *Hathor and Thoth: Two Key Figures of the Ancient Egyptian Religion*, Bleeker, 1973:98
[382] *Hathor and Thoth: Two Key Figures of the Ancient Egyptian Religion*, Bleeker, 1973:90
[383] *The Temple of Edfu*, Kurth, 2004:63
[384] *Hathor and Thoth: Two Key Figures of the Ancient Egyptian Religion*, Bleeker, 1973:89
[385] *Sekhmet et la Protection du Monde*, Germond, 1981:209 (My translation)

The *Return of the Distant Goddess*

The *Return of the Distant Goddess* was a joyful time. Not only had she returned to Egypt she had brought the inundation with her. The *Festival of the Navigation of Hathor* was celebrated during 19-21st *Tobe* (1st month of *Peret*, Emergence). It was created for her by Ra to celebrate the return of his daughter *"that the Nile-flood may be (given) to Egypt...and that she might turn her back on Nubia"*.[386] The fact that Hathor goes to her festivals by boat is significant in terms of the inundation which made the Nile navigable once more but all deities travelled by boat. Water was the principal means of transport in Egypt so it was logical for the Egyptians to view their deities using the same means of transport.

At Philae the Hathor temple is referred to as the *"the place of imploring"* where rituals were held to plead for the return of the Goddess.[387] It was said to be in the place where Hathor first set foot on Egyptian soil. The *Return of Hathor* as the Distant Goddess was particularly important at the temple of Medamud. The temple is dedicated to the Theban War God Montu. One of his consorts is the Solar Goddess Raet, who is aligned with Hathor. At Medamud the forecourt the Goddess returns to is a representation of the primaeval marshes. This alludes both to creation and to the inundation she brought with her; it also welcomes the Hathor Cow back to her original home in the marshes.

A hymn on the wall of the central kiosk at the entrance to the temple describes the festival which is thought to date to the 13th dynasty. The hymn is addressed to Hathor as Gold and as Raet. The hymn describes her entourage who accompany her back to Egypt which included Libyans, Nubians and other foreigners. When the Goddess is safely back on Egyptian soil the Egyptians greet her. *"Let us take for her feathers off the backs of ostriches...let us dance, and let us cry for our mistress."* They are mindful that the Goddess is not obliged to be with them and she can never be restrained or totally pacified. It could also mean that even if the inundation was late or had failed the role of the Goddess still had to be acknowledged. *"One behaves towards the Mistress of the Two Lands such that she will settle there, though she be yet in the desert."*[388]

---

[386] *Temple Festival Calendars of Ancient Egypt*, el-Sabban, 2000:174
[387] *Hathor Returns to Medamud*, Darnell, 1995:47-97
[388] *Hathor Returns to Medamud*, Darnell, 1995:47-97

The festival is one of celebration and music and dance were prominent. This was to pacify the Goddess and assure her that the people were delighted to see her again. *"The whole world rejoices for you, the animals dance for you in joy."* The Medamud hymn describes the accompanying musicians as *"those who placate the malevolent one"*. A hymn to Hathor in the tomb of Kheruef says *"come, arise, come that I may make for you jubilation at twilight and music in the evening"*. Texts at Medamud describe the activities during the festival. The officials consecrate offerings, the lector priest intones hymns and the priests read rituals and *"drunken celebrants drum for you during the cool of night"*.[389] There is a lot of emphasis on coolness as it is needed to cool the rage of the Goddess. She is received by royal women who pacify her by shaking *sistra* and *menats* before offering flowers.

Many temples had festivals to celebrate the *Return of the Distant Goddess*. The festival lasted 14 days and involved dancing and music to celebrate her arrival from Nubia. Graffiti and inscriptions on rocks were made by people going into the desert to help bring her home. This may have been done seriously as a pilgrimage. Certainly walking in the desert wasn't to be undertaken lightly but a short walk in a group as part of the celebrations may have been viewed as part of the fun or at least part of the ritual.

Pacification

When Ra sends his Eye to destroy his enemies, in the *Destruction of Mankind*, he is attempting to ensure that the original equilibrium of creation is restored, that is people respect and worship their Creator and *maat* is maintained. The Eye Goddess has a dual aspect and Ra has no control over the destructive force he has unleashed. When order is finally restored Ra doesn't punish or even chastise Sekhmet so he must have been conscious of his responsibility in unleashing such dangerous primaeval power. The Distant Goddess also has to be pacified by Thoth or Shu.

The rituals to pacify Sekhmet were a way of regulating her vital but dangerous original power and were an essential component of the maintenance of creation and Egypt. The Eye myths illustrate the Egyptians' belief in the fragility of creation which was seen in the

---

[389] *Hathor Returns to Medamud*, Darnell, 1995:47-97

corresponding fragility of everything they held dear; peace, health, social order, the monarchy, agricultural and economic wellbeing and of the country of Egypt itself. Is this part of the reason why Ancient Egypt endured so long? They were well aware that it requires constant hard work to maintain such things and in doing so they tried to accommodate and accept dualities and work with them.

The dangerous aspect of the Eye and Lioness Goddesses and their partnership with Ra illustrates the essential collaboration needed if the Creator is to maintain *maat*. The forces of Sekhmet and the other Goddesses may appear anti-social at first but they form an essential component in the ongoing battle against chaos. The rites of appeasing Sekhmet, *shtp*, helped at the critical times when passing from one cycle to another. A list of books held in the temple of Edfu was inscribed on the temple walls. These include the *Book of Appeasing Sekhmet* and the *Book of Driving Away Lions*.[390] It was said that Thoth created the *shtp* ritual to calm the Distant Goddess and this ritual was repeated on a daily basis in temples throughout Egypt. There were also feasts of pacification. The papyrus *Sallier* warns against travelling on the festivals which "*Ra made to pacify Sekhmet*".[391] A calendar of lucky and unlucky days gives the 3rd day of the year as "*lucky – feast of Sekhmet, instituted for her by Re when he had pacified her*".[392]

The ritual might have been designed for Sekhmet but all deities needed appeasing during rituals, if only to minimise the effects of their divine power to make it safer for people. The papyrus sceptre was frequently offered in pacification rites. This emphasised the aspects of the pacified Goddess as nourisher and protector. Hathor in particular would be reminded of her Cow aspect and her home in the swamps. The *menat* and the *sistrum* had pacifying qualities. The *sistrum* was used to "*cool her rage*". It "*banishes the irritation, it dispels the rage that is in the heart of the goddess and makes her affable after her grimness*".[393] Wine and beer were offered and drinking was an important part of many festivals. At Karnak during the *Festival of the Valley* red beer was offered to Hathor to appease her.

---

[390] *The Priests of Ancient Egypt*, Sauneron, 2000:135
[391] *Egyptian Myth: A Very Short Introduction*, Pinch, 2004:107
[392] *Egyptian Magic*, Raven, 2012:106
[393] *Hathor and Thoth: Two Key Figures of the Ancient Egyptian Religion*, Bleeker, 1973:60

Fragments of a relief from Samannud refers to a ritual of *"pacifying the Raging One"* which in this temple may refer to Mehit.[394] One relief from Mut's temple at Karnak shows the king and two priestesses playing music before Mut and Sekhmet. This appears to illustrate the pacification ritual as Sekhmet stands behind Mut. As the Goddess becomes calm her Sekhmet persona fades into the background.[395] At Edfu the king is shown offering incense, the *wedjat* eye, *sistra*, *menat*, geese, antelopes and jugs. At Philae he offers a sacrificed antelope before Tefnut. The geese may have been a substitute for the humans Sekhmet killed. The oryx and antelopes were desert animals and represented the chaos of Seth (the desert was his domain) and the prey of the Goddess whilst she prowled the deserts. At Queen Tiy's temple at Sedeinga she associated herself with Hathor as the Solar Eye. Rituals to pacify her angry aspect were held turning her from a raging lioness into the benevolent Hathor and perfect queen.

The Distant Goddess bathed in the Nile when she returned to Egypt so water was an important part of the pacification rituals. Mut was rowed on the *isheru*-lake at Karnak during the annual appeasement ritual and at Dendera there was a *Festival of Rowing Hathor* to pacify her when she was the angry Distant Goddess. The need to appease the Goddess is a constantly recurring theme. Benson, excavating at Karnak in1890, commented on some local lore. If a single man walked alone into the temple at night a beautiful woman was said to approach him. She then turned into a lion and attacked him.[396]

Drinking

In the myth of the *Destruction of Mankind*, Sekhmet is given beer dyed red to give it the appearance of blood. The calendar of the temple of Mut records that special red beer was served at the *Festival of Drunkenness* to commemorate the pacification of the Angry Eye. Offerings to the deities tended to be of wine as it was more expensive and prestigious. Wine symbolised new growth (of the vine) after the arrival of the inundation and alluded to rebirth through Osiris. Egyptian wine was red and the flood water was a reddish colour due to the silt it carried. Before the Distant Goddess returned to Egypt she was wild and

---

[394] *The Epigraphic Survey of Samanud*, Spencer, 1999:55-83
[395] *What's New in Luxor?* Betz, 2016:24-33
[396] *Egypt's Ageless Goddess*, Pinkowski, 2006:44-49

ferocious. After contact with civilisation (which according to the Egyptians included music, dance and wine) she became benevolent. This parallels the inundation. It is dangerous and violent when it first arrives, destroying land and property and drowning animals and people, but it becomes benevolent when it settles, providing a means of navigation, water and fertilised fields. Wine generates the reverse transformation, from a normal fruit and juice into an intoxicating and potentially dangerous drink.

Wine was an important component of most rituals and was offered to all deities. Its offering is a common theme on temple reliefs and on *stelae*. The offering of *maat* represented the offering of an abstract principle, but the offering of wine was a practical way of maintaining *maat* by appeasing the deity. Wine was particularly significant in the cults of Mut, Bastet, Tefnut, Hathor and Sekhmet as these are the Eye Goddesses who require pacification. A lot of wine was offered to Hathor who is *"Mistress of Wine"*.[397] In the Hathor-Tefnut versions of the Distant Goddess myth Thoth of Pnubs is in charge of the wine offering to Hathor and so he becomes the Lord of Wine.

The earliest scene of wine offering is in the pyramid temple of Sahure. Here the king offers *"wine and libation for the ka of the mistress of the Two Lands, Sekhmet of Sahure"*.[398] A common expression in the wine offering liturgy is *"may you be powerful through it"* which is a probably a pun on the name of Sekhmet.[399] *"How sweet is its taste to the nose of the Leader of the gods, Sekhmet, in happiness."*[400]

Drinking re-enacted the pacification of Sekhmet in the *Destruction of Mankind* and was seen as a way of communing with deities. Drunkenness was considered the equivalent to a state of ecstasy in honour of the Goddess. Sacred drunkenness said to be calming as well as exciting as Sekhmet cooled her rage when she was drunk on beer. *"May you drink, may your heart rejoice, may your anger be removed from your face."*[401] The drunkenness given by Seth causes turmoil as he is a Chaos God. When it is given by the Eye Goddess it brings peace and benevolence as she is at heart a benevolent Goddess.

---

[397] *Wine and Wine Offering in the Religion of Ancient Egypt*, Poo, 1995:66
[398] *Wine and Wine Offering in the Religion of Ancient Egypt*, Poo, 1995:39
[399] *Wine and Wine Offering in the Religion of Ancient Egypt*, Poo, 1995:161
[400] *Wine and Wine Offering in the Religion of Ancient Egypt*, Poo, 1995:121
[401] *Wine and Wine Offering in the Religion of Ancient Egypt*, Poo, 1995:142

It is no surprise that festivals of drunkenness were popular, a Goddess-given opportunity to overindulge. Hathor's *Festival of Drunkenness* is known from at least the Middle Kingdom and was especially popular during the Greco-Roman Period. The *Festival of Inebriety* for Hathor was held on the 20th day of *Thoth*. "*One celebrates for this goddess. It is her father Re who created it for her when she came from Bugwn, so that the inundation is given to Egypt...so that she may turn her back to Nubia.*"[402] Jugs of wine were offered to Hathor, and then consumed as a reversion offering. Bes is shown dancing at this festival at Hathor's temple at Philae.

Hatshepsut (18th dynasty) commissioned a "*monument for her mother Mut, making for her a columned porch of drunkenness*".[403] Worshipers got drunk and slept there until they were woken by drummers to 'commune' with Mut. One amulet shows a king offering wine or beer to Sekhmet with the inscription "*causing drunkenness*".[404] 19th dynasty graffiti at Abusir reads "*It is as we stand drunk before you, Sekhmet of Sahure, that we utter our petition*".[405]

The Festival of Bastet

The festival of Bastet at Bubastis is very well-known and the description given by Herodotus (484-425 BCE) is frequently quoted.[406] It involved a convoy of boats whose occupants played instruments and sang. As the retinue passed through towns the women shouted abuse at the residents, danced and lifted their skirts. Assuming that Herodotus gives a relatively accurate account it appears a drunk and debauched festival (hence seen as enjoyable to its supporters) and this will have boosted its popularity regardless of which Goddess was involved. There was an official element as well. A relief from the mortuary temple of Userkaf (5th dynasty) shows the king taking part in a ritual with Bastet and Shesmetet. He is shown "*returning from the temple of Bastet in the ship*".[407] The 18th dynasty tomb of AahMose explains that he was a supervisor of these mysteries. "*Hereditary Prince and Count, who*

---

[402] *Wine and Wine Offering in the Religion of Ancient Egypt*, Poo, 1995:155
[403] *The Story of Egypt*, Fletcher, 2015:181
[404] *The Apotropaic Goddess in the Eye.* Darnell, 1997:35-48
[405] *Ancient Egypt*, Oakes & Gahlin, 2004:479
[406] *The Histories*, Herodotus & Selincourt, 2003:119
[407] *Texts From the Pyramid Age*, Strudwick, 2005:83

conducteth the festival of Bastet."[408] The festival was also celebrated at Esna and Thebes but the Bubastis one was the largest and most popular and included a ceremonial procession of the sacred statue of Bastet.

The Festival of Sokar

Sokar was the hawk-headed God of the necropolis at Memphis and was seen as a manifestation of Osiris. As such he was connected with resurrection and the fertility of the earth. During the Old Kingdom he was associated with Ptah as Ptah-Sokar and as a result could have Sekhmet as his consort. His festival was a very old and important one, especially in Thebes. Scenes from the festival procession are depicted on the walls of Rameses III's (20th dynasty) temple at Thebes. Although it is not a festival of the Eye Goddesses they are prominent. The full procession is shown round the walls. Led by priests burning incense and musicians are the five barques of Hathor, Wadjet, Shesmetet, Bastet and Sekhmet. On the upper band of the relief the first barque is called *"the one who navigates gloriously for Hathor"*. The third is called *"the one who prospers the people for Shesmetet...the lady of diadems, mistress of the Two Lands"*. The scene is repeated on the lower band, the first barque is the *"one who pacifies lands, protecting the Two Lands for Bastet"*. The second is *"the one who opens to the secret cavern, who protects the Two Lands for Sekhmet"*.[409]

Scenes of the festival from Medinet Habu also show the barques of Hathor, Wadjet, Shesmetet, Bastet and Sekhmet. A priest offers incense to the *uraeus* and two Goddesses personifying the double crown of Egypt. Shesmetet also has epithet *Sekha'bau-s*. Gaballa suggests that in this context Shesmetet is an aspect of Hathor. This festival is also included in the *Bremner-Rhind* papyrus. Hathor is the most prominent Goddess and the other Eye Goddesses are mostly presented as epithets of her. In the festival of Sokar in the *Louvre* papyrus there is reference to *"the Hathors"*. Under the calendar entry for the *Festival of the Two Uraeus Goddesses* there is reference to Osiris summoning seven Goddesses; Isis, Nephthys and Five Hathors. The Five Hathors correspond to the barques of the Goddess and appear to be aspects of Hathor. Are these different to the Seven Hathors? Is the number five significant in this context or is

---

[408] *The Tomb of AahMose, Supervisor of the Mysteries in the House of the Morning,* Shorter, 1930:54-64
[409] *The Festival of Sokar,* Gaballa & Kitchen, 1969:1-76

it just that the Five Hathors and Isis and Nephthys produce the magical seven?

The two *uraei* referred to in the festival are Isis and Nephthys. They accompany Sokar-Osiris (or Ra) at dawn. Together the Goddesses may be comparable with the Seven Cobras in the text of *Amenirdis*, who are described as uniting *kas* and making a slaughter of foes in the Lake of Flames.[410] The Feline Goddesses are present as they represent the life-giving power of the sun as well as providing protection. Hathor is also present in her afterlife capacity as the Goddess of the West who cares for and guides the deceased.

Worship by Ordinary People

Religious life for the ordinary person was carried on at home, at work and in small shrines. The official state religion offered few roles for anyone else apart from the festivals and processions so there is little information about their religious practices. There is reference to a ritual of Mut in which *"the towns of Pe, Dep and...all wreathed with vines are dancing for you"*.[411] In one funerary text it says that *"you will hear the voices of the crowds of nomadic tribeswomen on the day of acclaiming Sekhmet"*. [412] Does the reference to nomadic women emphasise the untamed aspect of Sekhmet who presides over the desert?

There is relatively little evidence of the worship of the Feline Goddesses by the ordinary people although we know that they were popular, especially Bastet. The cult of Sekhmet of Sahure is an exception and is covered in chapter 19. Most of the evidence of worship of the Feline Goddesses is in the form of votive offerings. These were an important part of cultic devotions. The act of buying and donating the object to the temple brought merit to the donor and showed their devotion and brought important income to the temple. The offering of sacrificed animals is covered in chapter 20. Amulets were popular at all periods and amongst all classes although the rich obviously had the greater number. They were worn for protection and to bring fortune and fertility as well as to show devotion. But was wearing a Sekhmet amulet, for example, an expression of devotion to her or was it merely seen as a very

---

[410] *The Festival of Sokar*, Gaballa & Kitchen, 1969:1-76
[411] *Ancient Egyptian Dances*, Lexova, 2000:40
[412] *Traversing Eternity*, Smith, 2009:424

effective form of protection? In polytheist society it was expected that any deity would help you if it was in their nature.

CHAPTER 19

TEMPLES

"Mighty ruler in her Theban temple. She whose spirit exists because her temple endures. She whose temple and city will exist for millions of years."[413]

Introduction

There are not many temples dedicated to any of the Feline or Eye Goddesses with the exception of Hathor who was very popular but worshipped more in her other aspects than as an Eye Goddess. The other Goddesses will have had shrines within temples to other deities. Was this partly because the Eye Goddess didn't exist in isolation from the Sun God? Sekhmet was closely associated with other Goddesses such as Mut and Hathor and thus co-shared temples as she did with her consort Ptah. Bastet appears to have had more dedicated temples and this may have been because she was seen as more approachable and possibly more independent.

---

[413] *Excavating the Temple of Mut*, Fazzini & Peck, 1983:16-23

Egyptian Temples and the *Isheru*

Temples in the Pharaonic Period were models of creation. Major temples had sacred lakes which were used for purification and ceremonial processions, and these are normally square or rectangular but sacred lakes in temples associated with the Eye Goddesses are called *isheru* and are crescent-shaped. The temple of Bastet at Bubastis was surrounded by a horse-shoe shaped *isheru* and it is one of the main features of the temple of Mut at Karnak. Mut's is the only *isheru* which has been preserved. When approaching the temple from the south side it appears to be enclosed by the lake. This shape, enclosing the temple on three sides, reinforces the concept of containment and appeasement. Totally enclosing the temple by the lake may have been impractical or considered unnecessary. It could have been feared dangerous in case it provoked the Goddess by its attempt to constrain or trap her. The hieroglyph *hepet*, which was used as a determinative in words such as embrace and enclose, consists of two arms reaching out. Figures in protective poses often hold their arms in a similar way. The shape of the *isheru* might have been intended to imitate this pose. Mut's *isheru* was said to have been made for her by the Creator. "*Atum came and dug the isheru for her...surrounding her in order to cool the ferocity of her flame.*"[414] Other texts say she came to settle in the *isheru* "*in her form of Sakhmet*" at the time of creation.[415]

The Angry Goddess returned to the *isheru* and bathed in it. One text refers to the *isheru* extinguishing her flame and alludes to her pacification when she bathed in the waters of the Nile. The *isheru* was used in pacification rituals where priests extinguished torches representing the flame of the Angry Goddess. Mut was said to have given birth to her divine child in the safety of the *isheru*. This might have been referenced by a statue of her on a secluded island or just symbolically as the lotus flower emerging from its waters. The *isheru* also had a protective function acting as a barrier between the sacred temple and the outside world, between order and chaos. This parallels creation arising from the watery *nun*. Was the *isheru* also intended to contain or isolate any aggressive or dangerous divine power and protect the surrounding area? Divine power was considered to flow into the temple but it was too

---

[414] *The First Pylon of the Mut Temple, South Karnak: Architecture, Decorations, Inscriptions*, Fazzini & van Dijk, 2015:38
[415] *Excavating the Temple of Mut*, Fazzini & Peck, 1983:16-23

potent to be allowed to seep unregulated into the secular world. The energy of the Lioness Goddess was that of *sekhem*, the original power, a very potent and fiery power. It had to be treated with respect and the enclosing water would have provided a counterbalance. The hieroglyph spelling of *isheru* contains the symbol of a recumbent lion, a common guardian of temples.

The Temple of Bastet at Bubastis

Tell Basta in the Delta is ancient Bast, known to the Greeks as Bubastis. Its name derives from *per* Bastet, the house or domain of Bastet. By the Old Kingdom Bubastis was an important trading settlement due to its location, it was close to two branches of the Nile and near Wadi Tumilat which was the route into Sinai. Unlike cities such as Thebes its economy wasn't dependent upon the presence of the temple. Bubastis was home to the 22nd dynasty kings and reached the height of its political power at this time and the temple of Bastet was greatly extended.

It is assumed that there was a temple of Bastet here from the Old Kingdom but the surviving remains of the temple date to the 3rd Intermediate Period and the Late Kingdom. The site of the temple, covering an area of 80m by 220m, is now just a field of blocks of granite, basalt and quartzite. It is thought that the temple collapsed in an earthquake about 2,000 years ago. Stone is very valuable in the Delta and about half of the masonry has been taken and reused. It is very difficult to determine the outline and structure of the temple but some of the blocks contain enough information to piece together some details.

To the east was a courtyard and palm leaf column capitals have been found. Osorkon I (22nd dynasty) is shown offering to Bastet and a number of other deities. He built the hall and decorated some existing walls and built a small temple to Atum outside the main precinct. Close to this a duplicate Canopus decree from Ptolemy III (246-221 BCE) was found. The decree concerns the introduction of the leap year into calendar for the first time. The fact that the edict was displayed here shows the importance of the temple. Osorkon II (22nd dynasty) added a *hypostyle* hall to the main temple when he celebrated his *sed*-festival and built a *mammisi* for Mahes as the son of Bastet. A *mammisi* is a shrine which celebrates the birth of the Child Gods. Nectanebo II (30th dynasty) made the last additions to the temple. This was the main building which housed the sanctuary and at least eight shrines. At the front of the building was a large border of *uraei* and an inscription naming Nectanebo II, Bastet and other deities.[416]

Herodotus (c 484-425 BCE) describes the temple in the 5th century BCE. He describes the temple as almost an island. *"Two canals have been led from the Nile and sweep round it, one on each side, as far as the entrance, where they stop short without meeting; each canal is a hundred foot wide and shaded with trees. The gateway is sixty feet high and is decorated with remarkable carved figures, some nine feet high...It is surrounded by a low wall with carved figures and within the enclosure stands a grove of very tall trees around the actual shrine, which is large and contains the statue of the goddess."*[417]

Herodotus' accuracy has been questioned in many instances but excavation has proved him correct in this case, locating two canals which formed the sacred *isheru*. On columns of the *pronaos* at Edfu Bastet is referred to as *"this goddess, the noble one, under whom the Nile flows"* in a reference to this canal. The *Brooklyn* papyrus recounts a myth from the Bubastis area. The papyrus dates to the 7th century BCE but the myth is thought to be older. *"She was rowed within the Oryx-Antelope on the isheru in the very moment as she rescued the Udjat Eye from him; as Seth created his appearance, stealing the Udjat Eye in Mehet. He came to Bubastis, carrying the things he swallowed but Horit (Bastet) rescued the Udjat Eye of her father."*[418] A Late Period *stele* from the cat cemetery illustrates this scene. A lioness-headed Goddess sits enthroned in a shrine on the sacred barque. Zigzag lines under the barque show the waters of the *isheru*. The barque has the head of an oryx at the prow and stern, as the oryx is one of Seth's animals this probably shows the defeated Seth turned into a boat. The sacred statue of Bastet, or a priestess taking her role, will have been rowed along the sacred canals in a re-enactment of this myth.

Bubastis is also the site of the *ka*-chapels of Teti and Pepy I (6th dynasty) and the jubilee chapels of Amenemhat III (12th dynasty) and Amenhotep III (18th dynasty). The *ka* is the vital essence of a person and the *ka*-chapel held a statue in which the *ka* could reside. Some structures remain from the *ka*-chapel of Pepy I and a relief shows a

[416] *The Domain of the Cat-Goddess, Bastet*, Rosenow, 2008:27-33
[417] *The Histories*, Herodotus & Selincourt, 2003:152
[418] *Goddess on the Water: the Sacred Landscape of Bubastis*, Lange & Ullmann, 2015:17-19

lioness-headed Bastet holding an *ankh* to Pepy's nose. Hathor of Dendera stands behind the king. To the north of the city were the cat cemeteries.

The Temple of Mut at Karnak

Mut had a presence in Karnak since at least the 17th dynasty. Her temple, within the Precinct of Mut, lies to the south of that of her consort Amun. A ceremonial causeway linked the temples of Amun and Mut. Leaving the temple of Amun the avenue ran south out of the 18th dynasty pylons and through a line of ram-headed sphinxes (the ram was a sacred animal of Amun). Most of these have been destroyed. The precinct was enclosed by a brick wall. For over 1,600 years a succession of rulers built, restored and rebuilt it ending with Tiberius (14-37 CE). "*I renewed the temple of Mut the Great, lady of Isheru, so that it is more beautiful than it was before.*"[419] Most of the temple was built by Amenhotep III (18th dynasty) on the site of an earlier temple. The precinct of Mut was probably rebuilt by Hatshepsut (18th dynasty) as a "*monument for her mother Mut, Mistress of Isheru…so that she might do as one who is given life forever*".[420]

A chapel for Mut and Sekhmet was built in the Ptolemaic Period. At the entrance to the precinct of Mut is an inscription in which an unknown king says "*I am the perfect sistrum player for the Golden Lady, who pacifies the heart of my mistress every day*".[421] He is shown as the lead musician playing before Sekhmet and Mut. The temple is of the normal Pharaonic design with open colonnaded forecourts, a *hypostyle* hall, sanctuary and associated chambers. The Mut precinct was the setting for various rituals relating to the birth of Mut's child, *the Return of the Goddess* and *the Pacification of the Goddess*. It is here that Amenhotep III set up the statues of Sekhmet in two colonnaded courts and two corridors along the east and west sides of the precinct.

---

[419] *Writings from Ancient Egypt*, Wilkinson, 2016:26
[420] *Hatshepsut: From Queen to Pharaoh*, Roehrig, 1960:195
[421] *Mistress of the House, Mistress of Heaven: Women in Ancient Art*, Capel & Markoe, 1997:136

The Sekhmet Statues from the Temple of Mut

Although the statues of Sekhmet are of a standard form they do show some variation. On some the finger and toe nails are shown in detail but they are lacking on others. Some of the statues are not as well finished as others. They might have been finished in a hurry if they were needed for a specific event or possibly they were destined for a back row so didn't merit such a fine finish. There is also a variation over time. Most of the seated Sekhmet statues are thought to date to the reign of Amenhotep III but some of the standing ones have proportions more common to the 26th Dynasty and the uniform matt finish which was popular at that time. Their inscriptions are fairly standard giving the names and titles of the king and various epithets of Sekhmet. In general the inscriptions on statues from the reign of Amenhotep III make statements about her natures, refer to other deities and to geographical locations. 109 different epithets were recorded by Yoyotte, mostly from the temple of Mut.[422]

The number of Sekhmet statues shows both how important Sekhmet was to Amenhotep III and how wealthy he was. More than anything else it is the volume of these statues which are so unusual, no other deity had so many statues produced during one king's reign. No-one seems able to produce a definitive count; estimates have ranged from 730 to 1,000. In 1875 Mariette counted 498 at Karnak and the Mut precinct, and he estimated that there were originally at least 572 in the Mut precinct.[423] Many must have been destroyed when the site was used as a quarry or in the following centuries.

Statues, or fragments thereof, are still being uncovered. It is thought that they were buried when the temple either collapsed or was abandoned. There may have been too many statues for rehousing and they were considered unsuitable for reuse, either due to their condition or through the fear and awe attached to them for they still would have contained the power of Sekhmet. The Amenhotep III Temple Conservation Project has been working on the site since 1998. In 2005-6 they found a large destruction pit filled with statues of Sekhmet. 41 were found, either whole or in fragments, bringing the total found in 2006 to 62.[424] Eight statues were excavated in 2015. Six are of a seated

---

[422] *A Seated Statue of Sekhmet and Two Related Sculptures in the Collection of the San Antonia Museum of Art,* Scott, 2008:224
[423] *Travellers from an Antique Land: Statues of the Goddess Sekhmet in the British Museum,* Draper-Stumm, 2012.
[424] *The Theban Funerary Temple of Amenhotep III,* Sourouzian, 2006:21-24

Sekhmet and are 1.9m high, the other two are incomplete.[425] By March 2017 they had found another 66, most of which were complete.[426] The project's aim is to restore the statues and eventually return them to their original location at the temple. It is wonderful that so many statues of Sekhmet the Solar Eye Goddess are being released from the dark earth and brought back into the sunlight.

The Sekhmet statues are well travelled. In the Pharaonic Period they came from the quarries at Aswan to Thebes. Later Rameses II (19th dynasty) and Shesonk I (22nd dynasty) appropriated some of the statues. In more recent times they headed out of Egypt ending up in museums all over the world. The earliest record of their removal from Egypt is in 1760 when an Arab sheikh excavated some Sekhmet statues for a Venetian priest. The British Museum (London) has six on display and holds 37 in total, some complete others fragmentary. The earliest arrived in 1802. The Egyptian Museum in Turin (Italy) has a very good collection of 22 statues of Sekhmet most of which are beautifully displayed in a dedicated room. There is a well-illustrated book about them, in Italian, by Connor (2017).

The San Antonio Museum of Art (Texas) has one of these statues inscribed as "*Sekhmet, Lady of Aaget*". This place is unknown and has not been attested to elsewhere. It is a particularly well-travelled statue originating from the mortuary temple of Amenhotep III at Luxor. During the Pharaonic Period it was transferred to the temple of Mut at Karnak and was excavated in 1817. Brought to London it sat on Waterloo Bridge as a display for an auction of antiquities. Once purchased it went to Hartwell House (Buckinghamshire) then Didlington Hall (Norfolk) before heading to the New York Metropolitan Museum and then to San Antonio.[427]

Until hieroglyphics were deciphered no-one knew whom the statues represented and they were usually just described as lion-headed. Some of the Egyptian Goddesses were known through the Classical writers but Sekhmet wasn't. An auction catalogue of 1833 called the statue a representation of Isis with "*the mystical key of the waters of the Nile, or perhaps the portals of hell*" and referred to it as an idol "*superseded by*

---

[425] *News*, Griffiths, 2016:6-14
[426] *66 New Sekhmet Statues in Luxor*, Burzacott, 2017:8-11
[427] *A Seated Statue of Sekhmet and Two Related Sculptures in the Collection of the San Antonia Museum of Art*, Scott, 2008:

the light of Christianity".[428] One man's light is another's destructive fire. That aside, the description serves as a reminder that even with the best of intentions interpretation of an ancient culture is always at risk of misunderstanding and incorrect interpretation. Knowledge is constantly unfolding and it is wise to keep up to date with current discoveries and reinterpretations.

An early description of the site says that the statues were "*crowded together…presenting the appearance of a regiment drawn up in battle array*".[429] This may well have been the desired effect. In his plan Mariette shows double rows of statues to the north, east and west and a single row in the south of the first court. The second court has single rows. This suggests that most of the perceived threat came from the north, east and west or has the second row been moved from the south?

Simpson and Yoyotte both suggest that the statues of Sekhmet at Karnak represent the *Litany of Sekhmet* in stone. This litany invokes Sekhmet "*in all her names and all her places*" to protect the king and Egypt from various natural disasters including diseases.[430] It has been suggested that the statues were commissioned by Amenhotep III in response to a series of plagues in the hope of warding off any future occurrences. Others disagree, one argument being that if the country had been very badly affected by natural disasters such as plague they would not have been able to produce the vast number of statues with diminished wealth and manpower.

Bryan examined the Sekhmet statues in the funerary temple of Amenhotep III in context with its other statues and suggests that the collection represented a map of the heavens and a ritual calendar. Some statues represented the constellations and those of Sekhmet represented the stars, appropriately enough for a Solar Goddess as stars are suns.[431] As well as Sekhmet there were statues of a variety of deities in animal form; such as an ibis-headed Thoth, hippos, jackal, sphinx, crocodile and a giant scarab. Many of these animals represent the solar and lunar deities which may reflect a desire to have a solar-lunar balance. Both of the Eyes of Heaven need to be present and appeased to ensure *maat*. The

---

[428] *Statues of the Goddess Sekhmet*, Lythgoe, 1919:3-23
[429] *Statues of the Goddess Sekhmet*, Lythgoe, 1919:3-23
[430] *Mistress of the House, Mistress of Heaven: Women in Ancient Art*, Capel & Markoe, 1997:135
[431] *Travellers from an Antique Land: Statues of the Goddess Sekhmet in the British Museum*, Draper-Stumm, 2012.

Nile flood would have reached the courtyard of the funerary complex of Amenhotep and surrounded the Sekhmet statues. Water flowing around the statues would have brought rebirth to the king and to the heavens as represented by the statues.

Fletcher believes that the statues were a *"three-dimensional astronomical calendar to guarantee a propitious festival year"*.[432] She suggests that the 365 Sekhmet statues were set behind the columns of the solar court of Amenhotep's funerary temple to represent each night of the year and that they worked in conjunction with the 365 statues in Mut's temple which represented each day of the year. The temple of Kom Ombo depicts the ritual of the *Litany of Sekhmet* and mentions 730 statues. Sekhmet was *"she who his majesty follows, in the number of 730, lady of years, sovereign of months and days"*.[433] Sekhmet was depicted having power over every day. The *Litany of Sekhmet* is recorded in Greco-Roman temples and it may not have been in this form during the 18th dynasty when the Sekhmet statues were set up. Most scholars agree that we are not seeing the original layout and that they were moved to Mut's precinct later.

Despite much research we still don't know for certain the original function of the statues. They were certainly connected with processions and ceremonies and probably intended to protect the king and Egypt in some way. They will have worked at multiple levels: protecting the king, Egypt, and *maat* as well as enhancing the king's status and power. The statues of Sekhmet in the precinct of Mut received offerings as part of the *Litany of Ra*. Each separate statue was honoured on one specific day of the year. Later kings and religious leaders may well have used them in different ways for different purposes. They were definitely very important given their quality and quantities. Ongoing excavation and research may further our knowledge. Whatever their original purpose it is thanks to Amenhotep's generosity and devotion to Sekhmet that enough have survived to grace museums around the world.

In a sad reversal to the Ancient Egyptians' belief in Sekhmet's protective powers, there are reports from the early 20th century of statues of Sekhmet in the temple of Ptah being broken by superstitious locals in case they harmed their children. This won't have been a recent practice; once Pagan religion had been outlawed all divine statues and depictions

---

[432] *The Story of Egypt*, Fletcher, 2015:211
[433] *The Story of Egypt*, Fletcher, 2015:211

were deemed evil and thus a target. There is also a story that seven boys (the magical number) working to remove rubble from the statue of Sekhmet at the temple of Ptah at Karnak were buried at her feet by a rock-fall and their bodies were never found.[434]

The Feline Goddesses were increasing in importance during the New Kingdom before Amenhotep III. He had a special empathy with these deities which accelerated this rise. Kozloff suggests that Amenhotep spent part of his childhood being educated at the Mut temple, hence his affection for the site and for Sekhmet. He also closely identified himself with the Sun God giving himself the epithet "*the Dazzling Sun Disk of all lands*".[435] If he viewed himself as Ra it is not surprising that he had a close relationship with Sekhmet seeing her as his daughter and protector.

The Cult of Sekhmet of Sahure

No doubt there were hundreds of small cults which we have no knowledge of, but one of Sekhmet's has survived and this provides a glimpse into a local cult. Sahura (5th dynasty) had his funerary monument built at Abusir, the necropolis of Memphis. It consists of a valley and mortuary temple, causeway and pyramid. It was excavated in the early 1900s and produced reliefs of Bastet. For some reason a cult of Sekhmet developed in the New Kingdom, this seems to have been a spontaneous response by local people and pilgrims rather than a purposely established official cult.

There is nothing to indicate why the cult emerged but it was certainly well established by the reign of Amenhotep III. Pilgrims and other travellers will have come to the site which was already over 1,000 years old at the start of the New Kingdom. The cult might have arisen after reports of answered prayers, healing miracles, visions or by some unusual and impressive natural phenomena in the vicinity. Possibly there had always been a local cult of Sekhmet here. The corridor surrounding a palm-columned court was reroofed and turned into the sanctuary. For some reason the old northern stairs to the temple roof were not used, a brick staircase was built instead.

---

[434] *Gods of Ancient Egypt*, Watterson, 2003:154
[435] *Egypt's Dazzling Sun: Amenhotep III and his World*, Kozloff & Bryan, 1992:5

Stelae and graffiti give an insight into the followers of Sekhmet of Sahure. Analysis of these showed the cult had adherents at all levels of society; a few very high officials, a considerable number of middle-rank officials and many ordinary people. The highest-ranking visitor was Prince Khaemwaset, the fourth son of Rameses II. He may have been on an inspection tour, whatever the reason he presented a statute of Sekhmet and had this donation engraved on her shrine. *Stelae* were dedicated by a treasury scribe, a king's scribe, the chief chiseller of Ptah and a servant of the estate of the temple of Amun. The majority of middle-rank devotees seem to have been lay employees of temples. This is interesting in itself. Why did they become attached to Sekhmet of Sahure rather than the deities in their own temples? Were temple employees more likely to go on pilgrimages? Or was it just that people in such employment formed the majority of those well paid enough to be able to afford such donations and excursions?

Less wealthy people couldn't afford inscriptions, instead they offered ear *stele* (plaques shaped like an ear as to encourage the deity to listen to and respond to their prayers) or faience and sandstone plaques bearing the figure or head of Sekhmet or Sekhmet and Ptah. Many of these were inserted into the wall of the temple. During the reign of Rameses II two sailors came here on a pilgrimage and left graffiti asking for a long life. *"Blessings, blessings, O Sekhmet of Sahure, it is while we stand before you we say 'as sure as the sun lives, we are before our sovereign."*[436]

Faience lampstands, used for oil lamps or incense burners, and bowls as gifts or for the presentation of offerings were found. These date to the reign of Amenhotep III and the rest of the 18th dynasty. There was an abundance of ordinary pottery on the site, including wine jars, from offerings presented to Sekhmet. Most invoke Sekhmet, the rest Ptah or Thoth with a few to Amun. There were also faience inlays which seem to have come from a wooden structure, possibly a shrine. Small glazed plaques and faience throw sticks or wands were also donated.

The cult had its own clergy; there is a broken *stele* dedicated by a prophet of Sekhmet of Sahure. As soon as the heretic Akhenaten (18th dynasty) died the cult was restored. It may have become part of the official religion. A fine quality *stele* is attributed to Ay (18th dynasty) and

---

[436] *Sekhmet et la Protection du Monde*, Germond, 1981:343 (My translation)

8 - Ptah and Sekhmet

possibly the corniche to Horemhab (18th dynasty). There is also a dedication in the name of Sety I (19th dynasty) and Rameses II involving the High Priest of Ptah at Memphis. Graffiti shows that the cult continued into the 26th dynasty and may have survived into the Greco-Roman Period. The latest dated graffiti was made in 566 BCE by the son of the Prophet of Sekhmet of Sahure. His maternal grandfather worked for the cult and his mother was attached to a nearby cult of Bastet.[437] Sekhmet was called by her usual string of epithets as well as Sekhmet of Sahure and Sekhmet-Bastet.

The Temple of Pakhet at Speos Artemidos

Hatshepsut (18th dynasty) ruled for over 20 years, defying tradition to establish herself as king of Egypt. The country prospered during her reign but after her death her image and name were erased. Despite a stable government, successful trade missions, architectural achievements and internal peace her gender is still seen as the most important and outstanding characteristic of her 20 years as a monarch. Hatshepsut was particularly devoted to Hathor, Sekhmet and Pakhet. This may have arisen during her time as queen consort as the 17th and 18th dynasty queens were strongly associated with Hathor. She funded repairs to many temples which had been damaged during the 2nd Intermediate Period including Hathor's temple at Cusae which had fallen into disuse. Hatshepsut also adopted Pakhet and refurbished her temple at Speos Artemidos. It is not clear why Hatshepsut selected Pakhet's temple as she was a little-known Goddess. It might be that Pakhet was considered the aggressive form of Hathor in that area. Pakhet is very independent and does not have any recorded relationship with the other deities. Hatshepsut may have felt the same degree of isolation hence her identification with Pakhet.

Hatshepsut endowed two temples to Pakhet in the Beni Hasan area. One is less well known, the smaller Speos Batn el-Bakarah. This was badly defaced in the reign of Thutmose III (18th dynasty). The other is Speos Artemidos. It survived the reigns of Thutmose III and Akhenaten and then was taken over by Sety I (19th dynasty) who again didn't complete it. Why should both rulers not complete work on the temple? Perhaps the wild Goddess Pakhet preferred it in an unfinished state.

---

[437] *Popular Religion in Egypt During the New Kingdom*, Sadek, 1988:34

Inscriptions in the Speos Artemidos temple tell how Hatshepsut funded mass restoration of temples fallen into ruin under Hyksos rule and how she *"made her temple worthy...the doors of acacia inlaid with copper...and the priest knew her time"*.[438] Pakhet's temple is cut into the living rock on the south side of a small rocky valley called the Valley of the Knife. This whole area was considered sacred to Pakhet. The rock-hewn cave *"which she hewed out herself"* was a liminal place which formed the entrance to the underworld. The temple consists of a larger vestibule and an inner sanctuary. One of Pakhet's epithets is Mistress of Sro. The word *Sro* is written with the hieroglyph signs of knife, valley and thorn.[439]

The hall has Hathor-head pillars and a short passage leads to the inner sanctuary which is cut into the rock face. The focus was a niche which would have held the cult statue. An image of Pakhet is carved into the wall. Hatshepsut was especially keen to show that she ruled with divine consent. All kings did this to some extent but Hatshepsut was particularly vulnerable as a woman. In the sanctuary a relief shows Amun-Ra proclaiming Hatshepsut's kingship whilst Werethekau-Pakhet extends her left arm to the kneeling Hatshepsut. *"I place fear of thee in all lands. I rear myself up between thine eyebrows, my fiery breath being as a fire against thine enemies and thou art glad through me."* Thoth then announces her accession. Hatshepsut is referred to as the daughter of Amun and Pakhet. In another relief Hatshepsut offers incense and libations to an enthroned Pakhet who responds. *"O my beloved daughter...I give thee all strength, all might, all lands and every hill country crushed beneath thy sandals."* Pakhet wears the cow horn sun disc topped by a feather and holds a papyrus sceptre and *menat* in each hand which she offers to Hatshepsut. Each sceptre is crowned by a pair of *uraei* one wearing the Red Crown of Lower Egypt the other the White Crown of Upper Egypt. Pakhet says *"I give thee the two uraei upon thy brow...the mnit is with thee, protecting thee, thou having appeared upon the throne of Horus...I give thee all valour, all might, all provisions, and all offerings"*.[440]

Sety I was also a devotee of Pakhet and of the Lioness Goddesses in general. Inscriptions in the temple describe him as *"Born of Pakhet,*

---

[438] *Davies's Copy of the Great Speos Artemidos Inscription*, Gardiner, 1946:43-56

[439] *Texts of Hatshepsut and Sethos I inside Speos Artemidos*, Fairman & Grdseloff, 1947:12-33

[440] *Texts of Hatshepsut and Sethos I inside Speos Artemidos*, Fairman & Grdseloff, 1947:12-33

reared by the Sorceress...brought up by Edjo". He also states that he is the son of Sekhmet and Bastet, a king can never have too many powerful protectors. It is not clear if the Sorceress refers to Pakhet or another one of the Goddesses such as Weret-Hekau. Sety further aligns himself with Pakhet by describing himself as the *"claw of the lion that kills instantly"*. Like Hatshepsut, he records how he rebuilt the temple.[441]

Some Other Temples

As mentioned earlier there are not many temples dedicated to the Feline Goddesses. There are even less to the Feline Gods. These are the others that I have found.

Alexandria

In 2010 the remains of a temple dating to the reign of Queen Berenike II, the wife of Ptolemy III, were found. There was a large number of statues of reclining cats which suggest that the temple was dedicated to Bastet.[442]

Kellis

The only known temple to the God Tutu is as Kellis. Built in the Roman Period this small village temple stood until 1920 but it is now in ruins.[443] Here Tutu was venerated as the son of Neith. He is shown as a man with two heads, one human and one lion. The lion head faces towards Neith. Is she too powerful for a human to view? The temple also depicted deities from the Dakhla Oasis as well as principle ones from the Nile Valley.[444]

Kom el-Hisn

At Kom el-Hisn, in western Delta, was a temple dedicated to Sekhmet-Hathor who was the patron Goddess of the city. All that remains is the outline of the rectangular enclosure wall.[445]

---

[441] *Texts of Hatshepsut and Sethos I inside Speos Artemidos*, Fairman & Grdseloff, 1947:12-33
[442] *From Our Own Correspondent*, Taher, 2010:9-16
[443] *The Complete Temples of Ancient Egypt*, Wilkinson, 2000:235
[444] *Restoring Wall Paintings of the Temple of Tutu*, Kaper, 2009:3-7
[445] *The Complete Temples of Ancient Egypt*, Wilkinson, 2000:108

Leontopolis

There was a temple to the local God Mahes here. Most of the stone has been removed and reused so it can't be dated.[446]

Memphis

A large sacred complex, known to the Greeks as the Bubasteon, was dedicated to Bastet at the entrance to the Memphis necropolis of Saqqara. Here she was known as Lady of Ankhtawy. The only surviving structure is part of the large enclosure wall. From the Late Period the catacombs were filled with cat mummies. There are also the ruins of the temple to Ptah and Sekhmet built by Rameses II. In Memphis there was a palace with a shrine of Sekhmet, known through an 18th dynasty reference to a master craftsman *"of the barque of Sekhmet in the lake (or garden) of the Pharaoh"*.[447]

---

[446] *The New Cultural Atlas of Egypt*, Gray, 2009:143
[447] *The Garden in Ancient Egypt*, Wilkinson, 1998:67

CHAPTER 20

SACRED FELINES

"To the Cat of the Lady of Heaven."[448]

What Animals Meant to the Egyptians

Egyptian theology didn't consider humans to be superior to and apart from the rest of the natural world. The *Shabaka* text tells how the creative forces of Ptah are present *"in all gods, all people, all cattle, all crawling creatures, in all that lives"*. Animals were considered partners and caring for sacred animals appeared to have been comparable to caring for humans. *"I have given bread to the hungry…food to the ibis, the falcon, the cat."*[449] The papyrus *Zenon* states that the feeders of the sacred cats were exempt from liturgical services.[450] If an animal had an aspect which was particularly feared or admired it was considered a direct link to the divine. The animal's features would emphasise an aspect of a deity and so became a symbol for that deity. Egyptians believed that the divine could manifest on earth in animals, natural features and man-made objects such as statues. An animal could

---

[448] *The Cat in Ancient Egypt*, Langton, 2002:4
[449] *A Few Remarks on the Religious Significance of Animals*, te Velde, 1980:76-82
[450] *The Cat in Ancient Egypt*, Langton, 2002:38

therefore house the *ba* of a deity when they manifested on earth, and so as a sacred animal it would receive adulation both as a symbol of the deity and as their earthly manifestation. In theory the animal wasn't as important as the divine power it contained, but this line became blurred, especially during the Greco-Roman Period.

The Rise of the Sacred Cat

Cats are unusual in Egyptian religion in that they weren't associated with a deity at the beginning but their popularity as a sacred animal eventually overtook all others. They enjoyed a particularly important place in the religion of ordinary people. In addition to being popular pets they were believed to have apotropaic aspects. More importantly, they could house the *ba* of the popular Bastet. If Bastet was present in the cat even the poorest people could have access to her, even if they didn't actually own one, because cats became so widespread and common. Cats, and so the Goddess, lived with ordinary people rather than in temples. Because of this a unique cult developed focused on the cat which in general was considered an animal of Bastet but could also be sacred to Mut.

From the evidence we have, individual cats weren't seen as living deities, unlike the Apis bull which was believed to be the living image of Ptah at Memphis. During the late New Kingdom the role of sacred animals became increasingly important in the religion of ordinary people. This is illustrated by the prominent place animals take in iconography especially on private *stele* and tomb decorations. After the Hyksos invasion from the east in the 15th dynasty Seth was increasingly associated with invasion and the much hated foreign enemy. One text accuses him of a long list of crimes including "*he has desired to eat the sacred Cat in the presence of its mother Bastet*".[451]

Animal Sacrifice

Animal sacrifice was not uncommon in the ancient world, but the Egyptians took the practice to extremes during the Ptolemaic Period. The first animal sacrifices would have occurred in the Pre-dynastic Period but the first votive offerings of animal mummies, including cats, don't

---

[451] *Men and Gods on the Roman Nile*, Lindsay, 1968:180

appear until the 3rd Intermediate Period. Cats were buried in the tombs of senior officials of the late 18th and early 19th dynasties. Not all animals buried with the deceased were votive offerings. They may have been included for their symbolism or because the deceased was attached to them in life and wished them to be present with them in the afterlife. The mummified remains of horses have been found but these have no religious symbolism as they weren't introduced to Egypt until the 2nd Intermediate Period.

During the Late Period there was a widespread increase in animal cults and the 3rd Intermediate Period brought great social and political change which was reflected in changing religious practise, the increased popularity of local cults being one such change. The upsurge is thought to have begun in the 26th dynasty. The cause has been debated and many think it was a response to foreign invasion and immigration. This was a time of nostalgia, looking back to a glorious past when Egypt had been a major world power. It was also an era of commercialism in religious life which saw the upsurge in animal cults and in animal mummy offerings. There was a lot of contact with the rest of the Mediterranean and Egypt became a tourist destination. Either the animal cults were seen as a popular way of emphasising Egyptian culture or people had taken the invasions and social and economic upheavals as a sign that the deities were displeased and offering animal sacrifices was a method of appeasing them. The continued rapid growth in the animal cults during the Ptolemaic Period could be seen as an expression of Egyptian nationalism in the face of foreign rule. Some of the donors had Greek names which might have been a way for the ruling Greeks to placate the feelings of the Egyptians, or the Greek immigrants might just have adopted some of the local practices.

Breeding animals for sacrifice was an important revenue earner for the temples and it will have been encouraged and promoted, especially when other sources of revenue were declining. It was a deliberate policy of the 26th and 27th dynasties and the early Ptolemies to encourage the cult of animal sacrifices. This gave a huge boost to temple income and through that of taxes to the state. There was an organised industry in the production of animal mummies. For ordinary people the mummified animal was viewed as a direct link to the deity as the animal would act as an intermediary offering thanks or transmitting prayers.

The Cat Mummies

Although not the only mummified animals cats were amongst the most frequently mummified, along with ibis, because they were easy to breed and so made a cheap offering affordable to most people. The numbers can never be known but it will have been in the order of hundreds of thousands, possibly millions. During the 19th century excavated animal mummies were shipped to Europe to be ground up for use as fertiliser. One shipment of cat mummies to London weighed 19 tons. Of these just one cat mummy went to the British Museum.[452]

Herodotus reported that all cats were mummified and taken to Bubastis *"where they are embalmed and buried in sacred receptacles"*.[453] In reality wherever there were temples to any of the Feline Goddesses there tended to be cat cemeteries. The cat cemeteries of Bubastis date from 900 BCE and may have been some of the earliest but they were destroyed before they could be properly studied. Many of the bronze cats in museums around the world came from here. There was a large cat cemetery connected to the cult of Pakhet at Speos Artemidos. At Saqqara mummified cats are buried close to the Bubasteon, the precinct of Bastet. The connection with Bastet in this area may go back as far as the New Kingdom but no temple remains have yet been found. Other cat cemeteries are found at Abydos, Chemmis, Dendera, Giza, Koptos, Tanis, Thebes, and in the Dakhla Oasis. Small numbers will have been buried at other sites throughout Egypt. Cat mummies were not solely deposited in shrines for Bastet or the other Feline Goddesses, some were found at the ibis galleries of Tuna el-Gebel dedicated to Thoth. At Saqqara there were underground galleries (called the Houses of Rest) for various deities. Those for cats were dedicated to Bastet, Lady of Ankhtawy. The majority of cats were killed at 2-4 months or 9-12 months; this was done by breaking their necks.[454] On the whole the cats appear to have been well treated in life. Studies on 270 cat mummies from Saqqara found that a third of the bundles contained no parts of cats at all.[455] There were also some very small cats in large cases. Was this fraud by some of the temple staff to make or save money or because demand was too high to be satisfied? Or was it just a cheaper option chosen by the donor?

---

[452] *Cat Sense*, Bradshaw, 2014:47
[453] *The Histories*, Herodotus & Selincourt, 2003:122
[454] *The Cat in Ancient Egypt*, Malek, 1993:133
[455] *The Gayer-Anderson Cat*, Spencer, 2007:36

The money paid would determine the type of mummification. The majority of the mummy packets were elongated, some were plain whilst others were wrapped in elaborate geometric patterns. A stylised image of a cat's head was created in linen or drawn in ink. These faces were often painted with quizzical or humorous expressions. Sometimes a bronze bust of a cat was sewn onto the mummy packet. Some of the mummies then went into coffins, either in the shape of a cat or in a rectangular box. As usual these vary in quality. The standard coffins were made of wood or bronze but the cat models were bronze. The *Archive of Hor* explains how the mummies were sold to pilgrims then stored in the Hall of Waiting before being transferred in bulk to the catacombs each year.[456] Analysis of large volumes of the cat mummies showed that the majority were domesticated, as expected, but there were some wild cats. The mummified cats were about 15 percent larger than modern domestic cats but the DNA showed a link to modern Egyptian cats.

Today we cannot understand how someone could venerate a cat, love it as a pet yet be quite willing to sacrifice it. Before it was possible to neuter animals the only way to control a population of cats was to routinely kill their kittens and this was accepted as a necessary action. Farmers also care for their animals then kill them. What we see as a conflict wasn't an issue to the Ancient Egyptians. Logically this may be so, but the thought of people breeding animals purely to kill them as an offering to a deity whose sacred animal they happen to be is not a comfortable one for us today.

Sacred Lions

Very few remains of lions have been found from the Pre-dynastic and early Dynastic Periods. This is not unexpected given their scarcity and the low survival rates of early material. Lion bones were found in the grave of the 1st dynasty king Aha and these may have come from one kept in a royal menagerie. The remains of seven lion cubs were found around another 1st dynasty tomb near Abydos. They too may have come from a menagerie. As seven is an important number they no doubt had some symbolic meaning unavailable to us.

Given the religious significance of lions it would be expected that the Egyptians considered them sacred. There is little evidence of this,

---

[456] *The Quest for Immortality: Treasures of Ancient Egypt*, Hornung & Bryan, 2002:191

perhaps a reflection of the rarity of lions. When Rameses IV denies ritual wrongdoing he says *"I have not contended against a god; I have not affronted a goddess...I have not shot against a lion on the feast of Bastet"*.[457] Royal lion hunts were permitted at all other times. Amenhotep III (18th dynasty) was a devotee of Sekhmet, but this did not deter him from being an enthusiastic lion hunter. Texts from the Late and Greco-Roman Period suggest that there were sacred lions in temple precincts in Leontopolis (Lion city) and in Heliopolis. In 2001 the excavation of the tomb of Maia in Bubastis uncovered the skeleton of a lion which had been mummified.[458] It is no surprise that lion burials are rare. Cats were easy to breed and hence were cheap compared to the rare and expensive lions.

The Mongoose

The mongoose is depicted from the Pre-dynastic Period, one is shown on a pottery vase from the Naqada II Period and it was important to the Early Dynastic kings. It wasn't until the Late and Ptolemaic Periods that it really came to prominence as a sacred animal. Its first cult seems to appear in the 22nd dynasty. Killing snakes was an important theme in the solar myths so the mongoose became associated with the solar deities. The mongoose was a sacred animal in a number of cities. It was linked to Ra, Atum, Horus and Osiris and in Heliopolis was considered a form of the setting sun. Because of this solar association the mongoose sometimes has a solar disc or *uraeus*.

Many mongoose amulets and bronze figurines were produced in the Late and Greco-Roman Periods, often as votive offerings. One example is a pair of mongooses on a shrine shaped pedestal. They stand upright with their front paws raised. One wears a *uraeus* on its head. The mongoose was considered sacred to Wadjet of Buto. Late Period bronze statues of a lioness-headed Wadjet have been found which contain the mummified remains of mongooses. Figurines and mummified mongooses were given as votive offerings to Bastet and they have been found with the mummified cats at Bubastis.

---

[457] *The Oath in Ancient Egypt*, Wilson, 1948:129-156
[458] *Divine Creatures Animal Mummies in Ancient Egypt*, Ikram, 2005:114

Conclusion

To our minds, the term sacred animal means one that is treated with love and respect because it is favoured by the deity. No doubt some of the sacred animals were treated this way but not all would have been. Human nature unfortunately remains constant in its tendency towards cruelty. The killing of a sacred and loved animal is anathema to most of us today especially when this favoured animal of the deity was meant to take prayers with them. The gulf between us and the Ancient Egyptian's beliefs and practices is rarely wider than it is over animal sacrifice. I do suspect that the earlier Egyptians would have been bemused if not distressed by the volume of animal sacrifice in the Greco-Roman Period. A prime example of good intentions gone badly astray.

CHAPTER 21

FELINES IN ART AND ARTEFACT

"The beautiful cat of Mut...an offering the king gives to Mut."[459]

Decorative Felines

It is not easy to tell if the lion or cat motif on everyday objects is purely decorative or has religious symbolism. This is really the wrong question to ask as the Egyptians didn't differentiate between the sacred and the secular in the way that we do.

Depictions of Lions in the Pre-dynastic and Early Dynastic Period

Statues of lions have been found dating to the Pre-dynastic Period. A statuette of a limestone lion was found in a Naqada grave; other graves had statuettes of different animals. These might have been used to denote tribes in a similar way to a clan totem. It is not possible to determine if they were associated with deities or had the apotropaic

---

[459] *A Cat, a Nurse and a Standard Bearer. Notes on Three Late Eighteenth Dynasty Statues*, van Dijk, 2010:321

qualities they acquired in later periods. As lions became a more important symbol through their connection to royalty lion statues were installed in shrines. Several early limestone lions have been excavated at Koptos and Gebelein. All have a fierce expression and many bare their teeth. Even the statues of cubs do not look approachable or friendly. The idea was to convey the savagery and aggression of the king.

The depiction of lions on the Pre-dynastic palettes is unusual and some say that the style is Mesopotamian. Barbary and Asiatic lions did have a longer and extended mane than the African ones. The lions depicted on these, and other palettes, show the mane extending over its shoulders and along its belly.[460] Another interesting example of such lions is found on an ivory knife handle dating to Naqada II. On one side a man is shown between two long-maned lions. The literature says he is subduing them but it is hard to tell if he is doing this, separating them or interacting in another way. He has his hands on the lions' chins and they have their paws on his waist. Both the man and the lions have features common to Mesopotamian art and some have suggested that the knife was traded from Mesopotamia.[461] Are these lions the forerunner of the double lion symbol of Aker and Ruty? Does it depict a lost myth? We can only speculate.

With the start of the 3rd dynasty the form of the lion changes. They lose their long and extended mane and from that period onwards the Egyptians always depicted lions with a short mane. Were the longer manes just an artistic convention? Did the artists begin look to the more Egyptian African lion as their model rather than the foreign Barbary and Asiatic lions? There is also a change in the character of the lions. These early statues of lions do not display the consistency in style or material of their later counterparts but they appear much friendlier than the Pre-dynastic ones. The image the king wanted to portray had changed. Now more confident the kings realised that they didn't have to look so aggressive and threatening, a dignified watchfulness would suffice. It also hints at a degree of self-control more suitable for a king or deity than a look of uncontrollable rabid anger. A 3rd dynasty statuette of a seated lion modelled in clay was found in a temple at Hierakonpolis and was probably a votive offering. From the

---

[460] *The Mammals of Ancient Egypt,* Osborn, 1998:2
[461] *Egyptian Wall Paintings,* Tiradritti, 2007:93

same area a temple cache included a pottery lion coated with a haematite wash, giving it a red colouring. It sits upright, its face and body are realistic but his mane is very geometrical. It might have been one of a pair of guardians at the entrance to the temple site.[462] It is tentatively dated to the 6th dynasty.

Lions attacking their prey was a popular motif in the early Dynastic. Lions dominate but there are some images of lionesses. One ivory knife sheath shows hunting dogs and lions attacking herbivores. A carved ivory spoon, used for the preparation of incense, depicts a lion and a hunting dog. Lion-shaped gaming pieces, dating to the 1st dynasty, were found in and around elite tombs of Hierakonpolis. They include lionesses wearing decorative collars. This does suggest their role as royal pets from an early date.

The earliest depiction of a lioness, which isn't a hieroglyph, may be on fragments from a ceremonial gateway at Djoser's 3rd dynasty pyramid complex at Saqqara. The central column consists of twelve panels which alternatively depict a recumbent jackal (representing Anubis) and a recumbent lion or lioness. Hawass believes this is a lioness despite having a sparse mane. The tail is shown as non-tufted and held erect which is the traditional way the Egyptians depicted a lioness. Prior to this, the earliest non-disputed representations of a lioness are on reliefs in the 4th dynasty temple of Sneferu at Dahshur and the 5th dynasty reliefs of Sahura and Nyuserra.[463]

Lions in Art of the Dynastic and Greco-Roman Periods

Lions are less widespread in Egyptian art than cats and tend to appear more on monumental architecture. I have not come across any lioness statues, they all appear to be of lions. This is not unexpected given that it is the male which is more instantly recognisable. If they had intended to portray Sekhmet, or one of the other Lioness Goddesses, the Egyptians would have chosen her lioness-headed form. The lion statues tended to be large sculptures, representing either the king or acting as temple guardians. One example is the lion of Nectanebo I (30th dynasty) probably from Hermopolis Parva in the Delta. Carved from grey granite

---

[462] *Ancient Egypt and Nubia*, Whitehouse, 2009:51
[463] *A Fragmentary Monument of Djoser from Saqqara*, Hawass, 1994:45-56

it has its front paws crossed and its head turned sideways. During the Greco-Roman Period it was taken to Rome as a trophy and is now in the Vatican Museum.[464] Ptolemaic sculptures of lions lined the processional way to the Middle Kingdom temple of Renenutet at Medinet Maadi. Other significant statues have been mentioned earlier in this book.

One exception to these large-scale depictions of lions is a finely carved wooden lion, about 3cm high, dating to the Middle Kingdom which was found at Lahun. It is fragile, so is unlikely to have been intended as a toy, and has peg holes on the base. A crocodile of a similar size was found with it.[465] Such figures would probably have been placed on a rod or wand. A rod with similarly carved pieces of lions, crocodiles, frogs and turtles was found at Iunu.

Lion imagery by itself is less common in amulets and jewellery compared to other symbols. Lion amulets appear in the late Old Kingdom and were made of faience, carnelian, amethyst and lapis lazuli. Many had a suspension loop on the back. One Late Period spell has to be recited over a *"lion of glazed composition threaded to red linen"*.[466] Lions appear on bezel rings made of glass from the 6th dynasty through to the Greco-Roman Period. During the New Kingdom there was a Lion of Gold valour award for soldiers. There are records of 18th dynasty soldiers given gold as a reward by the king; one was given *"three lions"* another *"one lion"*.[467] A very fine bracelet came from the tomb of a 12th dynasty royal woman from Dahshur. Composed of gold, granite, lapis lazuli, carnelian and faience it includes two crouching lions made of gold.[468] Back to back lions, symbolising Aker or Ruty, occur from the 6th dynasty. Early ones tend to be crude and just show the forepaws or two heads, by the 26th dynasty they appear in the well-known back to back form.

Lioness-headed amulets are more common because they portray one of the Feline Goddesses, but there are also depictions of lionesses. One problem is that lioness heads are not easily distinguished from leopards at the small scale which will have changed the symbolism of the piece. One 12th dynasty princess had girdle components in the form

---

[464] *Egypt: 4000 Years of Egyptian Art*, Malek, 2003:305
[465] *Excavating Egypt*, Trope et al, 2005:66
[466] *Amulets of Ancient Egypt*, Andrews, 1994:64
[467] *Accessions to the Egyptian Department During 1914*, Reisner, 1915:29-36
[468] *The Quest for Immortality: Treasures of Ancient Egypt*, Hornung & Bryan, 2002:105

9 - Lion Statue

of lioness heads. A carnelian lioness head was found with an ivory lion both dating to the Old Kingdom or the 1st Intermediate Period. Lion-headed *uraeus* amulets first appear in the Saite Period and are thought to represent Sekhmet, Wadjet or Tefnut.

Cat Statues

Not all cat statues are a representation of Bastet. Some are her sacred cats while others are just cats. How do we distinguish them apart? It is thought that those engraved with the scarab and *wedjat* eye represent Bastet. Figurines of cats have been found in Middle Kingdom tombs. The earliest one comes from Thebes; it is a crouching cat with a black spotted coat made of blue faience. From Heliopolis comes a stalking cat and from Abydos one with its back arched. Figurines of cats were put in these tombs as protection for the deceased from the numerous snakes of the underworld.

From the 3rd Intermediate Period thousands of bronze votive offering statues were produced. Statues of cats in materials other than bronze are very rare and there are very few large stone statues comparable to those of lions and falcons found in temples. The vast numbers of cat statues are a reflection of both the popularity of Bastet and the move to a more industrialised process in the production of bronze casting. Votive offerings were given to the deity, usually with a request or to give thanks for a request granted. Periodically, when the volumes posed a storage problem, they were cleared out from the temple and buried in the temple grounds. It is very difficult to date these later bronzes. The earliest is thought to be about 900 BCE but the majority are from the Ptolemaic Period. Inscribed ones are rare, probably because the inscriptions were usually on the statue's wooden pedestal. What inscriptions that remain are usually simple. *"May Great Bastet, the Mistress of Bubastis, give life to Horemheb forever"* or *"May Bastet, Mistress of Ankh-Tawy, make life and protection"*.[469]

The bronzes range in size from a few centimetres to life-size. The smaller ones are solid and the larger ones hollow cast. Most are anatomically correct, but they vary in workmanship, with the most popular pose being that of the cat hieroglyph with its tail lying along the right side of the body. Sometimes the details were picked out in gold and

---

[469] *The Cat in Ancient Egypt*, Malek, 1993:107

the eyes inlaid with rock-crystal or a similar substance. Most cats are seated but there are examples in all poses, including a small bronze cat washing its face with its paw. Despite the individuality the heads tend to conform to one of two types. They either have long ears and a sharp nose or short ears and a blunt nose. This is also found in the cat-headed statues.

On some of the statues a sun disc, *uraeus* or scarab was carved between the ears and a winged scarab on the chest. A pendant was sometimes inscribed in the form of a *wedjat* eye, *aegis* or a small figure of a deity. A scarab between the ears is common, especially on the Late Period bronze statues. Some are engraved others cast with the statue. It is very rare to get such a scarab on the statues of the cat-headed Bastet. The scarab is a manifestation of Khepri as the rising sun and alludes to rebirth so its inclusion is not surprising but why are they never depicted on the heads of lions? It has been suggested that it was due to the markings on the Egyptian cats' forehead. Stripes often run down the forehead and the outer ones diverge until the upper eyelids. If these stripes are pronounced it produces a pattern suggestive of a scarab with the centre of the forehead making the body and the outer stripes the legs. Khepri represented the rising sun which was gentle and warming compared to the hot midday sun. Thus it is more appropriate to depict it on the gentler, more benevolent cat than the lion and equally on Bastet rather than Sekhmet. Sekhmet does have one epithet *"Beautiful Noon"* which means that she wouldn't be depicted as Khepri.[470] The fact that domestic cats display the sacred scarab would have emphasised their divine connections.

In one tomb painting a man sits on a chair holding a statue of a seated cat. It is thought to come from Bubastis and is a priest or worshiper offering a cult statue of Bastet in Cat form. Devotees will have bought such statues at temples as a votive offering or to take home for private devotion.

One of the most well-known statues is that of the Gayer-Anderson Cat now in the British Museum (London). It is a 42cm high bronze of a seated cat and the workmanship is excellent. Unlike most of the other bronze cats its head is held slightly down. It has a very serene gaze. The eyes were probably made of inlaid glass, faience or rock-crystal. The eyebrows and other eye markings are thinly incised giving the eyes a

---

[470] *Les Statues Thebaines de la Desses Sakhmet*, Gautier, 1920:117-207

hieroglyph-like appearance. Both its whiskers and ears are incised. The fur inside the ears is shown in the shape of the feather of Maat. This is a common motif on cat statues but it never appears on the cat-headed ones. The ears and nose have been pierced and it wears gold earrings, though probably not the original ones. A scarab is carved between the ears.

The cat wears a four strand collar with drop shaped pendants, this type of necklace is frequently worn by both men and women in tomb scenes. Over this is another common amulet, a silver plaque depicting the *wedjat* eye, worn on a string. Below the amulet is incised a winged scarab holding a sun disc which is inlaid with silver. A tomb painting from Deir el-Medina shows a cat wearing earrings and necklace. Did cats really wear jewellery or is this just artistic licence, wishing the pet cat to be shown in its finery alongside its owners? It is more likely that jewellery was only placed on cat statues. Attaching and keeping jewellery on a cat would have been problematic. Valuable jewellery would have been easy to steal, especially as the cat would have been more than happy to get rid of the encumbrances. Was jewellery put on the statues as adornment for special occasions? The cat is the only animal shown wearing earrings, other animal statues just wear collars or necklaces. Earrings tend to be present on the single cat figurines rather than the compositions.

The Gayer-Anderson cat sits upright and the tail is drawn up on the right-hand side. At the end of the tail are incised six rings which indicate striping on the tail. The individual claws have been delineated. The cat sits on a wooden base which is a replica of the ones used in Egypt. It is shaped in the form of the *menat* counterpoise which has associations with Hathor.[471] It is believed to be a Late Period piece but the lack of inscription makes more accurate dating impossible.

Despite its beauty is it unlikely that the Gayer-Anderson cat was the main cult image in a temple. Images and inscriptions show that the cult statues would have been much larger and were usually inlaid with precious stones and were gilded. Their value means that they haven't survived. Unfortunately the provenance of this particular statue is unknown. It is most likely to have been a votive offering dedicated by a wealthy person as a mark of piety. It may even have come from a cemetery rather than a temple.

---

[471] *The Gayer-Anderson Cat*, Spencer, 2007:15

Another bronze cat in the Louvre (Paris) differs in style from the Gayer-Anderson cat in having its head held high and its tail bending around its front paws. Around its neck is a pearl necklace with a feline-headed *aegis* as a pendant. Many bronze cats have an *aegis* hanging from a necklace, another common amulet is a figure of a Goddess. The inscription bears the name of Psamtek I (26th dynasty) and its donor, the official Mer-sopdu. The dedication asks Bastet for protection and also specifies that a temple dancer called Djed-bastet-iwefank is responsible for looking after the statue in the temple.[472] A model barque from the Louvre has a small bronze cat sitting on the deck. Did such statues accompany the cult statue on the barque for protection?

Cat statues vary greatly in composition and cats are often shown in groups. The simplest is a cat and one kitten, usually positioned between the mother's legs or protected by her paws. Smaller statues depicting a cat nursing kittens were popular. Up to 10 kittens can be shown and with this number some are positioned on her head and back. The kittens highlight Bastet's fertility and maternal protection aspects. One such example is in the Cairo Museum (Egypt). The cat is nursing two kittens. Another sits between her hind legs while the fourth stands on its rear legs stretching out a paw to its mother's face.[473] Some compositions allude to myths. One faience piece consists of a baboon sitting on top of a papyrus column with a cat on his lap - this is Thoth bringing home the Distant Goddess.

Paintings

Cats appear in paintings from the 18th Dynasty but it wasn't until about the end of the 20th Dynasty that a cat under the woman's chair became a standard motif. The cat is only ever a small element of the composition of the painting. Its presence may indicate that it was a popular pet and a regular feature in houses but the paintings all come from elite tombs. Owning a pet cat may have been the preserve of the wealthy in the earlier periods. The deceased may never have owned a cat, it being depicted because it was a desirable pet or fashionable accessory as well as for its important symbolism.

---

[472] *The Gayer-Anderson Cat*, Spencer, 2007:28
[473] *The Treasures of Ancient Egypt from the Egyptian Museum in Cairo*, Bongioanni & Crose, 2001:552

Hunting Scenes

Some Middle and New Kingdom tombs depict scenes of fowling and fishing in the marshes. The earliest is in the 12th dynasty tomb of an official at Beni Hasan. A cat, probably the swamp cat, is shown climbing among the papyrus stems. During the New Kingdom the deceased were depicted with their family in recreational fowling expeditions in the marshes, often bringing along their pet cat. The cats are shown enjoying themselves stalking and catching birds. The best known is the 18th dynasty Theban wall painting from the tomb of Nebamun, now in the British Museum (London). The cat is tawny with huge whiskers and golden eyes. It balances on a papyrus stem with one bird in its mouth, one under its back paws and one in its front paws.[474] Some commentators have said that this shows that cats were used in hunting. I think that this is highly unlikely given the trainability of cats. The cat would be more likely to wander off and hunt for its own amusement.

Wetlands are productive lands and were especially so in Egypt before modern methods of agriculture, drainage and overuse degraded them. Marshes were a symbol of fertility as they were teeming with life; fish, insects, birds and the less popular crocodiles, hippos and snakes. The marsh could be a mysterious and dangerous place but it was a place of fertility and regeneration and considered the equivalent of the *nun*. It was a liminal place of permanent duality, lying between the deserts and the cultivated land neither solid ground nor open water. The flocks of wild birds flying around and calling represented the forces of chaos and so fowling could be seen as symbolic of the fight against chaos. The cat killing the wild birds, the symbols of chaos, was paralleled with the Great Cat of Ra killing Apophis. The golden eyes of the cat in Nebamun's tomb emphasises its solar connection.

The paintings depict a stylised ideal family outing and the family cat was included as part of the family as well as for its symbolism. The other components of the painting are not realistic. No-one dresses up in their finery and expensive jewellery to go fowling. It is comparable to fashion shoots where models waft through the wilderness in high heels and flowing ball-gowns. Some scholars see deep erotic symbolism with these scenes. As the tomb paintings depicted the idealised life the deceased hoped for in the afterlife, it is fair to say that this probably did include

---

[474] *The Painted Tomb-Chapel of Nebamun,* Parkinson, 2008:129

sexual activity but the scenes probably have more religious symbolism than that.

Cats in Other Tomb Scenes

In tomb paintings of the New Kingdom, particularly in Thebes, it was common to show a cat under the wife's chair and some scholars have suggested that this evokes fertility and sexuality and the hope that the woman will be 'available' for sex in the afterlife. Was this what it meant to the Egyptians or is it a reflection of the mindset of some modern commentators? Dogs are often depicted under men's chairs as are monkeys and geese. What are we to interpret these animals as symbolising? If a cat implies sexual or fertility aspects then surely the dog or monkey under the man's chair should be read in the same fashion. Dogs had been shown under men's chairs for 1,000 years before the cat was depicted which meant that the cat had to take the default position under the wife's chair. Did this theme arise mainly due to artistic convention? Cats also like to sit under chairs.

In a wall painting in the 19th dynasty tomb of Ipuy and his wife Duammeres, at Deir el-Medina, a cat sits under the chair of Duammeres. Ipuy is depicted with a kitten on his lap and a cat beneath his chair. The cat wears one earing and is shown facing the viewer, a very unusual pose in Egyptian art.[475] Cats depicted this way occur in several of the Ramesside tombs at Deir el-Medina. Was it a quirk of the same artist or a local tradition? Is there an erotic connotation here or is Ipuy just being portrayed as a cat lover? Perhaps a cat under the chair shows it as a favourite pet or the desirability of a pet cat. The cats are depicted in a variety of poses many of which are humorous as well as realistic; they are shown sleeping, chewing on bones and eating fish. One is shown spitting at a goose and other has its paw around a goose. One is tied to the leg of the chair, possibly to keep her in place for the portrait.

The Egyptian artists had quite a formulaic approach in formal works because the composition, in terms of proportion, was very important. A well-balanced composition was a visual expression of *maat*. For this reason they liked symmetry and avoided empty spaces. The convention was to show the wife behind the husband and so her feet occupied the space under the husband's chair but there was nothing under her chair

---

[475] *The Animal World of the Pharaohs*, Houlihan, 1996:85

so why not add a popular pet with afterlife associations? Was the cat under the woman's chair in part showing a connection to Bastet or Mut? During the reign of Akhenaten (18th dynasty) no cats are shown in the tombs of the elite. After his reign the cat doesn't appear with the same frequency. Malek suggests that it was originally a space filler and desirable motif but when the Memphite School began to dominate they used other methods and traditions.[476]

Humour

"*Do not laugh at a cat*" ordered the *Instructions of Onchsheshonqy*[477], but not all the artists followed his advice. *Ostraca* are fragments of limestone or pottery used for writing or drawing on and hundreds of these from the New Kingdom have been found at Deir el-Medina. Some were used for rough work and jottings but a number are illustrated with drawings showing animals in human situations. They were produced by the artists who worked on the tombs in the Valley of the Kings and are also found in papyri of the Ramesside Period. Cats and mice were very popular. One cat carries a pack on a stick over its shoulder. Other examples include a cat dressed as a woman smelling a lotus flower, a servant cat fanning an enthroned cat and a tabby cat herding ducks. Another shows servant cats waiting on lady mice and a cat acting as a nursemaid to a baby mouse. In an attempt to make arithmetic more interesting one set problem in the Middle Kingdom *Rhind* mathematical papyrus refers to seven houses, 49 cats and 343 mice. Other animals were also depicted in humorous situations. The *Turin* papyrus shows a band made up of animals with a lion as the lead vocalist. In another a lion plays a *senet* (a popular board game which was symbolic of the deceased's passage through the underworld) with a worried-looking antelope.

Was this irreverent social satire with angry undertones? Feline power could represent the abuse of royal power and satirical cartoons of mice defeating cats might allude to the hopes of ordinary people that royal tyranny would eventually be overcome. This was the only safe way in which way the disempowered but literate could retaliate - a way of mocking the elite in an innocent way where the dissolute ruling classes were represented as beleaguered cats and the virtuous mice (the honest

---

[476] *The Cat in Ancient Egypt*, Malek, 1993:69
[477] *The Literature of Ancient Egypt*, Simpson et al, 2003:516

workers) ruling for a change. In one example warrior mice attack cats in a castle. Some may have just been for fun or to illustrate animal fables or myths. One depicts a monkey seated in front of a large cat and is probably an illustration of the Distant Goddess myth. It may have been a popular theme at the time, comparable with the Victorians' depictions of clothed animals performing human activities.

Cats in Amulets and Jewellery

Amulets in cat form appear in late Old Kingdom burials and in the 1st Intermediate Period there are small cat and cat-headed amulets. They are believed to be protective but it is not clear which deities they relate to. In the early New Kingdom cat insignia became increasingly popular with royal women. This reflects the rise in popularity of the solar cults as well as that of the domestic cat. One example is a broad collar of the 17th dynasty Queen Ahhotep which included 18 gold pendants of a seated cat. In the tombs of the wives of Thutmose III (18th dynasty) were bead armlets with gold bars inlaid with figures of recumbent cats, depicted with their front paws crossed and heads turned. This is a similar posture to some of the large lion statues. Following the trend set by royalty, amulets of faience cats became very common in the New Kingdom. They probably had a protective function as well as showing that the owner liked cats. They were often carved in semiprecious stones and formed the ring bezel or back of a scarab. There are also gold earrings in the form of cats. More elaborate designs don't appear until the 3rd Intermediate Period.

Bronze amulets of a seated cat, with a loop at the back, became common in the 3rd Intermediate Period. As well as being threaded on a necklace they could be attached to a wall or sacred object. There is also a seated cat carved from black and white diorite. Not all the amulets were intended to be worn, some being set up on a plinth. Examples of these tend to be the more complex compositions with cat and kittens. The Late Period saw a further increase in cat amulets in bronze and semi-precious stones such as amethyst, calcite and carnelian. One example is a blue-green faience amulet of Bastet as a cat with a litter of kittens. A small amulet of a cat-headed Bastet shows her carrying a *sistrum*, *menat* and basket. A more unusual form is a small faience quadriform (representing four figures) amulet of the cat-headed Bastet

10 - Lion Statue

from Abydos. One lapis lazuli amulet from the Late Period is in the form of a cat-headed cobra and is thought to represent Bastet.

A common 22nd dynasty composition was a pendant in the form of a pillar surmounted by one or more cats. The pillar is in the form of the capital of a column, probably a lotus capital rather than a papyrus capital. One was inscribed *"Utterance by Bastet, Lady of Bubastis"*[478]. Another faience amulet has two cats seated on a papyrus column. It may have been attached to a stick used as a mark of rank or it may have been part of a decorative finial. The pillar form occurs from the 3rd Intermediate Period; there is an example of a blue-green cat sat on the top of a papyrus column. What is the reason for this combination of columns and cats? One simple explanation is that cats love to sit on top of things and for a protective cat it would give it the best viewpoint. This form of amulet may have been inspired by temple scenes. There are temple reliefs which show bronze cats (from two to 40) positioned around the base of Hathor-head columns. Columns are associated with Hathor,

---

[478] *Notes on Some Small Egyptian Figures of Cats*, Langton, 1936:115-120

Osiris and Min. Hathor has an association with cats and their protective role in the afterlife would have linked them with Osiris. There is a Ptolemaic amulet of Osiris with a seated cat.

Cats on Other Objects

Cats, like the other apotropaic animals such as lions, are carved into the armrests of chairs. They are depicted on large bowls decorated with Hathor Heads. The cat sits next to the Hathor Head showing its connection to her. Another connection to Hathor is on the handle of a mirror, an object closely associated with her, which is carved with a nude girl holding a kitten. There is a wooden hairpin from the New Kingdom topped with a seated cat. A bronze 3-*deben* weight in the form of a recumbent cat dates to the Late or Greco-Roman Period. One *deben* is 90g of bronze. The *Archive of Hor* refers to transactions paid in the *"portion of the god"* which is believed to be a reference to these weights.[479]

The Importance of Symbolism

Felines are popular subjects in all forms of artwork over many periods and cultures. They are present for purely aesthetic reasons as well as for the wealth of symbolism attached to them. Some cultures included lions as a way of emphasising the braveness of heroes. Young men wrestling lions was a common theme in ancient Cypriot and Near Eastern art. Here the lion has no religious or spiritual symbolism, he exists only to enhance the superiority of the young man. Excavations of the sunken Ptolemaic city of Naukratis have yielded many such figures which are often referred to as lion-tamers. For the Egyptians cats and lions were present because of their solar symbolism and to indicate the presence of a particular deity. The decorative appeal of cats is obvious but to the Egyptians they were so much more than that, transmitting many religious concepts as well as being pleasing to look at.

---

[479] *Soulful Creatures. Animal Mummies in Ancient Egypt*, Bleiberg, Barbash & Bruno, 2013:100

CHAPTER 22

CONCLUSION

"I am Sekhmet, Great of Magic. I sit at the western side in the sky."[480]

Egypt is the land of the Feline Goddesses; there is little evidence for them elsewhere. However, we do need to be aware that other cultures used iconography in a different way to the Egyptians as they tended to represent the deity accompanied by an animal rather than as an animal. The Great Mother Goddess of Catal Huyuk is shown with lions, Cybele rides a chariot drawn by lions and Ishtar *"drives seven lions"*. Inanna has the epithet *"Divine Lioness"*[481]. None of these Goddesses show the same feline temperament as Sekhmet and Bastet though. Near Eastern Gods are often compared to lions and shown as having power over lions. No-one has power over Sekhmet. So why did the Egyptians have Feline Goddesses? Being unashamedly biased I could suggest that the Egyptians were the more perceptive and sensible. The fact that they viewed the Solar Eye as feminine had a great bearing on the dominance

---

[480] *The Cat in Ancient Egypt*, Malek, 1993:69
[480] *The Literature of Ancient Egypt*, Simpson et al, 2003:516
[481] *Notes on Some Small Egyptian Figures of Cats*, Langton, 1936:115-120

of the Feline Goddesses as does the fact that *sekhem*, the original power, was seen as a female energy. It also explains the nature of the Lion Gods and their powers of earth rather than of fire.

Are all Eye Goddess and Feline Goddess individual or are they merely aspects of one Goddess? They can appear simply as differing aspects of one Goddess given how easily they interchange with each other, yet they have very distinct personalities in their own right. The Egyptian approach is the best to adopt – both views are equally valid and can be held simultaneously. After all who can understand their Goddesses better than the Egyptians themselves? I believe that the duality and transferability of these Goddesses is due to the nature of their feline power which is itself a reflection of the original power from the instant of creation. Power weaves and merges and changes form and this is reflected in its manifestation in the various Feline Goddesses.

No-one needs science to tell them that our sun is both essential to life and dangerous but solar physics provides us with new insights as well as ungraspable statistics about the Solar Disc; 15 million degrees at its core, solar prominences looping hundreds of thousands of miles into space. Its magnetic field protects us from lethal cosmic rays and solar flares disrupt modern telecommunications and delight us with the aurora borealis and aurora australis. Images of the sun show a boiling, turbulent surface where contorted magnetic fields twist until they snap sending bursts of plasma into space. Volatile yet constant, dangerous yet protective. Totally essential. Images provided by solar physics reveal one of the faces of the Eye of the Sun. Sekhmet illuminated by modern science not veiled by it. *"Its fire is blue…fifty cubits along its side are fire, the tip of its flame crosses the land from the sky…it has gone forth from the hands of Sakhmet.*[482]

And what of Bastet *"lady of the shrine and eye of Horus…pre-eminent of the god's field"*?[483] She has merely moved from *"the god's field"* into our gardens and our homes. Not always loved and respected as she should be but still *"the Good Cat, well established"*.[484]

---

[482] *Soulful Creatures. Animal Mummies in Ancient Egypt*, Bleiberg, Barbash & Bruno, 2013:100

[483] *Sunken Cities Egypt's Lost Worlds*, Goddio & Masson-Berghoff, 2016:61

BIBLIOGRAPHY

Abt, T. & Hornung, E. (2003) *Knowledge for the Afterlife.* Zurich, Living Human Heritage Publications

Abt, T. & Hornung, E. (2007) *The Egyptian Amduat.* Zurich, Living Human Heritage Publications

Allen, J. P. (2005) *The Art of Medicine in Ancient Egypt.* New York, Metropolitan Museum of Art

Allen, T. A. (1974) *The Book of the Dead or Going Forth by Day.* Chicago, University of Chicago Press

Andrews, C. (1994) *Amulets of Ancient Egypt.* London, British Museum Press

Armstrong, C. H. (2015) *The Two Non-Blue Amuns of the Shrine of Taharqa at Kawa.* In *Journal of Egyptian Archaeology,* Vol 101:177-195

Betz, H. D. (Ed.) (1996) *The Greek Magical Papyri in Translation. Volume I: Texts.* Chicago, University of Chicago Press

Betz, R. (2016) *What's New in Luxor?* In *Ancient Egypt,* Vol 16.4:24-33

Blackman, A. M. & Fairman, H. W. (1944) *The Myth of Horus at Edfu: II. C. The Triumph of Horus over His Enemies a Sacred Drama (Concluded).* In *Journal of Egyptian Archaeology,* Vol 30:5-22

Blackman, A. M. (1918) *The Funerary Papyrus of Nespeher'an (Pap. Skrine, No. 2).* In *Journal of Egyptian Archaeology,* Vol 5:24-35

Blackman, A. M. (1945) *The King of Egypt's Grace before Meat.* In *Journal of Egyptian Archaeology,* Vol 1945:57-73

Bleeker, C. J. (1973) *Hathor and Thoth: Two Key Figures of the Ancient Egyptian Religion.* Leiden, E J Brill

Bleiberg, E., Barbash, Y. & Bruno, L. (2013) *Soulful Creatures. Animal Mummies in Ancient Egypt.* New York, Giles

Bomhard, A. S. (1999) *The Egyptian Calendar: A Work For Eternity*. London, Periplus Publishing

Bongioanni, A. & Crose, M. S. (Ed.) (2001) *The Treasures of Ancient Egypt from the Egyptian Museum in Cairo*. New York, Universal Publishing

Bourghouts, J. F. (1972) *The Evil Eye of Apophis*. In *Journal of Egyptian Archaeology*, Vol 59:114-150

Bourghouts, J. F. (1978) *Ancient Egyptian Magical Texts*. Leiden, E J Brill

Boylan, P. (1922) *Thoth or the Hermes of Egypt*. Kessinger Publishing (Reprints)

Bradshaw, J. (2014) *Cat Sense*. London, Penguin Books

Buhl, N. (1947) *The Goddesses of the Egyptian Tree Cult*, In *Journal of Near Eastern Studies*, Vol 6:80-97

Burzacott, J. (2017) *66 New Sekhmet Statues in Luxor*. In *Nile Magazine*. No. 7:8-11

Caminos, R. A. (1982) *The Rendells Mummy Bandages*. In *Journal of Egyptian Archaeology*, Vol 68:145-155

Capel, A. K. & Markoe, G. E. (1997) *Mistress of the House, Mistress of Heaven: Women in Ancient Art*. Easthampton, Hudson Hills Press Inc.

Clark, R. T. (1978) *Myth and Symbol in Ancient Egypt*. London, Thames & Hudson

Connor, S. (2017) *Le Statue della Dea Sekhmet*. Turin, Museo Egizio di Torino

Darnell, J. C. (1995) *Hathor Returns to Medamud*. In *Studien zur Altägyptischen Kultur*, Vol 22:47-97

Darnell, J. C. (1997) *The Apotropaic Goddess in the Eye*. In *Studien zur Altägyptischen Kultur*, Vol 24:35-48

Darnell, J. C. (2004) *The Enigmatic Netherworld Books of the Solar-Osiran Unity*. Fribourg, Academic Press

David, R. (2013) *Egyptian Medicine: Science and Superstition in the Ancient World*. In *Current World Archaeology*, No. 59:38-40

David, R. (2016) *Temple Ritual at Abydos*. London. Egypt Exploration Society

De Wit, C. (1951) *Le Role et le Sens du Lion dans L'Egypte Ancienne*. Leiden, Brill.

Diodorus Siculus & Booth, G. (1814) *The Historical Library of History of Diodorus Siculus*. London, McDowall

Draper-Stumm, T. (2012) *Travellers from an Antique Land: Statues of the Goddess Sekhmet in the British Museum*. www.academia.edu accessed 12/08/2016

Duffy, J. S. (2012) *Artefacts of Stone*. In *Ancient Egypt*, Vol 13.1: 44-49

el-Sabban (2000) *Temple Festival Calendars of Ancient Egypt*. Liverpool, Liverpool University Press

el-Sayed, M.A. (1978) *A New Temple for Hathor at Memphis*. Warminster, Aris & Phillips Ltd.

Eyre, C. (2002) *The Cannibal Hymn*. Liverpool, Liverpool University Press

Fairman, H. W. & Grdseloff, B. (1947) *Texts of Hatshepsut and Sethos I inside Speos Artemidos*. In *Journal of Egyptian Archaeology*, Vol 33:12-33

Faulkner, R. O. (1937) *The Bremner-Rhind Papyrus II*. In *Journal of Egyptian Archaeology*, Vol 23:10-16

Faulkner, R. O. (1937) *The Bremner-Rhind Papyrus III*. In *Journal of Egyptian Archaeology*, Vol 23:166-185

Faulkner, R. O. (1938) *The Bremner-Rhind Papyrus IV*. In *Journal of Egyptian Archaeology*, Vol 24:41-53

Faulkner, R. O. (1958) *An Ancient Egyptian Book of Hours*. Oxford, Griffith Institute

Faulkner, R. O. (1989) *The Ancient Egyptian Book of the Dead*. London, British Museum Publications

Faulkner, R. O. (2007) *The Ancient Egyptian Coffin Texts*. Oxford, Aris & Phillips

Faulkner, R. O. (2007) *The Ancient Egyptian Pyramid Texts*. Kansas, Digireads.com Publishing

Fazzini, R. A. & Peck, W. H. (1983) *Excavating the Temple of Mut*. In *Archaeology*, Vol 36:16-23

Fazzini, R. A. & van Dijk, J (2015) *The First Pylon of the Mut Temple, South Karnak: Architecture, Decorations, Inscriptions*. Leuven, Peeters

Fischer-Elfert, H. (1996) *Two Oracle Petitions Addressed to Horus-khau with Some Notes on the Oracular Amuletic Decrees* (P. Berlin P. 8525 and P. 8526). In *Journal of Egyptian Archaeology*, Vol 82:129-144

Fletcher, J. (1999) *Oils and Perfumes of Ancient Egypt*. New York, Harry N Abrams Inc.

Fletcher, J. (2015) *The Story of Egypt*. London, Hodder & Stoughton

Foreman, W. & Quirke, S. (1996) *Hieroglyphs & the Afterlife in Ancient Egypt*. London, Opus Publishing Ltd

Foster, J. L. (1992) *Echoes of Egyptian Voices*. Oklahoma City, University of Oklahoma Press

Foster, J. L. (1995) *Hymns, Prayers and Songs*. Atlanta, Scholars Press

Foster, J. L. (2001) *Ancient Egyptian Literature*. Austin, University of Texas Press

Frankfurter, D. (1998) *Religion in Roman Egypt*. Princeton, Princeton University Press

Gaballa, G. A. & Kitchen K. A. (1969) *The Festival of Sokar*. In *Orientalia*, Vol 38:1-76

Gaballa, G. A. (1969) *Minor War Scenes of Ramesses II at Karnak*. In *Journal of Egyptian Archaeology*, Vol 55:82-88

Gardiner, A. H. (1938) *The House of Life*. In *Journal of Egyptian Archaeology*, Vol 24:157-179

Gardiner, A. H. (1946) *Davies's Copy of the Great Speos Artemidos Inscription*. In *Journal of Egyptian Archaeology*, Vol 32:43-56

Gautier, H. (1920) *Les Statues Thebaines de la Desses Sakhmet*. In *Annales du Service des Antiquités de l'Egypte*, Vol 19:117-207

Germond, P. (1981) *Sekhmet et la Protection du Monde*. Geneva, l'Université de Genève.

Germond, P. (2001) *Ancient Egyptian Bestiary*. London, Thames & Hudson

Ghalioungui, P. (1963) *Magic and Medical Science in Ancient Egypt*. Amsterdam, Hodder & Stoughton

Goddio, F. & Masson-Berghoff, A. (Ed.) (2016) *Sunken Cities Egypt's Lost Worlds*. London, Thames & Hudson

Gozzoli, R. B. (2000) *The statue BMEA 37891 and the Erasure of Necho II's Names*. In *Journal of Egyptian Archaeology*, Vol 86:67-80

Graves-Brown, C. (2010) *Dancing for Hathor: Women in Ancient Egypt*. London, Continuum

Gray, L. (Ed.) (2009) *The New Cultural Atlas of Egypt*. London, Brown Reference Group

Griffith, F. L. & Thompson, H. (1974) *The Leyden Papyrus*. New York, Dover Publications

Griffiths, S. (2016) *News*. In *Ancient Egypt*, Vol 16.6:6-14

Hart, G. (2005) *The Routledge Dictionary of Egyptian Gods and Goddesses*. Abingdon, Routledge

Hawass, Z. (1994) *A Fragmentary Monument of Djoser from Saqqara*. In *Journal of Egyptian Archaeology*, Vol 80:45-56

Herodotus & Selincourt, A. (Trans.) (2003) *The Histories*. London, Penguin Books

Hill, M. (Ed.) (2007) *Gifts for the Gods: Images from Egyptian Temples*. New York, Metropolitan Museum of Art

Holmberg, M. S. (1946) *The God Ptah*. Lund, C W K Gleerup

Horapollo & Boas, G. (1950) *The Hieroglyphics of Horapollo*. New Jersey, Princeton University Press

Hornung, E. & Bryan, B. M. (Eds.) (2002) *The Quest for Immortality: Treasures of Ancient Egypt*. London, Prestel Publishers

Hornung, E. (2001) *The Secret Lore of Egypt: Its Impact on the West*. Ithaca, Cornell University Press

Houlihan, P. F. (1996) *The Animal World of the Pharaohs*. London, Thames & Hudson

Hussein, H. (2016) *Searching for Ptolemy XII: Inscriptions from Sinai*. In *Egyptian Archaeology*, No. 48:28-29

Ikram, S. (Ed.) (2005) *Divine Creatures Animal Mummies in Ancient Egypt*. New York, American University in Cairo Press

Jackson, D. (2010) *Lion*. London, Reaktion Books

Jacquet-Gordon, H. K. (1960) *The Inscriptions on the Philadelphia: Cairo Statue of Osorkon II*. In *Journal of Egyptian Archaeology*, Vol 46:12-23

James, T. G. H. (1982) *A Wooden Figure of Wadjet with Two Painted Representations of Amasis*. In *Journal of Egyptian Archaeology*, Vol 68:156-165

Janssen, J. J. (1968) *The Smaller Dakhla Stele (Ashmolean Museum No. 1894. 107 b)*. In *Journal of Egyptian Archaeology*, Vol 54:165-172

Jasnow, R. & Zauzich, K (2005) *The Ancient Egyptian Book of Thoth*. Harrassowitz Verlag 2005.

Johnson, S. B. (1990) *The Cobra Goddesses of Ancient Egypt*. London, Kegan Paul International

Johnson, W. R. & McClain J. B. (2008) *A Fragmentary Scene of Ptolemy XII Worshiping the Goddess Mut and Her Divine Entourage*. In *D'Auria, S. (Ed.) (2008) Servant of Mut. Studies in Honour of Richard A Fazzini*. Leiden, Brill

Kakosy, L. (1967) *Egyptian Healing Statues in Three Museums in Italy (Turin, Florence, Naples)*. Turin, Egyptian Museum of Turin

Kakosy, L. (1980) *A Memphite Triad*. In *Journal of Egyptian Archaeology*, Vol 66:48-53

Kakosy, L. (1996) *The Ptah-Shu-Tefnut Triad and the Gods of the Winds on a Ptolemaic Sarcophagus.* In *van Dijk, J. (Ed,) (1996) Essays on Ancient Egypt in Honour of Herman te Velde.* Groningen, Styx Publications

Kaper, O. A. (1995) *The Astronomical Ceiling of Deir el-Haggar in the Dakhleh Oasis.* In *Journal of Egyptian Archaeology,* Vol 81:175-195

Kaper, O. E. (2009) *Restoring Wall Paintings of the Temple of Tutu.* In *Egyptian Archaeology,* No. 35:3-7

Kaster, J. (1993) *The Wisdom of Ancient Egypt.* New York, Barnes & Noble Books

Kawai, N. (2011) *An Early Cult Centre at Abusir-Saqqara? Recent Discoveries at a Rocky Outcrop in Northwest Saqqara.* In *Friedman, R. F. & Fiske, P. N. (Ed.) (2011) Egypt at its Origins, Proceedings of the Third International Conference.* Leuven, Peeters

Kemp, B. (2006) *100 Hieroglyphs: Think Like an Egyptian.* London, Granta Books

Kemp, B. (2007) *How to Read the Egyptian Book of the Dead.* London, Granta Books

Kirby, C. J., Orel, S. E. & Smith, S. T. (1998) *Preliminary Report on the Survey of Kom el-Hisin, 1996.* In *Journal of Egyptian Archaeology,* Vol 84:23-43

Klotz, D. (2010) *Two Overlooked Oracles.* In *Journal of Egyptian Archaeology,* Vol 96:247-254

Kozloff, A. P. & Bryan, B. M. (1992) *Egypt's Dazzling Sun: Amenhotep III and his World.* Cleveland, Cleveland Museum of Art

Kurth, D. (2004) *The Temple of Edfu.* Cairo, The American University in Cairo Press

Lamy, L. (1986) *Egyptian Mysteries: New Light on Ancient Knowledge.* London, Thames & Hudson

Lange, E. & Ullmann, T. (2015) *Goddess on the Water: the Sacred Landscape of Bubastis.* In *Egyptian Archaeology,* No. 47:17-19

Langton, N. (1936) *Further Notes on Some Egyptian Figures of Cats.* In *Journal of Egyptian Archaeology,* Vol 24:54-58

Langton, N. (1936) *Notes on Some Small Egyptian Figures of Cats.* In *Journal of Egyptian Archaeology,* Vol 22:115-120

Langton, N. B. (2002) *The Cat in Ancient Egypt.* London, Kegan Paul

Lesko, L. H. (1977) *The Ancient Egyptian Book of Two Ways.* California, University of California Publications 1977.

Lexova, I. (2000) *Ancient Egyptian Dances.* New York, Dover Publications

Lezno, G. (2015) *A Xoite Stela of Ptolemy VIII Euergetes II with Cleopatra II (British Museum EA 612).* In *Journal of Egyptian Archaeology,* Vol 101:217-237

Lichtheim, M. (2006) *Ancient Egyptian Literature Volume I.* California, University of California Press

Lichtheim, M. (2006) *Ancient Egyptian Literature Volume II.* California, University of California Press

Lichtheim, M. (2006) *Ancient Egyptian Literature Volume III.* California, University of California Press

Lindsay, J. (1968) *Men and Gods on the Roman Nile.* London, Frederick Muller

Lord, C. (2010) *How Now Sick Cow.* In *Ancient Egypt,* Vol 11.1:20-34

Lurker, M. (1986) *The Gods and Symbols of Ancient Egypt.* London, Thames & Hudson

Lythgoe, A. M. (1919) *Statues of the Goddess Sekhmet.* In *The Metropolitan Museum of Art Bulletin,* Vol 14:3-23

Malek, J. (1993) *The Cat in Ancient Egypt.* London, The British Museum Press

Malek, J. (2003) *Egypt: 4000 Years of Egyptian Art.* London, Phaidon Press Ltd

Markowitz, Y. J. & Doxey, D. M. (2014) *Jewels of Ancient Nubia.* Boston, MFA Publications

Mead, G. R. S. (2002) *Plutarch: Concerning the Mysteries of Isis and Osiris.* Montana, Kessinger Publishing (Reprints)

Meeks, D. & Favard-Meeks, C. (1999) *Daily Life of Egyptian Gods.* London, Pimlico

Myers, O. H. & Fairman, H. W. (1931) *Excavations at Armant, 1929-31.* In *Journal of Egyptian Archaeology,* Vol 17:223-232

Nelson, H. H. (1949) *Certain Reliefs at Karnak and Medinet Habu and the Ritual of Amenophis I (Concluded).* In *Journal of Near Eastern Studies,* Vol 8.4:310-345

O'Roukre, P. F. (2016) *An Ancient Egyptian Book of the Dead.* London, Thames & Hudson

Oakes, L. & Gahlin, L. (2004) *Ancient Egypt.* London, Hermes House

Osborn, D. J. (1998) *The Mammals of Ancient Egypt.* Warminster, Aris & Philips

Parkinson, R. (1991) *Voices from Ancient Egypt.* London, British Museum Press

Parkinson, R. (2008) *The Painted Tomb-Chapel of Nebamun.* London, British Museum Press

Parkinson, R. B. (1998) *The Tale of Sinuhe and Other Ancient Egyptian Poems.* Oxford, Oxford University Press

Patch, D. C. (2011) *Dawn of Egyptian Art.* New York, Metropolitan Museum of Art

Peet, T. E. (1925) *The Legend of the Capture of Joppa and the Story of the Foredoomed Prince. Being a Translation of the Verso of Papyrus Harris 500.* In *Journal of Egyptian Archaeology,* Vol 11:225-229

Piankoff, A. (1964) *The Litany of Re.* New York, Pantheon Books.

Pinch, G. (1993) *Votive Offerings to Hathor.* Oxford, Griffith Institute

Pinch, G. (2002) *Egyptian Mythology.* Oxford, Oxford University Press

Pinch, G. (2004) *Egyptian Myth: A Very Short Introduction.* Oxford, Oxford University Press

Pinch, G. (2006) *Magic in Ancient Egypt.* London, The British Museum Press

Pinkowski, J. (2006) *Egypt's Ageless Goddess.* In *Archaeology,* Vol 59:44-49

Poo, M. (1995) *Wine and Wine Offering in the Religion of Ancient Egypt.* London, Kegan Paul International

Raven, M. (2012) *Egyptian Magic.* Cairo, American University in Cairo Press

Raven, M. J. (1997) *Charms for Protection During the Epagomenal Days.* In *van Dijk, J. (Ed,) (1996) Essays on Ancient Egypt in Honour of Herman te Velde.* Groningen, Styx Publications

Reisner, G. A. (1915) *Accessions to the Egyptian Department During 1914.* In *Bulletin of the Museum of Fine Arts,* No. 76:29-36

Roberts, A. (2001) *Hathor Rising.* Rottingdean, Northgate Publishers

Roehrig, C. H. et al (ed.) (2005) *Hatshepsut: From Queen to Pharaoh.* New York, Metropolitan Museum of Art

Rogers, K. M. (2013) *Cat.* London, Reaktion Books

Rosenow, D. (2008) *The Domain of the Cat-Goddess, Bastet.* In Ancient Egypt, Vol 9.1: 27-33

Rosenow, D. (2017) *The Naos of 'Bastet, Lady of the Shrine' from Bubastis.* In *Journal of Egyptian Archaeology*, Vol 94:247-266

Sadek, A. I. (1988) *Popular Religion in Egypt During the New Kingdom.* Hildesheim, Gerstenberg

Sauneron, S. (2000) *The Priests of Ancient Egypt.* Ithaca, Cornell University Press

Schweizer, A. (2010) *The Sungod's Journey Through the Netherworld.* Ithaca, Cornell University Press

Scott, G. D. (2008) *A Seated Statue of Sekhmet and Two Related Sculptures in the Collection of the San Antonia Museum of Art.* In *D'Auria, S. (Ed.) (2008) Servant of Mut. Studies in Honour of Richard A Fazzini.* Leiden, Brill

Scott, N. E. (1951) *The Metternich Stele.* In The Metropolitan Museum of Art Bulletin, Vol 9:201-217

Shaw, G. J. (2014) *The Egyptian Myths.* London, Thames & Hudson

Shaw, I. & Nicholson, P. (2008) *The British Museum Dictionary of Ancient Egypt.* London, British Museum Press

Shorter, A. W. (1930) *The Tomb of AahMose, Supervisor of the Mysteries in the House of the Morning.* In *Journal of Egyptian Archaeology*, Vol 16:54-62

Shorter, A. W. (1932) *Two Statuettes of the Goddess Sekhmet-Ubastet.* In *Journal of Egyptian Archaeology*, Vol 18:121-124

Simpson, W. K. et al (2003) *The Literature of Ancient Egypt.* New Haven, Yale University Press

Smethills, J. (2014) *Playing with Fire.* In *Ancient Egypt*, Vol 15.1:12-16

Smith, M. (2009) *Traversing Eternity.* Oxford, Oxford University Press

Sourouzian, H. (2006) *The Theban Funerary Temple of Amenhotep III.* In *Egyptian Archaeology*, No. 29:21-24

Spalinger, A. (2000) *The Destruction of Mankind: A Transitional Literary Text.* In *Studien zur Altägyptischen Kultur*, Vol 28:257-282

Spencer, N. (2007) *The Gayer-Anderson Cat.* London, The British Museum Press

Spencer, N. A. (1999) *The Epigraphic Survey of Samanud.* In *Journal of Egyptian Archaeology*, Vol 85:55-83

Stewart, H. M. (1971) *A Crossword Hymn to Mut.* In *Journal of Egyptian Archaeology*, Vol 57:87-104

Strawn, B. A. (2005) *What is Stronger than a Lion?* Fribourg, Academic Press

Strudwick, N. (2005) *Texts From the Pyramid Age.* Atlanta, Society of Biblical Literature

Szpakowska, K. (2008) *Daily Life in Ancient Egypt.* Oxford, Blackwell Publishing

Taher, A. W. (2010) *From Our Own Correspondent.* In *Ancient Egypt*, Vol 10.5:9-16

te Velde, H. (1971) *Some Remarks on the Structure of Egyptian Divine Triads.* In *Journal of Egyptian Archaeology*, Vol 57:80-86 te Velde, H. (1980) *A Few Remarks on the Religious Significance of Animals*. In *Numen*, Vol 27:76-82

te Velde, H. (1982) *The Cat as a Sacred Animal of the Goddess Mut*. In *Van Voss, H. et al (Ed.) (1982) Studies in Egyptian Religion: Dedicated to Professor Jan Zandee*. Leiden, Brill

te Velde, H. (2008) *The Goddess Mut and the Vulture*. In *D'Auria, S. (Ed.) (2008) Servant of Mut. Studies in Honour of Richard A Fazzini*. Leiden, Brill

Teeter, E. & Johnson, J. H. (Eds.) (2009) *The Life of Meresamun*. Chicago, University of Chicago

Teeter, E. (2011) *Before the Pyramids*. Chicago, Oriental Institute Museum Publications

Teeter, E. (2011) *Religion and Ritual in Ancient Egypt*. Cambridge, Cambridge University Press

Tiradritti, F. (2007) *Egyptian Wall Paintings*. New York, Abbeville Press

Torok, L. (2002) *The Image of the Ordered World in Ancient Nubian Art*. Leiden, Brill

Torok, L. (2009) *Between Two Worlds*. Leiden, Brill

Trope, B. et al (2005) *Excavating Egypt*. Atlanta, Emory University

Troy, L. *Mut Enthroned*. (1996) In *van Dijk, J. (Ed,) (1996) Essays on Ancient Egypt in Honour of Herman te Velde*. Groningen, Styx Publications

Tyldesley, J (2010) *Myths & Legends of Ancient Egypt*. London, Allen Lane

Tyldesley, J. (2012) *Atum: Creating the World*. In *Ancient Egypt*, Vol 12.3:25-27

van Dijk, J. (2010) *A Cat, a Nurse and a Standard Bearer. Notes on Three Late Eighteenth Dynasty Statues. In D'Auria, S. H. (Ed.) (2010) Offerings to the Discerning Eye.*

van Ryneveld, M (2008) *The Use of Leopard Skin in Ancient Egypt*. In *Ancient Egypt*, Vol 9.2: 30-32

Vernus, P. (1998) *The Gods of Ancient Egypt*. London, Tauris Parke Books

Watterson, B. (2003) *Gods of Ancient Egypt*. Stroud, Sutton Publishing Ltd

Wente, E. (1990) *Letters from Ancient Egypt*. Atlanta, Scholars Press

Whitehouse, H. (2009) *Ancient Egypt and Nubia*. Oxford, Ashmolean Museum

Widmer, G. (1999) *Emphasizing and Non-Emphasizing Second Tenses in the "Myth of the Sun's Eye"*. In *Journal of Egyptian Archaeology*, Vol 85:165-188

Wilkinson, A. (1998) *The Garden in Ancient Egypt*. London, The Rubicon Press

Wilkinson, R. H. (2000) *The Complete Temples of Ancient Egypt*. London, Thames & Hudson

Wilkinson, R. H. (2003) *The Complete Gods and Goddesses of Ancient Egypt*. London, Thames & Hudson

Wilkinson, R. H. (2008) *Egyptian Scarabs*. Oxford, Shire Publications

Wilkinson, T. (2016) *Writings from Ancient Egypt*. London, Penguin Books

Wilkinson, T. A. H. (1999) *Early Dynastic Egypt*. London, Routledge

Wilson, J. A. (1948) *The Oath in Ancient Egypt*. In *Journal of Near Eastern Studies*, Vol 7:129-156

Wilson, J. A. (1952) *A Note of the Edwin Smith Surgical Papyrus*. In *Journal of Near Eastern Studies*, Vol 11:76-80

Wilson, R. (2009) *KV-63 Update: the 2009 Season*. In *Ancient Egypt*, Vol 9.6:30-38

Zabkar, L. V. (1988) *Hymns to Isis in Her Temple at Philae*. Hanover, University Press of New England

Zandee, J. (1960) *Death as an Enemy*. Leiden, Brill

INDEX

Lightning Source UK Ltd.
Milton Keynes UK
UKHW030615220519
343122UK00007B/656/P